G000274459

NUTSHELLS

Criminal Law

FOURTH EDITION

Round Hall's Nutshell, Nutcase, Exam Focus, and Legal Skills Series

NUTSHELL TITLES

Specially written for students of Irish law, each title in the **Nutshell Series** from Round Hall is an accessible review of key principles, concepts and cases. Nutshells are both the ideal introductory text, and the perfect revision aid.

- **Administrative Law** by Matthew Holmes
- **Company Law** – 3rd edition by Catherine McConville
- **Contract Law** by Fergus Ryan
- **Constitutional Law** – 2nd edition by Fergus Ryan
- **Criminal Law** – 4th edition by Cecilia Ní Choileáin
- **Equity and Trusts** – 2nd edition by Miriam Dowling
- **Employment Law** – 2nd edition by Dorothy Donovan
- **Evidence** by Ross Gorman
- **EU Law** by Matthew Holmes
- **Family Law** by Louise Crowley
- **The Irish Legal System** by Dorothy Donovan
- **Land Law** – 2nd edition by Ruth Cannon
- **Succession Law** by Karl Dowling and Robert Grimes
- **Tort** – 2nd edition by Ursula Connolly

NUTCASE TITLES

Round Hall Nutcases are written to give you the key facts and principles of **important cases** in core legal subject areas. Straightforward, no-nonsense language makes Nutcases an easy way to understand and learn key cases.

- **Criminal Law** by Majella Walsh
- **Evidence** by Neil Van Dokkum
- **Tort** – 2nd edition by Val Corbett

EXAM FOCUS TITLES

The series is especially designed to support students in the weeks coming up to exams by providing a unique tutorial approach to answering questions.

- **Criminal Law** by Sarah Carew

LEGAL SKILLS TITLES

The Legal Skills Series helps students master the essential legal and research skills needed to succeed in their studies and in their future careers.

- **How to Think, Write and Cite: Key Skills for Irish Law Students**, 2nd edition by Jennifer Schweppe, Rónán Kennedy and Lawrence Donnelly.

NUTSHELLS

Criminal Law

FOURTH EDITION

by

CECILIA NÍ CHOILEÁIN
BA (Hons)(NUI), LLB (Hons)(NUI),
LLM (Hons)(Trinity College, Dublin),
BL (King's Inns)

ROUND HALL

Published in 2017 by
Thomson Reuters Ireland Limited
(Registered in Ireland, Company No. 80867. Registered Office
and address for service 12–13 Exchange Place, Dublin 1)
trading as Round Hall.

Typeset by Carrigboy Typesetting Services

Printed and bound in the UK by
CPI Group (UK) Ltd, Croydon, CR0 4YY

ISBN 978-0-41406-172-9

A catalogue record for this book is available from the British Library.

All rights reserved. No part of this publication may be reproduced or transmitted
in any form or by any means, or stored in any retrieval system of any nature
without prior written permission.

Thomson Reuters and the Thomson Reuters Logo are trademarks of
Thomson Reuters. Round Hall is a registered trademark of
Thomson Reuters Ireland Limited.

© Thomson Reuters Ireland Limited, 2017

Do John agus mo theaghlach, Betty, Seán Cathal, agus Tara,
le meas, míle buíochas agus grá.

"í gcuimhne ar Sandra agus Caroline."

Acknowledgments

As with previous editions, there are a number of people to whom I owe a debt of gratitude for their help with this book. In particular, I would like to thank all at Thomson Reuters, past and present, for their assistance, patience, and unfailing good humour. I am especially grateful to Sami Long, Beth Fitzgerald, Alana Gerring, Pauline Ward, and Pamela Moran.

I am grateful to my colleagues who have helped with all editions of this book and I would like, in particular, to thank Anna Bazarchina BL.

Finally, I would like to thank my family and, in particular, my husband, John Tully.

I am stating the law as I understand it as of 2 March 2017.

Cecilia Ní Choileáin

Biography

Cecilia Ní Choileáin BA (NUI), LLB (NUI), LLM (Trinity College, Dublin), BL (King's Inns) is a barrister and former lecturer in the Department of Legal Studies, DIT. She has worked as a researcher in the Judicial Researchers' Office in the Four Courts, the Parliamentary Legal Advisor's Office, and in the Library and Research Service of the Houses of the Oireachtas.

Contents

Table of Cases

IRELAND

UNITED KINGDOM

Australia

Canada

Europe

Table of Legislation

THE IRISH CONSTITUTION

Irish Statutes

Pre-1922 Statutes

English Statutes

EU LEGISLATION

EUROPEAN CONVENTION ON HUMAN RIGHTS

Introduction

1

It is impossible in a book of this nature to cover all aspects of an area of law as broad and diverse as the criminal law in any great depth. Its objective, then, is to set out the most fundamental principles of criminal law as they operate in this jurisdiction and to update the previous editions of this book in light of subsequent changes in the law.

Before looking at the substantive areas covered by the criminal law which are contained in subsequent chapters, a few general points need to be made about the criminal law itself and its function in this, or indeed any, society.

The Function of the Criminal Law

The behaviour of individuals in any society is subject to regulation in a number of ways. Social norms and customs, religion, and the laws of any jurisdiction are just some of the methods through which the behaviour of human beings can be curtailed in an attempt to establish and maintain a peaceful and ordered society. Of all these methods, the criminal law is unique in that it is the only method of social control which is enforced by means of State-imposed sanctions on the transgressing individual. The criminal law of any jurisdiction sets out the various types of behaviour which are deemed to be unacceptable to the members of that society and which are considered to be sufficiently serious to warrant the involvement of the State. Unlike other areas of law, such as the law of contract and the law of tort, both of which involve disputes between private individuals, the criminal law is an area of public law in which the individual against whom allegations of criminal activity are made is prosecuted by the State in the name of the People and, if convicted, will be subject to court-imposed sanctions which are prescribed by law and enforced by the Executive.

In this jurisdiction, criminal activity is that which is expressly prohibited by statute. In addition, there are numerous offences recognised by the common law and a very small number which are provided for by Bunreacht na hÉireann. Regardless of the source of the offence, all remain subject to the requirements of Bunreacht na hÉireann, which imposes a number of obligations on the State in respect of individual rights. Society's interest in the suppression of criminal activity and the effective operation of its criminal justice system requires a coherent body of rules, an impartial and independent judiciary, and adequately resourced and trained police, prison and probation services. On the other hand, the seriousness of the consequences to the individual charged with a criminal offence requires that at all stages from the investigation of an offence through to the outcome of a criminal trial, the individual is possessed of numerous rights provided for by law. Anyone charged with a criminal offence in this jurisdiction is entitled by law to be presumed innocent until the contrary is proven beyond a reasonable doubt before an impartial judge and, subject to certain exceptions, a jury. While it will normally be in society's interests to prosecute criminal activity, there are instances in which this interest must yield to a greater interest in protecting the individual. The clearest example of this occurs where the accused person is deemed not fit to stand trial, in accordance with the provisions of the Criminal Law (Insanity) Act 2006, as amended. In addition, there are various defences available to the individual charged with a criminal offence. These can operate in such a way as to either excuse or justify the behaviour of the defendant. The right of an accused person to be presumed innocent places the burden of proof on the prosecution, who must not only prove all the elements of the charge(s) against the accused beyond a reasonable doubt, but also negative any defence(s) and/or explanations put forward by the defence which are consistent with the innocence of the accused.

Primary Sources of Criminal Law

2

The primary sources of Irish criminal law are legislation and common law, both of which will be discussed briefly. The role played by Bunreacht na hÉireann is of fundamental importance, since it provides the framework within which the criminal law must operate. In addition to domestic law, criminal law in Ireland is increasingly influenced by external factors. Criminal activity has become more globalised and, as a result, efforts to combat it require co-ordinated efforts and co-operation across international borders. As a Member State of both the European Union (EU) and the Council of Europe, Ireland's criminal law is also derived, at least in part, from treaties entered into with both of these bodies.

Statute

As provided for by Art.15 of Bunreacht na hÉireann, sole legislative power is vested in the Oireachtas. This power is not unfettered and comes with the caveat that any legislation enacted must comply with constitutional requirements. An exception to this general principle is set out in Art.29.4.6° of Bunreacht na hÉireann which gives EU law primacy over domestic law in matters necessitated by Ireland's membership of the EU.

Consequently, the Oireachtas is prohibited from enacting criminal legislation which is retrospective in effect or which is unconstitutional by virtue of its incompatibility with any of the provisions of Bunreacht na hÉireann. Criminal statutes may be enacted to create entirely new offences, to codify existing common law rules, or to add to existing common law offences.

Common Law

Since the enactment of Bunreacht na hÉireann, with its prohibition on law-making by any body other than the Oireachtas, judges have not been able to declare acts to be illegal as they had been able to for centuries. Nevertheless, the common law remains a very important legal resource, in that many of the rules and principles which are employed by the courts have been created by the common law courts. The decisions of courts in other common law jurisdictions, although not binding on Irish courts, are of persuasive value. At common law, offences were categorised as treasons, felonies and misdemeanours, the first two types being the most serious, and the latter being less grave in nature. The distinction between felonies and misdemeanours was abolished in this jurisdiction by s.3 of the Criminal Law Act 1997 which replaced the category of felonies with a new classification of offences, known as arrestable offences. An arrestable offence is defined as one which carries a potential sentence of five years or more. Offences are also categorised as "indictable" or "summary". Indictable offences are tried on indictment in the Circuit, Central or Special Criminal Courts or in some cases in the District Court if the offence in question is an "either/or" offence, subject to the conditions outlined in the paragraph in Ch.3 relating to the criminal jurisdiction of the District Court. Summary offences are less serious in nature and are dealt with in the District Court.

The Impact of Bunreacht na hÉireann 1937

Bunreacht na hÉireann 1937 is the primary source of law in this jurisdiction. A number of Articles in Bunreacht na hÉireann are of particular relevance to the criminal law. The following is a brief outline of those:

Article 15.2.1° vests sole law-making power in the Oireachtas. Due to the operation of the doctrine of the separation of powers, no other body, including the judicial arm of the State, has the power to make law.

Article 15.4.1° precludes the Oireachtas from enacting any law that is repugnant to any part of Bunreacht na hÉireann.

Article 15.5.1° forbids the enactment of any legislation that is retrospective in its effect. This is in keeping with the maxim *nullum crimen sine lege, nulla poena sine lege* which translates as "no crime without law, no punishment without law".

Article 15.13 provides immunity from arrest for criminal offences except treason, felony (now abolished) and breach of the peace for any member of either House of the Oireachtas going to, coming from, or while within, the precincts of either House of the Oireachtas.

Article 26 provides for the procedure by which the President may, after consultation with the Council of State, refer a Bill to the Supreme Court for a determination as to its constitutionality. If a Bill survives a challenge under the Article, it must be signed into law by the President and is immune from further challenge.

Article 29.4.6° provides for the supremacy of EU law in respect of "laws enacted, acts done or measures adopted by the State" that are necessitated by Ireland's membership of the EU.

Article 30.1 provides for the office of the Attorney General who is the legal advisor to the Government.

Article 30.3 provides that all crimes other than summary offences shall be prosecuted in the name of the People and at the suit of the Attorney General "or some other person authorised in accordance with law to act for that purpose". Since the establishment of the office of the Director of Public Prosecutions pursuant to the provisions of the Prosecution of Offences Act 1974, the vast majority of prosecutions are taken by the Director of Public Prosecutions (the "DPP"), although there appears to be nothing to stop the Attorney General from prosecuting any non-summary offence and there are a small number of offences that may only be prosecuted by the Attorney General.

Article 34 and its subsections relate to the courts. A number of changes have been made to this Article following a referendum in 2013 which paved the way for the establishment, in October 2014, of the Court of Appeal. The statutory basis for the Court of Appeal is set out in the Court of Appeal Act 2014 which abolished the Court of Criminal Appeal.

Under Art.34.3.1° the High Court is vested with "full original jurisdiction in and power to determine all matters and questions whether of law or fact, civil or criminal." Article 34.3.2° is of particular importance in that it provides that only the High Court has jurisdiction to determine the constitutionality of any law, subject to an appeal to the Court of Appeal or the Supreme Court. Article 34.5.3° provides that a decision of the Court of Appeal may be appealed to the Supreme Court provided that the Supreme Court is satisfied that the decision involves a matter of general public importance or that the interests of justice require that the appeal be heard.

Article 35 relates to the appointment and tenure of judges.

Article 37 provides that limited powers of a judicial nature may be exercised by a person or body of persons other than a judge or a court. Criminal matters are expressly *excluded* from this, which means that no person or body of persons other than a judge or a court can determine matters of a criminal nature.

Article 38 deals with the trial of offences and provides, in subs.1, that "[n]o person shall be tried on any criminal charge save in due course of law".

Article 38.2 states that minor offences may be tried by courts of summary jurisdiction.

Article 38.3.1° declares that "[s]pecial courts may be established by law for the trial of offences in cases where it may be determined in accordance with such law that the ordinary courts are inadequate to secure the effective administration of justice, and the preservation of public peace and order". The Special Criminal Court was set up under the Offences against the State Act 1939 pursuant to the terms of this Article and its subsections.

Article 38.5 provides that "[s]ave in the case of the trial of offences under section 2, section 3 or section 4 of this Article no person shall be tried on any criminal charge without a jury". This means that summary trials (Art.38.2), trials in the Special Criminal Court (Art.38.3) and trials before Military Tribunals (Art.38.4) are not required to be held before a jury and that the trial of an accused person in these circumstances is not unconstitutional by virtue of the absence of a jury.

Articles 40–44 deal with fundamental and personal rights. Many of these are enumerated, such as personal liberty (Art.40.1) and freedom of assembly (Art.40.6.1°(ii)). Others are unenumerated but are no less significant. Examples of unenumerated personal rights include:

- Privacy—recognised in *Kennedy v Ireland* [1987] I.R. 587.
- Bodily integrity—recognised in *Ryan v Attorney General* [1965] I.R. 294.
- Free legal aid in criminal cases—recognised in *State (Healy) v Donoghue* [1976] I.R. 325.

Article 40.4 provides for the procedure known as "habeas corpus" whereby a person may question the legality of his detention.

Article 50 provides that laws in force in Saorstát Éireann immediately prior to the enactment of Bunreacht na hÉireann will be deemed to have been carried over into the law of the new State provided that they are not inconsistent with the provisions of Bunreacht na hÉireann and that they have not been repealed. Any statutory provision or rule of common law that preceded the enactment of Bunreacht na hÉireann may be challenged under Art.50, a recent example of which was the challenge to s.1(1) of the Criminal Law Amendment Act 1935, which was deemed to be unconstitutional in *C.C. v Ireland* [2006] 4 I.R. 1.

In the context of the criminal law, two important factors should be noted:

(1) Breaches of the constitutional rights of an accused person may well lead to an arrest, detention, prosecution or trial being invalid. It must be said, however, that no right is absolute and even a constitutionally protected right may have to give way to a superior right or interest on occasion. *DPP v Shaw* [1982] I.R. 1 is one such example. In this case, a confession obtained at a time when the accused was being detained unconstitutionally was nevertheless admitted into evidence on the basis that the Gardaí had breached his constitutional right to liberty in order to vindicate the right to life of a woman who had been kidnapped by the accused. Unknown to Gardaí, the woman had, in fact, been murdered by the accused. In this case, it was held that the woman's right to life took precedence over the accused's right to liberty and the evidence was allowed. The decision to admit or exclude evidence obtained as a result of breaching the constitutional rights of the accused is subject to the so-called exclusionary rule. Until recently, the Irish courts operated a relatively strict version of this rule, in accordance with the decision of the Supreme Court in *DPP v Kenny* [1990] 2 I.R. 110. The effect of *Kenny* was that courts were obliged to exclude unconstitutionally obtained evidence unless there were extraordinary excusing circumstances which mitigated in favour of its inclusion. The rule applied regardless of whether the breach was deliberate or accidental. The rule in *Kenny* was overturned and replaced by a newly formulated exclusionary rule by the Supreme Court in *DPP v J.C.* [2015] IESC 31. Following *J.C.*, the test for admissibility of evidence is as follows:

   - The admissibility of all evidence is to be established by the prosecution.
   - If the defence argues that evidence was obtained in breach of the accused person's constitutional rights, the prosecution must establish beyond reasonable doubt that the evidence had not been obtained unconstitutionally *or* that, notwithstanding any violation of constitutional rights, the evidence should be admitted.
   - Evidence obtained as a result of a "deliberate and conscious" breach of constitutional rights should be excluded unless there are exceptional circumstances which warrant its inclusion.
   - The question of whether there had been a deliberate and conscious breach of the accused person's constitutional rights requires analysis of the state of mind or the conduct of the person who gathered the evidence, as well as any other officer who was involved in the investigation and any other senior officer who was involved in the decision.

- Where the prosecution establishes that the breach of constitutional rights was not deliberate and conscious, a presumption arises in favour of excluding the evidence. In order to rebut this presumption, the prosecution must establish, with evidence, that the breach was inadvertent or that it derived from subsequent legal developments.

(2) Legislation or rules of common law can be challenged using the process known as judicial review. The net effect of a finding of unconstitutionality is that the legislation or common law rule in question is of no legal consequence. Different considerations apply depending on the vintage of the impugned law. If the legislation or rule of common law predates the enactment of Bunreacht na hÉireann, the question for the court will be whether it was "carried over" into the law of the modern Irish State—such laws do not enjoy any presumption of constitutionality, and if they are found to be repugnant to the terms of Bunreacht na hÉireann, are deemed not to have been carried over and never to have been valid in this jurisdiction. See, for example, the decision of the Supreme Court in *C.C. v Ireland* referred to above.

Where the impugned law was passed after the enactment of Bunreacht na hÉireann, it is reviewed under Art.34. Any law passed since 1937 is presumed to be constitutional. Where such a law is then found to be unconstitutional, it is declared to have been void ab initio; in other words, it was never valid. Bills are also presumed to be constitutional unless/until they are challenged under Art.26 of Bunreacht na hÉireann. Only the President may refer a Bill to the Supreme Court for a ruling as to its constitutionality and this reference may only be made following a consultation by the President with the Council of State. A Bill that survives a challenge under Art.26 is then immune from further challenge, even if constitutional rights are subsequently infringed by it. In *Re Ó Laighléis* [1960] I.R. 93, the plaintiff had been interned without trial pursuant to the provisions of the Offences Against the State (Amendment) Act 1940. He challenged the Act on the basis that it infringed his constitutional rights. However, the Act had been passed following an unsuccessful Art.26 challenge in *Re Article 26 and the Offences Against the State (Amendment) Bill, 1940* [1940] I.R. 470 and was therefore immune from further challenge. In more recent times, the Supreme Court struck down as unconstitutional s.29 of the Offences against the State Act 1939, as amended, in *Damache v DPP* [2012] 2 I.R. 266. In this case, the applicant had been suspected of involvement in a conspiracy to murder a Danish cartoonist who had depicted the Islamic prophet Muhammad in a manner which led to serious unrest in a number of Islamic countries. A search warrant was issued pursuant to s.29 by a member of An Garda Síochána who had himself directed the investigation of the offence. The applicant issued judicial review proceedings which were successful on appeal to the Supreme Court. The Supreme Court held that the section was unconstitutional because it permitted a search warrant to be issued by an individual who was not independent. This lack of independence, coupled with the fact that the search was carried out at the applicant's dwelling, were two aspects of the case that were described by Denham C.J. as being "at the kernel of the Court's decision".

The European Convention on Human Rights

Prior to the incorporation of the European Convention on Human Rights (the "Convention") into domestic law by the European Convention on Human Rights Act 2003, Ireland did have international obligations under the Convention, and was amenable to the jurisdiction of the European Court of Human Rights. This, however, did not mean that the Convention could be invoked before the Irish courts due to the fact that while the Convention was binding upon the State, it was not binding within it. Consequently, an individual who alleged that his rights under the Convention had been breached had to take his case to the European Court of Human Rights in Strasbourg in order to have the right in question vindicated.

The European Convention on Human Rights Act 2003

Having opted to incorporate the Convention into domestic law at sub-constitutional level, the legislature has ensured that the status of the Constitution remains the same. However, s.2(1) of the European Convention on Human Rights Act 2003 (the "2003 Act") provides: "In interpreting and applying any statutory provision or rule of law, a court shall, in so far as is possible, subject to the rules of law relating to such interpretation and application, do so in a manner compatible with the State's obligations under the Convention provisions." The 2003 Act requires that judicial notice must be taken of all decisions and declarations of the European Court of Human Rights and that the courts must interpret legislation "in so far as is possible" in conformity with the provisions of the Convention. This is likely to mean that the courts will continue to interpret legislation in conformity with the provisions of Bunreacht na hÉireann, even where this might mean that to do so would not be in keeping with the terms of the Convention. This will mean that applicants will still have to go to Strasbourg to let the European Court of Human Rights adjudicate on the matter. The European Court of Human Rights may only exercise its jurisdiction in cases where domestic remedies have been exhausted and an application to the European Court of Human Rights must be made within six months of the decision under challenge. The High Court may declare that a statutory provision or a rule of law violates the Convention. An appeal against the High Court's ruling lies to the Court of Appeal but neither court is empowered to strike the offending legislation or rule of law down solely on this basis but may issue a declaration to the effect that the statutory provision or rule of law is incompatible with the Convention. Where a "declaration of incompatibility" is granted, an ex gratia payment may be made by the Government to a party who has suffered loss, damage or injury as a result of the violation of the Convention where an application has been made in this regard by the aggrieved party to the Attorney General.

The only obligation imposed by the 2003 Act is that where a rule of law or statutory provision is declared by a court to be incompatible with the terms of the Convention, the Taoiseach must cause a statement to be made in both Houses of the Oireachtas to that effect. The Oireachtas is not obliged to enact legislation that will accord with the provisions of the Convention, which could mean that legislation which is deemed to be incompatible with the Convention will remain on the statute book, although it will still be open to an aggrieved individual to pursue the matter before the European Court of Human Rights. In the context of criminal law, the most important rights covered by the Convention are:

- Life (art.2);
- Freedom from torture/inhuman/degrading treatment (art.3);
- Liberty (art.5);
- Fair trial (art.6);
- Non-retrospectivity in criminal legislation (art.7);
- Freedom of expression (art.8); and
- Freedom of peaceful assembly (art.11).

The Jurisdiction of the Irish Courts in Criminal Matters

3

The District Court

The country is divided into 24 districts: the Dublin Metropolitan District, and 23 others outside Dublin. The 23 districts outside Dublin are sub-divided into numerous smaller districts, each with its own District Court. Each District Court is a court of local and limited jurisdiction and, in the context of criminal offences, is a court of summary jurisdiction. The court is presided over by a judge who sits without a jury. Article 38.2 of Bunreacht na hÉireann provides that minor offences may be tried summarily, although it is silent on the issue of what constitutes a minor offence.

In *Melling v Ó Mathghamhna* [1962] I.R. 1, the Supreme Court stated that when deciding whether an offence is minor, particular regard should be had to two factors:

(1) The severity of the punishment attracted by the offence; and
(2) The nature of the offence itself.

See also *Conroy v Attorney General* [1965] I.R. 411.

Where an offence is provided for by statute, it will indicate whether the offence is one capable of being tried summarily.

The District Court is a court of limited and summary jurisdiction and may deal with:

- (i) Cases in the District Court area in which the alleged offence was committed;
- (ii) Cases in the area where the defendant lives or carries out business;
- (iii) Cases in the area in which the defendant was arrested;
- (iv) Cases involving certain offences contained in the First Schedule to the Criminal Justice Act 1951 (as amended), provided that:
  - (1) The District Court judge accepts jurisdiction.
  - (2) The accused consents to the offence being tried summarily, bearing in mind that he will forego his right to be tried by a jury.

(3) The consent of the DPP may also be required for the summary disposal of the offence in question.

(v) Indictable offences which are triable summarily.

Indictable offences will also be sent forward by the District Court for trial upon service of the Book of Evidence.

The Circuit Court

The country is divided into eight circuits, each Circuit Court being a court of local and limited jurisdiction. The Circuit Court has jurisdiction to try all indictable offences except murder, rape, aggravated sexual assault, treason, piracy, and related offences which may only be tried before the Central Criminal Court.

In addition to its first instance jurisdiction with regard to most indictable offences, the Circuit Court has appellate jurisdiction over decisions of the District Court. An appeal against conviction in the District Court may be made to the Circuit Court. The matter is then dealt with de novo (i.e. the case is heard again from the beginning) by the Circuit Court and no appeal lies from that decision.

This court sits with a judge and jury and may deal with:

(i) Cases in the Circuit Court area in which the alleged offence was committed;
(ii) Cases in the area where the defendant lives or carries out business;
(iii) Cases in the area in which the defendant was arrested;
(iv) Cases which are transferred from one part of a circuit to another. Where the DDP or the accused applies for a transfer of a case, the Circuit Court judge may, if satisfied that it would be manifestly unfair not to do so, transfer a trial from the Circuit Court sitting outside Dublin to the Dublin Circuit Court.

The High Court/The Central Criminal Court

Article 34.3.1° of Bunreacht na hÉireann provides that the High Court has "full original jurisdiction in and power to determine all matters and questions whether of law or fact, civil or criminal."

The High Court, when exercising its criminal jurisdiction, is known as the Central Criminal Court. The court is presided over by a judge sitting with a jury. The court deals with those criminal offences which are outside the jurisdiction of the Circuit Court. These are:

- Murder, attempted murder and conspiracy to murder;
- Treason—defined in Art.39 of Bunreacht na hÉireann and provided for by the Treason Act 1939;
- Piracy;
- Certain offences under the Offences against the State Acts 1939–1998;
- Rape, aggravated sexual assault and attempted aggravated sexual assault;
- Offences under the Genocide Act 1973, the Geneva Conventions Act 1962 and the Criminal Justice (United Nations Convention against Torture) Act 2000;
- Certain offences under the Competition Act 2002.

The High Court has jurisdiction to deal with questions sent to it on a "case stated" basis. Where the District Court refers a matter to the High Court while a case is ongoing, the procedure is referred to as a "consultative case stated".

The Special Criminal Court

This court was set up under Pt V of the Offences against the State Act 1939 and is one of the constitutionally permissible instances in which an accused person may be tried without a jury. The constitutional basis for the court is to be found in Art.38.3.1°, which provides that: "Special Courts may be established by law for the trial of offences in cases where it may be determined in accordance with such law that the ordinary courts are inadequate to secure the effective administration of justice, and the preservation of public peace and order." The Special Criminal Court sits with three judges and no jury.

Offences contained in the Schedule to the Offences against the State Act 1939 are dealt with by the court, as are offences in respect of which the DPP has issued a certificate declaring that, in her opinion, the ordinary courts are inadequate to secure the administration of justice. The Criminal Justice (Amendment) Act 2009 creates a number of new offences pertaining to criminal organisations. The jurisdiction of the Special Criminal Court has been extended to include these offences. In effect, therefore, any serious offence can come before the Special Criminal Court, even those which have no "subversive" element. See, for example, *DPP v Quilligan* [1986] I.R. 495. In *Savage v DPP* [1982] I.L.R.M. 385, the court stated that the decisions of the DPP are generally not amenable to judicial review.

THE COURT OF APPEAL

The Court of Appeal was established in 2014, following a referendum the previous year. In the hierarchy of the Irish courts system, the Court of Appeal is located between the High Court and the Supreme Court. The court sits with three judges and exercises the appellate jurisdiction formerly exercised by the Court of Criminal Appeal, which was abolished by the Court of Appeal Act 2014. The Court of Appeal can hear appeals against convictions from the Circuit, Central and Special Criminal Courts. An appeal is heard on the basis that the trial judge has granted leave to appeal or, where such leave to appeal has been refused, the Court of Appeal may itself grant leave to appeal. An appeal against conviction is premised on the assertion that the trial judge either erred in law or the trial was unsatisfactory for some other reason.

In cases involving appeals against conviction, the Court of Appeal can either:

(a) affirm the conviction;
(b) allow the appeal and order a re-trial; or
(c) allow the appeal and enter an acquittal.

The Court of Appeal also hears appeals against sentence. These appeals can be brought by either the convicted person, on the basis that the sentence is too harsh, or by the prosecution, who may appeal against the leniency of the sentence. In either case, the court looks at whether the sentence imposed deviated from the range of sentences usually handed down for that particular offence with regard to the circumstances of the convicted person and of the offence itself.

Both these types of appeal are dealt with on the basis of the transcripts from the trial courts. In cases in which a miscarriage of justice is alleged due to the existence of a newly discovered fact, the court will hear this new evidence. If the court is satisfied that a miscarriage of justice has taken place, it may issue a certificate to that effect which will then result in a payment of compensation to the aggrieved party. In *DPP v Pringle* [1997] 2 I.R. 225, it was held that there was no exhaustive definition of "miscarriage of justice" and that, furthermore, no such definition should be attempted. In *DPP v Wall* [2005] IECCA 140, the court gave some examples of situations which could amount to miscarriages of justice, but said that the list was not definitive. These examples include: where the innocence of the accused is established; where the prosecution ought not to have been pursued due to a lack of credible evidence; where the trial was conducted in a manner inconsistent with judicial or constitutional procedure; and where, as occurred in *DPP v Shortt (No.2)* [2002] 2 I.R. 696, there had been a grave defect in the administration of justice caused by the agents of the State.

The Court of Appeal was also granted jurisdiction by the Court of Appeal Act 2014 to deal with appeals brought by the DPP on a question of law arising out of trials which resulted in an acquittal. These cases would previously have been within the jurisdiction of the Supreme Court.

The Supreme Court

The Supreme Court is a court of appellate jurisdiction and has original jurisdiction in only two matters. The appellate jurisdiction of the Supreme Court was changed with the establishment of the Court of Appeal. A decision of the Court of Appeal may be appealed to the Supreme Court if the Supreme Court is satisfied that the matter is one of general public importance or that the interests of justice require that the appeal be heard. In exceptional circumstances, a decision of the High Court may be appealed directly to the Supreme Court by way of what is commonly called a "leap-frog appeal". This will only be possible where the Supreme Court is satisfied, as a precondition to hearing the appeal, that the decision is one of general public importance and/or that it is in the interests of justice.

Questions of law which would previously have been referred from the Circuit Court to the Supreme Court on a "case stated" basis are now within the jurisdiction of the Court of Appeal.

The original jurisdiction of the Supreme Court has not been altered by the establishment of the Court of Appeal. This jurisdiction arises in two situations: first, the determination, pursuant to Art.12 of Bunreacht na hÉireann, as to whether the President has become permanently incapacitated; and, secondly, the reference made by the President under Art.26 of Bunreacht na hÉireann for a determination as to the constitutionality of a Bill or part thereof.

The composition of the court varies depending on the type of proceedings but in general, the court comprises three or five judges. Additionally, since the Supreme Court is not a trial court, proceedings are based on transcripts and documentation which had been before the trial court.

KEY CASES AND LEGISLATION

Melling v Ó Mathghamhna [1962] I.R. 1—Factors determining whether an offence is minor.

DPP v J.C. [2015] IESC 31—New test set out by the Supreme Court governing the admissibility of unconstitutionally obtained evidence.

Court of Appeal Act 2014—Establishes the Court of Appeal on a statutory footing.

Arrest and Detention

Article 40.4.1° of Bunreacht na hÉireann provides that "[n]o citizen shall be deprived of his personal liberty save in accordance with law". Subsequent subsections of the Article lay out the procedure known as "habeas corpus", which is an investigation into the legality of detention. This chapter sets out the law relating to the arrest and detention of a suspect and the statutory provisions which prescribe the maximum duration of detention periods. The habeas corpus procedure is also briefly outlined.

ARREST

An arrest, at common law, was defined by O'Higgins C.J. in *DPP v Walsh* [1980] I.R. 294 as being, "the actual or notional seizure of a person for the purpose of imprisonment".

In *DPP v McCreesh* [1992] 2 I.R. 239, the Supreme Court defined an arrest in the following terms:

> "An arrest consists in or involves the seizure or touching of a person's body accompanied by a form of words which indicate to that person that he is under restraint. Whilst the older cases held that words alone would not suffice to constitute an arrest, nowadays words alone may amount to an arrest, if, in the circumstances they are calculated to bring, and do bring, to the person's notice that he is under restraint and he submitted to the compulsion."

A person may generally only be arrested for the purpose of bringing him before a court to be charged with an offence. It is essential that the person is told the true reason for his arrest and the fact that he is under arrest must be clearly communicated to him. Numerous statutes contain powers of arrest for specified offences and a general power of arrest is set out in s.4 of the Criminal Law Act 1997 (the "1997 Act"). Under s.4 of the 1997 Act, there must be a reasonable suspicion that the suspect is committing or has committed an arrestable offence.

An arrest may be carried out by any person who has reasonable cause to believe that an arrestable offence has been committed or is being committed by the suspect *and* where that person has reasonable cause to believe that the suspect could, or would attempt to, avoid being arrested by An Garda Síochána. An arrestable offence is defined in the 1997 Act as one which carries a maximum sentence of five years' imprisonment or more. This is commonly referred to as a "citizen's arrest", which had been permitted under common law. It is now, however, provided for by s.4 of the 1997 Act. In these circumstances, the suspect must be handed over to An Garda Síochána without delay.

Members of An Garda Síochána, unsurprisingly, have wider powers of arrest and may arrest, without warrant, any person whom the member believes, with reasonable cause, has committed an arrestable offence. Additional powers of arrest are granted to An Garda Síochána in respect of many statutory offences, such as those provided for by the Road Traffic Acts. The absence of reasonable suspicion that an arrestable offence has been committed will render the arrest invalid and any detention pursuant to that arrest, unlawful. In *State (Trimbole) v Governor of Mountjoy Prison* [1985] I.R. 306, an arrest was carried out in the absence of any reasonable cause to believe an offence had been committed. Gardaí arrested the individual for the sole purpose of detaining him pending the arrival of an extradition warrant. Due to the fact that there was no other reason to arrest him, his release was ordered on the grounds that his arrest was unlawful.

Members of An Garda Síochána may also, pursuant to s.6 of the 1997 Act, enter any premises for the purpose of arresting a suspect on foot of a warrant or order of committal. This permission extends to entry by An Garda Síochána into a dwelling, and reasonable force may be used to carry out the arrest, if necessary. The person whose arrest is sought must be on the premises or the member must have reasonable cause to believe that he is on the premises. Where there is no arrest warrant, s.6(2) of the 1997 Act provides that a member of An Garda Síochána may only enter a dwelling with the consent of the occupier or other person who appears to the member to be in charge of the dwelling *and* provided that one of the following criteria is met:

(a) The person to be arrested has been observed within the dwelling or entering the dwelling by the arresting officer or another member of An Garda Síochána;
(b) The arresting officer has reasonable grounds for believing that the person to be arrested will abscond in order to avoid justice or otherwise seek to obstruct the course of justice before an arrest warrant can be obtained;
(c) The arresting officer has reasonable cause to suspect that an arrestable offence would be committed by the person before an arrest warrant can be obtained;
(d) The person to be arrested ordinarily resides in the dwelling.

Once arrested, the suspect must be brought before the District Court to be charged with the offence, at the earliest practicable opportunity, even if this means that a special sitting of the District Court must be arranged. An exception to this occurs where the suspect is arrested after 5pm. In these situations, it is permissible to hold that person overnight until the court sits the following morning.

There is no general power of arrest for questioning. However, there are a number of statutory provisions which set out the maximum possible periods for which a suspect may be detained in custody. Once these periods have expired, the suspect must be either charged or released. The statutory detention periods are as follows:

(1) Although s.4 of the Criminal Justice Act 1984 (as amended) does not contain a power of arrest, it provides for the detention of a suspect after arrest. Under s.4, a suspect may be detained for questioning for an initial period of six hours. This initial period may be extended by another six hours by a Garda of the rank of Superintendent or higher. A further extension of 12 hours is permissible where directed by a Garda not below the rank of Chief Superintendent. The member authorising the extended periods of detention must have reasonable grounds for believing that the continued detention of the suspect is required for the proper investigation of the offence and not merely for questioning. The maximum permissible period of detention under s.4 (as amended) is 24 hours. The detention periods permitted under s.4 apply also to suspects who are arrested under s.42 of the Criminal Justice Act 1999 (as amended). Section 42 permits the arrest of prisoners in connection with the investigation of an offence other than the offence(s) for which the suspect is imprisoned. The arrest of the prisoner must be authorised by a District Court judge.

(2) Section 30 of the Offences against the State Act 1939 (as amended) permits the detention of a person arrested on suspicion of an offence "scheduled" to that Act for an initial period of 24 hours. A further period of 24 hours may be granted with the consent of a member of the Gardaí of the rank of Chief Superintendent or higher. Another period of 24 hours may be granted by a District Court judge. The maximum permissible period of detention under s.30 is therefore 72 hours. The constitutionality of s.30 was upheld by the Supreme Court in *DPP v Quilligan* [1986] I.R. 495.

(3) Section 2 of the Criminal Justice (Drug Trafficking) Act 1996 allows for a suspect to be detained for an initial period of six hours. Further extensions may be granted as follows:

- A further period of 18 hours may be granted with the consent of a Chief Superintendent.
- Another 24-hour period may subsequently be granted, again with the consent of a Chief Superintendent.
- A further period of 72 hours may be granted where a District or Circuit Court judge consents.
- Finally, another period of 48 hours may be granted with the consent of a District or Circuit Court judge. The maximum period of detention under the 1996 Act is 168 hours/seven days.

(4) Section 50 of the Criminal Justice Act 2007 also permits the detention of a suspect for up to 168 hours/seven days. The initial period permitted under the 2007 Act is six hours. This period may be extended for a further 18 hours on the authorisation of a Superintendent. A second period of extension of up to 24 hours may be granted on the authorisation of a Chief Superintendent. Thereafter, provision is made for applications for two further extensions. These may only be granted on application to the District Court or the Circuit Court. The first extension is for a period not exceeding 72 hours and the second period cannot exceed 48 hours.

Rights on Arrest and During Detention

(1) A suspect has the right to remain silent and to be made aware of that right. This right is seen as a corollary of the right to communicate recognised in *Attorney General v Paperlink* [1984] I.L.R.M. 373 and that of freedom of expression as provided for by Art.40.6.1°(i) of Bunreacht na hÉireann. The right to remain silent was held to be a constitutional right by the Supreme Court in *Heaney v Ireland* [1996] 1 I.R. 580.

(2) A suspect must be told why he is being arrested—*DPP v Walsh* [1980] I.R. 294. This does not necessarily mean that the precise provision of the Act in question must be cited to the suspect, but he must be given the true reason for his arrest.

(3) A suspect has the right to legal aid if he cannot afford legal representation —*State (Healy) v Donoghue* [1976] I.R. 325.

(4) A suspect has the right to consult with a lawyer and failure by the Gardaí to allow for this may render the suspect's detention unlawful. In *DPP v Healy* [1990] I.L.R.M. 313, the Supreme Court held that this was a fundamental constitutional right. This is not an absolute right and extends only as far as "reasonable access" to a solicitor—*DPP v Buck* [2002]

2 I.R. 268.There is no general right to be informed of the right to a solicitor although, under s.5 of the Criminal Justice Act 1984, a person arrested pursuant to certain statutory provisions must be informed of his right to access a lawyer. The right to consult with a solicitor *prior* to questioning was held to be a constitutional right under Art.38.1 by the Supreme Court in joined cases *DPP v Gormley*; *DPP v White* [2014] 2 I.R. 591. However, the Supreme Court held that this right did not extend to access to a lawyer prior to the taking of non-invasive forensic samples from a suspect. The rationale for this distinction was that evidence given by a suspect during questioning could be affected by the legal advice obtained from his lawyer whereas evidence obtained from forensic samples could not be and a lawyer cannot advise a client to refuse to comply with a lawful request for a sample. There is also no right to have a lawyer present *during* interrogation. This was held in *DPP v Pringle* [1981] 2 Frewen 57 and in *DPP v Doyle* [2017] IESC 1 where the Supreme Court held that the constitutional right to a fair trial includes the right of access to a solicitor but that this right does not extend to having a lawyer present during questioning.

(5) A suspect has the right to food, rest, medical treatment, and access to the courts.

Prior to the Supreme Court's ruling in *DPP v J.C.*, evidence obtained in breach of an accused person's constitutional rights was generally inadmissible under the exclusionary rule as set out in *DPP v Kenny* [1990] 2 I.R. 110. The Supreme Court in *J.C.* set out a new test to be applied to such evidence. Accordingly, it should be borne in mind that it is now likely that evidence which would have been excluded under *Kenny* will now be admitted.

Habeas Corpus

A person who wishes to question the validity of his detention may invoke the procedure known as habeas corpus. This procedure involves an inquiry under Art.40.4.2° of Bunreacht na hÉireann and involves an application to the High Court or any judge thereof, by the person detained or by someone on his behalf, for a conditional order compelling the person causing the detention to produce the detainee before the court and to provide the court with justification for the detention. Under the provisions of Bunreacht na hÉireann, the matter must be looked into "forthwith". The court must order the release of the detainee if it is not satisfied that the detention is in accordance with the law.

KEY CASES

DPP v Walsh [1980] I.R. 294 and *DPP v McCreesh* [1992] I.L.R.M. 239—Definitions of "arrest".

DPP v Walsh [1980] I.R. 294—Suspect must be told why he is being arrested.

State (Trimbole) v Governor of Mountjoy Prison [1985] I.R. 306—Absence of reasonable grounds renders arrest and subsequent detention invalid.

DPP v Doyle [2017] IESC 1—Constitutional right of access to legal advice does not extend to having a solicitor present during questioning.

Bail

5

Article 40.4.1° of Bunreacht na hÉireann states that "[n]o citizen shall be deprived of his personal liberty save in accordance with law." The issue of bail arises in two situations. The first of these is where an accused person has been charged with an offence and wishes to be released on bail pending the date of his trial. The second occurs where the accused, having been convicted, wishes to appeal against either his conviction or the sentence imposed by the court and applies to be released on bail until the hearing of his appeal. For the purposes of this chapter, the issue of bail will be dealt with in the context of the former of the two situations, this being the more usual of the two.

Essentially, bail is a form of conditional release, the main condition being that the accused person will turn up to face trial. Bail is granted upon the accused person entering into a recognisance, with or without sureties. What this means is that the accused person agrees to abide by whatever conditions the court may impose, and crucially, that he will show up to face trial. Breach of any bail conditions or failure to attend for his trial by the accused will lead to the issuing of a bench warrant for his arrest and the forfeiture of whatever sum of money has been lodged, either by the accused person himself or by a third party on his behalf. He may also be arrested without warrant. The main issue that arises in the context of bail is that of the valid grounds upon which bail may be refused. In addition to any impact on the accused person's constitutional rights, the refusal of bail has wide-reaching and very serious repercussions for the accused person in a number of respects. The loss of liberty brings with it loss of contact with family and community. It also takes the accused person out of the workplace, with the consequent impact on earnings. In addition, an accused person who is remanded in custody will find it more difficult to adequately prepare his defence. Whilst a large number of offences are committed by defendants whilst on bail, the law provides for harsher penalties upon conviction for these individuals. A person who has been refused bail and is subsequently acquitted, whether at his trial or on appeal, has no redress available to him. It must be borne in mind that at the bail application stage, the accused person has not yet been tried for the offence in question, much less convicted of it, and that unless/until he is convicted, he is entitled under the terms of Bunreacht na hÉireann to the presumption of innocence.

Jurisdiction to Grant Bail

Jurisdiction to grant bail is provided by s.31 of the Criminal Procedure Act 1967, as amended by the Criminal Justice (Miscellaneous Provisions) Act 1997 and by the Criminal Justice Act 2007. This procedure is known as "station bail". The Sergeant/Member in charge of a Garda station may, "if he considers it prudent to do so and no warrant directing the detention of that person is in force, release him on bail and for that purpose take from him a recognisance, with or without sureties, for his due appearance before the District Court at the appropriate time and place".

The jurisdiction of the District Court to grant bail is provided by s.28 of the Criminal Procedure Act 1967, as amended by the Bail Act 1997 and by the Criminal Justice Act 2007. The District Court is obliged to admit an accused person to bail provided that the case is one in which bail should be granted. The decision of the District Court may be appealed to the High Court, which also has jurisdiction to grant bail at first instance. In the case of certain offences, such as murder, piracy and treason, bail may only be granted on application to the High Court.

Admission to bail usually involves the accused and his sureties acknowledging that they are liable to forfeit a sum of money if bail conditions are disobeyed.

Valid Grounds for Refusal of Bail

The traditional view had been that if there was a possibility that the accused would commit another offence while on bail, the court would be entitled to take this into account when deciding whether to grant bail. The criteria governing the granting or refusal of bail were laid down by Hanna J. in *State v Purcell* [1926] I.R. 207. These were:

(a) The seriousness of the charge faced by the accused.
(b) The severity of the punishment imposed by law.
(c) The strength of the case against the accused.
(d) The prospect of a reasonably speedy trial.
(e) The opposition of the Attorney General.

In *Attorney General v Duffy* [1942] I.R. 529, Hanna J. added another criterion to the list, which was that if there was evidence that the accused was likely to interfere with the course of justice, the court would be entitled to consider this as a material ground for bail being refused.

The Supreme Court endorsed the criteria set down by Hanna J. in *Purcell* and *Duffy* in *People (Attorney General) v Crosbie* [1966] I.R. 426, where Ó Dálaigh C.J. summed up the position of bail in the following terms:

> "These applicants are charged with non-capital murder and counsel for the Attorney General has given an unqualified 'no' in answer to the Court's question, 'is it apprehended that the applicants will abscond if bailed?' Nor, moreover is it apprehended that there will be any interference with witnesses. In these circumstances it is the Court's duty to admit these untried prisoners to bail."

Ó Dálaigh C.J. also said that the only criterion or consideration for the court was whether the accused would abscond before trial or interfere with witnesses. The power to refuse bail on the basis that the accused might commit further offences was not included.

The following year, the Supreme Court revisited the issue of bail in *People (Attorney General) v O'Callaghan* [1966] I.R. 501. In this case, a bail motion had been refused in the High Court, where Murnaghan J. set out, without reference to either *Purcell* or *Duffy*, a new and more extensive set of "matters which may be, and should be where appropriate, taken into account by the Court in considering whether or not it is likely that the prisoner may evade justice".

Murnaghan J. then stated that the following were issues to which the court was entitled to have regard:

(1) The nature of the accusation/the seriousness of the charge. The heavier the charge, the greater the chance that the accused would not appear to face it;
(2) The nature of the evidence in support of the charge. The more cogent the evidence, the greater the chance of conviction and consequently, the greater the likelihood that the prisoner would try to evade justice;
(3) The likely sentence on conviction—in this instance, it was felt that the heavier the potential sentence, the more likely it would be that the prisoner would try to avoid it. The accused's previous record has a bearing on the probable sentence;
(4) The likelihood of more offences being committed while the accused was on bail. It was felt that a prisoner facing a long sentence would have nothing much to lose by committing further offences;
(5) The possibility of the disposal of illegally acquired property;
(6) The possibility of interference with witnesses and/or jurors;
(7) Failure to answer bail on a previous occasion;
(8) The fact that the prisoner was caught "red-handed";

(9) The objection of the Attorney General and/or the police authorities;
(10) The substance/reliability of the bailsmen offered;
(11) The possibility of a speedy trial.

It was also suggested that bail might be refused in order to protect the prisoner.

On appeal to the Supreme Court, Walsh J. recognised that grounds 1, 2, 3, 5, 6, 7 and 8 were acceptable, but with certain reservations. The remaining grounds were deemed not to be so. In particular, ground number 4—the likelihood of the commission of further offences while on bail—was held to be a matter which was in the view of the learned judge "quite unacceptable". He stated that, "this is a form of preventative justice which has no place in our legal system and is quite alien to the true purpose of bail".

The Supreme Court held that certain factors would be relevant in ascertaining the likelihood that the accused person would attempt to evade justice. These are as follows:

(1) The seriousness of the charge;
(2) The nature of the evidence of the accused;
(3) The likely sentence upon conviction;
(4) The likelihood that unlawfully acquired property would be disposed of/destroyed;
(5) Interference with witnesses/jurors;
(6) Previous failure to answer to bail;
(7) Whether the accused had been caught red-handed;
(8) The objections of the Attorney General/Gardaí;
(9) The reliability/substance of the bailsmen;
(10) The likelihood of a speedy trial.

It can be seen that most of these criteria can be categorised into two broad groups, namely the evasion of justice and interference with the trial. The Supreme Court rejected the argument that the commission of further offences in the event of bail being granted was a valid ground upon which bail could be refused.

In an attempt to deal with the situation, s.11 of the Criminal Justice Act 1984 provides for the imposition of mandatory consecutive sentences in respect of offences committed while the accused person was on bail.

In *Ryan v DPP* [1989] I.R. 399, an argument that bail could be refused in order to prevent the commission of further offences was similarly rejected. Here, it had been argued that the rights of those citizens who might become victims of crime should be taken into consideration when deciding whether or not to grant bail to an accused person. The argument was rejected because, according to Finlay C.J., "the criminalising of mere intent has usually been the badge of an oppressive or unjust legal system".

This remained the position until the passing of the 16th Amendment to Bunreacht na hÉireann following the bail referendum in 1996. Article 40.4.6° of Bunreacht na hÉireann now provides that "[p]rovision may be made by law for the refusal of bail by a court to a person charged with a serious offence where it is reasonably considered necessary to prevent the commission of a serious offence by that person."

The Bail Act 1997

The Bail Act 1997 (the "1997 Act"), in s.1(2), defines "serious offence" as any crime contained in the Schedule to the 1997 Act which attracts a possible custodial sentence of five years or more for an accused person of full capacity and with no previous convictions. The court is to have regard to factors outlined in s.2(2) when deciding whether bail ought to be denied. These are broadly similar to the list of grounds laid down in *O'Callaghan*, and in addition, the court may have regard to the fact that the accused person is addicted to a controlled substance. Effectively, therefore, the valid grounds upon which bail may be refused are those grounds which were upheld in *O'Callaghan*, together with the new grounds set out in the 1997 Act.

Refusal of Bail

Section 2 of the 1997 Act provides that "where an application for bail is made by a person charged with a serious offence", bail may be refused if the court is satisfied that such refusal is "reasonably considered necessary to prevent the commission of a serious offence". For bail to be refused under s.2 of the 1997 Act, the accused must be charged with a serious offence, as defined in s.1 and contained in the Schedule to the 1997 Act. Further offences have been appended to the Schedule by other pieces of legislation. In addition, the apprehended offence must also be a serious offence, although it is not required that the court be satisfied that the apprehended offence is a specific offence. Clearly though, s.2 cannot be invoked in the case of a person charged with a serious offence where the apprehended offence is of a minor nature. The court must also be satisfied that the refusal of bail is "reasonably considered necessary". The 1997 Act requires that in determining the issue of bail, the court *must* have regard to the following factors:

(1) The nature and gravity of the offence with which the accused is charged and the punishment likely to be imposed if he is convicted;
(2) The nature and gravity of the apprehended offence and the likely punishment;
(3) Previous convictions (if any) of the accused;
(4) Previous convictions (if any) in respect of offences committed whilst on bail;
(5) The nature and strength of the evidence against the accused;
(6) Any other offence with which the accused is charged and in respect of which he is awaiting trial.

Section 2 of the 1997 Act was amended by the Criminal Justice (Burglary of Dwellings) Act 2015 which applies when a court is deciding whether it is "reasonably considered necessary" to refuse bail to an adult accused with burglary or aggravated burglary in a dwelling. The 2015 Act sets out a list of circumstances which, if satisfied, oblige the court to consider the presence of these circumstances as evidence that the accused is likely to commit a domestic burglary if granted bail. These circumstances arise where a person has been convicted in the five years prior to the bail application of an offence under s.12 or s.13 of the Criminal Justice (Theft and Fraud Offences) Act 2001, committed in a dwelling *and*:

- has been convicted of at least two domestic burglaries committed in the period beginning six months before and ending six months after the alleged commission of the offence for which he is seeking bail; or
- has been charged with and is awaiting trial for at least two other domestic burglaries in that same period; or
- has been convicted of at least one domestic burglary and charged with at least one domestic burglary in the same period.

The stated purpose of this amendment to the 1997 Act is to tackle recidivist offenders although it is possible to deny bail on this ground to a person who has one conviction in the previous five years and who has been charged, but not yet convicted, of a further offence alleged to have been committed in the period starting six months prior and ending six months after the alleged commission of the offence for which bail is being sought.

The court is entitled to have regard to any other factors in addition to those listed above, including whether the accused is addicted to any controlled drug covered by the Misuse of Drugs Act 1977. In *Maguire v DPP* [2004] 3 I.R. 241, the Supreme Court rejected the argument that a court, in deciding whether to grant bail, was confined to a consideration of the factors set out in s.2 of the 1997 Act to the exclusion of other factors relevant to the application.

If bail is refused under s.2(1) of the 1997 Act, provision is made in s.3 for the right of the accused to have the application for bail renewed if his trial has not commenced within four months.

Section 4 of the 1997 Act provides that where bail is being opposed under s.2, the accused's previous convictions cannot be referred to in a way that would prejudice the accused's right to a fair trial.

Section 5 of the 1997 Act relates to recognisances and provides that where bail is granted subject to recognisances, the accused person will not be released on bail until at least one-third of the amount of the recognisance is paid into court.

Section 6 provides for conditions which the court may impose on bail. Failure on the part of the accused to comply with these will lead to the re-arrest of the accused and forfeiture of any recognisances.

Sentencing

Prior to the passing of the Criminal Justice Act 1984 (the "1984 Act"), judges were entitled to exercise discretion with regard to imposing the appropriate penalties in respect of offences committed while the accused had been on bail.

Section 11(1) of the 1984 Act curbed this discretion somewhat by requiring the judge to impose a consecutive sentence for such offences. Section 11(1) of the 1984 Act, as substituted by s.22 of the Criminal Justice Act 2007, provides as follows:

> "Any sentence of imprisonment passed on a person for an offence—
> (a) committed while on bail, whether committed before or after the commencement of section 22 of the Criminal Justice Act 2007, or
> (b) committed after such commencement while the person is unlawfully at large after the issue of a warrant for his or her arrest for non-compliance with a condition of the recognisance concerned,
>
> shall be consecutive on any sentence passed on him or her for a previous offence or, if he or she is sentenced in respect of two or more previous offences, on the sentence last due to expire, so however that, where two or more consecutive sentences as required by this section are passed by the District Court, the aggregate term of imprisonment in respect of those consecutive sentences shall not exceed 2 years."

Section 11 of the 1984 Act was also amended by s.10 of the 1997 Act. The effect of this amendment is that whereas s.11 of the 1984 Act required that mandatory consecutive sentences be imposed upon conviction for offences committed whilst on bail, s.10 of the 1997 Act additionally requires that a greater sentence be imposed in respect of such offences unless the offence is one which is punishable by a sentence of life imprisonment or where the court is satisfied that there are exceptional circumstances which justify it not doing so.

It might be argued, however, that both sections are rendered toothless by their failure to prevent the judge from suspending the second (or even the first) of the sentences. The Irish judiciary has traditionally been quite hostile to any intrusion by the legislature into its discretionary powers with regard to sentencing.

In *People (DPP) v Healy* [1989] 3 Frewen 188, the applicant was charged with a series of offences and was convicted and sentenced to concurrent terms of eight years on each count. He had been on bail when the offences were committed. When passing sentence, the judge took the total number of years which would be served into account and adjusted the sentence downwards. The applicant appealed against the severity of the sentence, arguing that he had received a much harsher punishment than his co-accused. During the appeal, counsel for the DPP submitted that the judge should disregard the duration of the sentence imposed for a previous offence and fix a sentence appropriate to the second crime—and not follow the English practice of taking account of the total number of years to be served. The Court of Criminal Appeal dismissed the application, holding that the sentence imposed on the accused was not excessive or founded on any error of principle, and that the comparison with the sentence handed down to the co-accused was inappropriate.

The question of suspending one of the consecutive sentences was raised in *DPP v Dennigan* [1980] 3 Frewen 253, in which case the accused pleaded guilty to a series of offences contained in two bills of indictment—the second of which referred to offences allegedly committed whilst the accused was on bail in respect of the charges contained in the first bill.

With regard to the first set of charges, the accused was convicted and sentenced to concurrent sentences, the longest of which was a term of four years. He was then sentenced to five years for the second list of offences, to run concurrently with the first term. Counsel pleaded for leniency on his behalf due to personal circumstances, and said that the court could suspend one of the sentences on the basis that nothing in the 1984 Act prevented the judge from doing so. The court held that it could suspend a consecutive sentence, but that in this case, the offences committed were too serious. The court did, however, reduce each sentence due to the fact that not enough consideration had been given to the accused's personal circumstances.

Hearsay Evidence

Following the decision of the Supreme Court in *DPP v McGinley* [1998] 2 I.L.R.M. 233, hearsay evidence may be adduced in support of an objection to bail under s.2 of the 1997 Act. The High Court had denied bail in that case on the basis of hearsay evidence from a member of the Gardaí. On appeal, the Supreme Court held that the accused retained the right to fair procedures, which included the right to test the evidence against him through cross-examination *unless* special factors existed which could justify the use of hearsay evidence. This was affirmed by the Supreme Court in *DPP v McLoughlin* [2010] 1 I.R. 590 where Denham J. (as she then was) stated:

> "There can be no question of hearsay being admitted in all bail applications as such. I wish to say that the rule against hearsay is of full force and effect in bail applications and that the exceptions which permit its use are just that: rare exceptions."

No provision is made in the 1997 Act or elsewhere for the compensation of an accused person who has been denied bail and who is subsequently acquitted. Finally, bail should not be set at such a high amount as to equate to a de facto refusal of bail.

Further Restrictions on Bail

Despite there being a constitutional presumption in favour of granting bail, numerous statutory incursions into that right have been enacted. In *DPP v McLoughlin* [2010] 1 I.R. 590, Hardiman J. commented that it was "virtually impossible to do justice to the increased numbers and increased complexity of bail applications in the very long lists which are currently the norm". At the time of writing, further statutory changes to the bail laws are planned in the Bail (Amendment) Bill 2016 which was introduced in Dáil Éireann in December 2016. This Bill proposes, inter alia, to increase the number of reasons for which bail may be refused and the number of conditions which may be attached to bail.

The Criminal Justice Act 2006 created a number of specific offences relating to the activities of criminal organisations. The 2006 Act refers to "serious offences" committed by, or in conjunction with, criminal organisations and for the purposes of that Act, a "serious offence" is defined as one which attracts a sentence of four years or more. The 2006 Act also adds three "organised crime" offences to the list of offences contained in the Criminal Procedure Act 1967, with the effect that bail in respect of those offences may only be granted on application to the High Court. Of significance to this issue is the decision of the Supreme Court in *McDonagh v Governor of Cloverhill Prison* [2005] 1 I.R. 394, where it was held that bail could not be refused solely on the basis that the applicant was involved in an ongoing feud.

Part 2 of the Criminal Justice Act 2007 (the "2007 Act") amends the law on bail in a number of respects. First, s.6 of the 2007 Act requires that an applicant for bail who is charged with a serious offence must furnish the prosecution with a statement containing details of any previous convictions and whether any of these convictions related to offences committed whilst on bail. Secondly, the statement must also set out any previous applications for bail made by the applicant and the grounds upon which such application(s) were based. Finally, the statement must contain specific information relating to the applicant's source of income, including details of any property owned by the applicant which is valued in excess of €3,000.

Section 7 of the 2007 Act provides that where the State objects to the granting of bail, the opinion evidence of a Garda holding the rank of Chief Superintendent or higher that bail should not be granted in order to prevent the commission of a further serious offence, may be admitted into evidence.

As previously stated, bail is a form of conditional release pending trial or appeal. The conditions to be attached to bail are determined by the court. Section 11 of the 2007 Act provides that among the conditions which may be imposed on the accused is that he wears an electronic monitoring device for the purpose of establishing his compliance, or non-compliance as the case may be, with the conditions of his bail. Section 11 applies to accused persons who are charged with a serious offence or those who are appealing against a custodial sentence imposed by the District Court. The commencement of this section is one of the measures proposed in the Bail (Amendment) Bill 2016 currently before Dáil Éireann.

Section 19 of the 2007 Act also provides that the DPP may appeal against the decision of the District Court to grant bail. The appeal lies to the High Court and was previously only available to an accused person who had been denied bail in the District Court.

KEY CASES AND LEGISLATION

People (Attorney General) v O'Callaghan [1966] I.R. 501 and s.2 of the Bail Act 1997 (as amended)—Valid grounds for refusal of bail.

Maguire v DPP [2004] 3 I.R. 241—Court may have regard to any relevant factors in determining the issue of bail.

Bail (Amendment) Bill 2016—if/when enacted will add to the number of reasons for which bail may be refused and the number of conditions which may be attached to bail.

6 Types of Punishment

Upon conviction for a criminal offence, the court must then determine the nature and severity of the punishment to be imposed. In deciding this, the court will have regard to certain factors, both aggravating and mitigating, and will adjust the sentence accordingly. Aggravating factors include the level of violence used, previous convictions, and where there was a serious impact on the victim. Mitigating factors include co-operation with the Gardaí, the personal circumstances of the accused, and where the accused entered a plea of guilty, particularly at an early stage. The sentencing court must also have regard to the severity of the offence and to the personal circumstances of the offender. A sentence may be custodial or non-custodial in nature. The imposition of a criminal sanction is a judicial function but the administration of that sentence is a matter for the Executive. Criminal sanctions may also be categorised as either primary or secondary punishment. Primary punishment is punitive in nature, whereas secondary punishment can be viewed as something that is ancillary or consequential to the primary sanction. An example of a secondary punishment occurs where an offender is disqualified from an activity as a result of his conviction.

Imprisonment

Custodial sentences may be mandatory or discretionary. A mandatory sentence is one which the court must impose, and the best example of this is the mandatory life sentence which must be handed down for murder. There is no judicial discretion in this case and, accordingly, mitigating or aggravating factors, which are taken into consideration when sentencing in other cases, are of no relevance. A conviction for murder will result in a mandatory life sentence regardless of any mitigating factors that may exist. The constitutionality of the mandatory life sentence for murder was upheld by the Supreme Court in *Lynch and Whelan v Minister for Justice, Equality and Law Reform* [2012] 1 I.R. 1. In the case of aggravated murder, s.3 of the Criminal Justice Act 1990 provides that a conviction for aggravated murder, which essentially replaces the offence of capital murder, attracts a mandatory life sentence with the stipulation that no fewer than 40 years be served. Possession of controlled drugs with intent to supply is an offence under s.15A of the Misuse of Drugs

Act 1977, as amended by the Criminal Justice Act 1999, and is subject to a mandatory *minimum* sentence of 10 years' imprisonment. Some discretion is allowed in this case; the mandatory minimum sentence need not be imposed where the judge is satisfied that there are sufficient reasons for not imposing it.

In most other cases, sentencing is a matter for the discretion of the trial judge. Sentences for multiple offences can run concurrently. This means that where, for example, an accused is being sentenced for two offences, with 12 months' imprisonment being imposed for each offence, he will spend 12 months in prison, subject to whatever period of remission he may be entitled to. If the sentences in the example just given were ordered to run consecutively, time will start to run in respect of the second of the two sentences when the first sentence has been served. A judge can also direct that a sentence, or a part thereof, be suspended for a specified amount of time. The power to suspend a sentence, in whole or in part, had always been exercised by the Irish judiciary but was placed on a statutory footing in s.99 of the Criminal Justice Act 2006 (the "2006 Act"), as amended by s.60 of the Criminal Justice Act 2007 and by s.51 of the Criminal Justice (Miscellaneous Provisions) Act 2009. Any custodial sentence, except one that is mandatory, may be wholly or partially suspended. Certain conditions must be attached, such as the requirement that the offender be of good behaviour and keep the peace. These conditions apply equally to any portion of the sentence that is not suspended. Further conditions may be imposed by the court as are appropriate in the circumstances. Breach of any of the conditions set by the court may result in the activation of the suspended sentence. In the case of offences committed while on bail, sentences in respect of these *must* run consecutively, as provided for by s.11 of the Criminal Justice Act 1984, as amended by s.10 of the Bail Act 1997.

A number of difficulties had been identified with s.99 of the 2006 Act, subsections of which provided for the circumstances in which a suspended sentence could be reactivated if a person was convicted of a subsequent offence during the period of suspension. In essence, the difficulty was that the conviction of the subsequent offence triggered the reactivation of the suspended sentence *prior to* sentence being passed in respect of the second offence, thus depriving the accused of the opportunity to appeal against his conviction for the later offence. In the event that an appeal later resulted in the conviction being overturned, the accused person would have been deprived of his liberty due to his being imprisoned on foot of the reactivation of the suspended sentence. The matter came before the High Court by way of judicial review in *Moore v DPP* [2016] IEHC 244 and resulted in the striking down of s.99(9) and (10) of the 2006 Act as unconstitutional. The Criminal Justice (Suspended Sentences of Imprisonment) Act 2017, which will amend the law in light of the *Moore* case, remains uncommenced at the time of writing.

Fines

A court may order that a convicted person may incur some financial penalty either in addition to, or instead of, a custodial sentence. The maximum amount to be imposed by the court will be laid down in the relevant Act. In accordance with the provisions of the Fines Act 2010 (the "2010 Act"), the maximum penalties that may be imposed in respect of summary offences are set down in the 2010 Act, which creates different categories of fines and the maximum amount which can be imposed in relation to each offence. In the case of fines imposed in respect of indictable offences, the 2010 Act set out a multiplier scheme to calculate the maximum amount applicable to offences committed after the commencement of the 2010 Act. Significant changes have been made to the law in relation to the payment and recovery of fines by the Fines (Payment and Recovery) Act 2014. The main provisions of the 2014 Act are as follows:

- The court must take the person's financial circumstances into account when determining the amount of the fine.
- Fines over €100 may be paid by instalments.
- A person who defaults may be made subject to an Attachment Order, a Recovery Order, or a Community Service Order.
- A person may be imprisoned for failure to pay a fine if it is not appropriate to make an Attachment Order, a Recovery Order, or a Community Service Order or where the person fails to comply with a Community Service Order. The term of imprisonment is to be determined by reference to the unpaid amount of the fine.

Community Service Orders

Community Service Orders were originally provided for in s.3 of the Criminal Justice Act 1983 (the "1983 Act") which permitted any court, other than the Special Criminal Court, to order an offender to carry out unpaid community work under the supervision of the Probation Service. This form of penalty was imposed in lieu of a custodial sentence and could be imposed at the discretion of the sentencing court on offenders who were over 16 years of age. The Criminal Justice (Community Service) (Amendment) Act 2011 amends the 1983 Act with the result that a court must now give consideration to the making of a Community Service Order if the term of imprisonment which would otherwise be imposed would be less than 12 months. In the case of potential custodial sentences of longer than 12 months, the court may consider making a Community Service Order in lieu of committal. A Community Service Order cannot be made as a simple alternative to imprisonment per se. It can only be granted in lieu of a specific term of imprisonment and the court must be satisfied that the offender is suitable for community service. The offender must consent to the making of the order, which will stipulate the number of hours to be worked. This number of hours cannot exceed 240. The 1983 Act has been further amended by s.19 of the Fines (Payment and Recovery) Act 2014 to provide for the making, in certain circumstances, of Community Service Orders in default of payment of fines.

Probation

The issue of probation is governed by the Probation of Offenders Act 1907 (the "1907 Act"). Where a person has been convicted of an offence punishable by a custodial sentence, the provisions of the 1907 Act may be invoked. There are two ways in which this might happen:

(1) Where the offender has been tried in the District Court, s.1(1) of the 1907 Act may be applied. If the District Court judge is willing, no conviction is recorded against the offender, although the court recognises that an offence has been committed.

(2) Where the offender has been convicted, the relevant court can order the release of the offender, under s.1(2) of the 1907 Act. The offender must, however, enter into a recognisance to be of good behaviour for a period of up to three years. He will then be assigned a Probation Officer who will supervise him for the duration of his probation. Failure to abide by the terms of probation will result in the offender being sentenced for the original offence.

Compensation

The Criminal Justice Act 1993 provides that courts have the power to order the payment of compensation by an offender to the victim of a crime. The amount of compensation is at the discretion of the court but it should not be greater than the amount that would be awarded in civil litigation for similar injuries. The court may still impose a custodial sentence notwithstanding the order to pay compensation.

Binding to the Peace

An offender may be ordered to enter into a bond to keep the peace and be of good behaviour. This is effectively a form of conditional release whereby the offender signs an undertaking to abide by such conditions as are set down by the court for a specified period of time. In the event that these conditions are not observed, the court may order that the bond be forfeited or that the offender be committed to prison.

The Court Poor Box

The court may dismiss the charge against the accused pursuant to the 1907 Act provided that the accused accepts responsibility for the offence and makes a donation to a charity. The charity and the amount to be donated are decided by the judge. It is most commonly used in the context of more minor public order offences. The jurisdiction to strike out proceedings on condition that the accused makes a donation to the court poor box was questioned in the High Court in *Kennedy v Gibbons* [2014] IEHC 67 where Hogan J. held: "Despite its obscure and uncertain origins, the existence of the poor box jurisdiction is of such long standing and is so widespread and inveterate, that it must be considered now to be part of the common law which was adopted by Article 50.1 following the coming into force of the Constitution on December 29th, 1937."

Consequential Orders

In addition to any primary sanctions which may be imposed upon conviction, there are a number of further orders which are a direct consequence thereof. These include:

(i) Notification requirements may be imposed on sex offenders pursuant to the Sex Offenders Act 2001 and on those convicted of drug trafficking offences pursuant to the Criminal Justice Act 2006.

(ii) Restriction on Movement Orders pursuant to the Criminal Justice Act 2006 which may be imposed upon conviction of specific offences set out in that Act.

(iii) A court may order that property, which it is satisfied was obtained as a result of criminal activity, be forfeited. For example, the Proceeds of Crime Acts 1996–2016 provide for the forfeiture of property over a certain value where the court is satisfied, on the civil standard of proof, that such property was obtained as a result of criminal activity. The Proceeds of Crime Act 1996 is enforced by the Criminal Assets Bureau, set up by the Criminal Assets Bureau Act 1996. A conviction is not required prior to the confiscation of any property. The constitutionality of the Proceeds of Crime Act 1996 was upheld by the Supreme Court in *Gilligan v Criminal Assets Bureau* [1998] 3 I.R. 185.

(iv) Property may also be subject to court-ordered confiscation under the Criminal Justice Act 1994 (as amended).

(v) Conviction for certain offences may lead to an offender being disqualified from activities such as driving under the Road Traffic Acts.

(vi) A court may opt to impose a curfew or an exclusion order as an alternative to a custodial sentence and such orders are often imposed as conditions of bail.

KEY CASES AND LEGISLATION

Fines (Payment and Recovery) Act 2014—New provisions dealing with the payment of fines.

Moore v DPP [2016] IEHC 244—Struck down s.99(9) and (10) of the Criminal Justice Act 2006 as unconstitutional.

Kennedy v Gibbons [2014] IEHC 67—Court poor box jurisdiction to be regarded as part of the common law.

7 Elements of a Criminal Offence

The component parts of a criminal offence are the "actus reus" and the "mens rea", both of which derive from the maxim *actus non facit reum nisi mens sit rea* (an act does not make a man guilty unless his mind be also guilty). If there is no actus reus, there is no crime, and where an act is carried out in the absence of any form of guilty intention, there generally can be no conviction. The exception to this is where an offence is one of absolute or strict liability, where mens rea is irrelevant, liability being imposed on proof that the prohibited conduct had been carried out. In the vast majority of cases, however, both elements of the offence must be established before criminal liability can be imposed.

The Burden of Proof

The burden of proof in a criminal trial is placed on the prosecution. This refers to what the prosecution must do in order to prove its case against the accused, and was described in the following terms in *Woolmington v DPP* [1935] All E.R. Rep. 1: "Throughout the web of the English criminal law one golden thread is always to be seen, that it is the duty of the prosecution to prove the prisoner's guilt".

To discharge this burden, the prosecution must: (a) prove all the elements of the offence with which the accused is charged; and (b) disprove/negative any defences that are consistent with the innocence of the accused. This flows from the right of the accused to be presumed innocent until proven guilty, which was held by the Supreme Court in *O'Leary v Attorney General* [1995] 1 I.R. 254 to be covered by Art.38.1 of Bunreacht na hÉireann. There are some exceptions to the general rule under the *Woolmington* principle, where the burden of proof shifts to the accused; an example is where the defence of insanity is being put forward by the accused. In this instance, it will be for the accused to prove that he was insane at the time of the commission of the offence.

THE STANDARD OF PROOF

In criminal cases, the standard of proof is "beyond reasonable doubt". This means that even where the jury believes that it is possible that the accused committed the offence with which he is charged, they must acquit him if there is a reasonable doubt in their minds as to his guilt. In *People (Attorney General) v Byrne* [1974] I.R. 1, the court stated that they must be satisfied beyond reasonable doubt that the accused committed the offence and also that the accused was entitled to the benefit of the doubt. Where, therefore, two interpretations of the accused's part in an alleged offence are possible, one being in his favour, the accused is entitled to be judged according to the more benign of the two, unless the jury is satisfied, beyond reasonable doubt, that the prosecution has established the contrary to the required standard. In *DPP v Wallace*, unreported, Court of Criminal Appeal, 30 April 2001, Keane C.J. held that there is no requirement that both (or more) explanations be equally reasonable.

It should be remembered that "beyond reasonable doubt" does not necessarily mean "beyond all doubt", but it is nonetheless a very high standard. This point was clearly articulated by Denning J. in *Miller v Minister for Pensions* [1947] 2 All E.R. 372 where he stated:

> "Proof beyond reasonable doubt does not mean proof beyond the shadow of doubt. The law would fail to protect the community if it admitted fanciful possibilities to deflect the course of justice. If the evidence is so strong against a man as to leave only a remote possibility in his favour which can be dismissed with the sentence 'of course it is possible but not in the least probable', the case is proved beyond reasonable doubt, but nothing short of that will suffice."

The standard of proof is lower in civil cases, where the plaintiff must prove his case on "the balance of probabilities". Where, in a criminal case, the burden of proof shifts to the defence (for example, the insanity defence), this burden is discharged on the civil standard, which is the balance of probabilities.

THE ACTUS REUS

The actus reus is sometimes referred to as being the physical or action element of an offence. It should be remembered, however, that the actus reus can also include inaction or an omission on the part of the accused. It can also include the result or consequences of the defendant's voluntary act or omission. The surrounding circumstances may also be of relevance. This is best illustrated by reference to the classification of offences as follows:

- Result offences: These require proof that the conduct of the defendant brought about a particular outcome or caused a particular harm. Murder is the clearest example of a result offence, insofar as it is the death of the victim that gives rise to liability. A defendant who intends to kill or seriously injure another person will not be guilty of murder unless the victim dies.
- Conduct offences: These do not require proof that the defendant's action caused any particular outcome. The defendant will be liable simply because he engaged in the prohibited conduct. A defendant who drives a car whilst intoxicated will be guilty of an offence under the Road Traffic Acts regardless of the outcome of his actions.
- Offences dependent on circumstances: Some forms of conduct are not unlawful per se, but will attract criminal liability if carried out in the presence of certain external circumstances. Sexual offences are an example of this: the conduct in question is not usually itself illegal, but becomes so if carried out in the absence of the victim's consent. The conduct in question might also be illegal. To kill a person intentionally is murder. If, however, the victim is a member of An Garda Síochána who has been killed in the course of duty, the offence is aggravated murder.

Without the actus reus, there is no offence. It is impossible to sustain a prosecution for any offence on the basis of mens rea alone. In *R. v Deller* (1952) 36 Cr. App. Rep. 184, the accused tried to sell a vehicle that he believed to be owned by a hire purchase company. He informed the purchaser that the car was legally his. Unknown to him, he was in fact the legal owner of the vehicle. He was acquitted of the offence of obtaining by false pretences because although he had the mens rea for the offence, there was no actus reus.

As stated previously, the actus reus need not necessarily be a positive act on the part of the accused, and can be established where there is a "state of affairs" or where the accused has omitted to act where he otherwise should have.

State of Affairs

In *R. v Larsonneur* (1933) 29 Cox C.C. 673, the accused was convicted under the Aliens Order 1920, having been found in the UK. She had been sent out of the UK and had come to Ireland whereupon she was returned to the UK and handed over to the police. In *Winzar v Chief Constable of Kent*, *The Times*, 28 March 1983, the accused was convicted of being found drunk on the highway.

He had been removed from a hospital by the police and had been put into a police car which had been parked on the highway. Despite the fact that in both these cases the offences could not be said to have been due to the voluntary actions of either accused, both resulted in convictions.

Omission

Criminal liability for omission arises where the accused is under some form of duty to act but fails to do so. In cases where there is no duty to act, no liability for failure to act will be incurred. A duty to act can arise in different circumstances:

(1) Statutory Duty. Where a duty is imposed by a statute, failure to perform the obligations imposed amounts to an offence.
(2) Contractual Duty. Where, by virtue of a contract or by virtue of holding a particular office, duties are imposed on an individual, failure to carry out those duties may lead to a conviction. In *R. v Dytham* [1979] 3 All E.R. 641, a police officer who failed to act to stop a brawl was convicted of misconduct. The Court of Appeal in *Dytham* stated that the neglect of duty had to be wilful and not merely due to inadvertence. The court stated that the culpability of the accused must be "of such degree that the misconduct impugned is calculated to injure the public interest so as to call for condemnation and punishment". *Dytham* was cited with approval in Ireland in *DPP v Bartley*, unreported, High Court, Carney J., 13 June 1997.
(3) Where the accused creates the danger, he may be convicted of an offence if he does nothing to mitigate its effects. In *R. v Miller* [1983] 1 All E.R. 978, the accused was convicted of arson. He had accidentally started a fire and had done nothing to try to put it out. It was held that having started the fire, albeit by accident, he was then under a duty to extinguish it.
(4) Voluntary Assumption of Duty. An accused can be convicted in circumstances where he has breached a duty owed to a third party in his care. In *R. v Stone* [1977] 2 All E.R. 341, both defendants were convicted of manslaughter where they had failed to provide medical assistance for an elderly relative of the first-named defendant who had lived with them. In that case, the duty had arisen in the case of the first-named defendant because he was related to the deceased. The duty was imposed on the second-named defendant because she had assumed responsibility for the deceased. Further examples of instances in which criminal liability has been imposed on the basis of a voluntary assumption of duty are *R. v Bubb* (1851) 4 Cox C.C. 455; *R. v Gibbins and Proctor* (1918) 13 Cr. App. Rep. 134; and *R. v Taktak* (1988) 34 A. Crim. R. 334.

Voluntariness

The action(s) of the accused must be voluntary. Accordingly, where the accused has no control over his actions, there will generally be no conviction. This is discussed further in the chapter on automatism.

The Mens Rea

This is the mental element of an offence and it refers to the state of mind of the accused in respect of the offence. Where the accused has no mens rea, he cannot be convicted unless the offence is one of absolute or strict liability. There are different degrees of mens rea, which will be discussed separately.

Intention

In the context of criminal law, the term "intention" means the conscious objective or purpose of the accused. Intention is often confused with other concepts, such as motive, and the desire to achieve a particular result. It is important to note that intention is not the same as either one. One's motive for acting in a particular way is his *reason* for doing so. The presence of a motive may well be a factor from which guilt may be easier to establish but the absence of a motive does not mean that the accused has not committed the offence. The desire to bring about a particular result is not the same as intention either. An accused can be convicted even if the result of his action(s) is not what he desired. Where the intention of the accused forms a part of the offence, this must be proved beyond a reasonable doubt. Intention, as a form of mens rea, can be either *direct* or *oblique*.

Direct intention

This is where the accused wanted to bring about a particular result and carried out a deliberate act in order to achieve it.

Oblique intention

This form of intention is a more nebulous concept than direct intention and is premised on what the accused foresaw as being the result of his conduct. The actions of the accused are deliberate, but a result other than the one anticipated or desired comes about. The English courts have formulated and modified the test to be applied in cases of oblique intent and the following is a brief summary of the most relevant of these authorities:

- In *Hyam v DPP* [1974] 2 All E.R. 41, the defendant put burning newspaper through a letterbox causing the deaths of two children. Her *motive* was to frighten the owner of the house. She appealed her conviction for murder arguing that she had no intention to kill anyone. The House of Lords held that the conviction should stand if the prosecution could establish that when she had committed the act, she had known that it was *highly probable* that death or grievous bodily harm would result. In *R. v Moloney* [1985] 1 All E.R. 1025, two men decided to compete with each other to see which of them was better at handling a shotgun. The defendant won and was then challenged by the deceased to fire the weapon. The accused duly fired and killed the deceased. In his defence, it was argued that because he was drunk, he had not considered the outcome of his actions. The House of Lords laid down a two-part test to be applied in cases such as this, and in doing so, departed from the "highly probable" test laid down in *Hyam*. The judge, in directing a jury, should where possible avoid prescribing a definition of "intention" and leave it to the jury to decide. Where, however, an explanation should be given, the jury should be asked to consider two questions:

  (1) Was the outcome a natural consequence of the voluntary act of the accused?
  (2) Was this result foreseen by the accused as being a natural consequence of his actions?

  If the answer to both was yes, then the jury would be entitled to infer that the accused intended to bring about the result.

- In *R. v Hancock and Shankland* [1986] 1 All E.R. 641, the two defendants were charged with murder, having thrown a concrete slab over a bridge resulting in the death of a driver in a car on the road below. The defence argued that they did not intend to kill the deceased and that they had acted as they did in a bid to prevent miners from breaking a picket. The trial judge directed the jury, in accordance with the ruling in *Moloney*, that intent could be inferred if the defendants had foreseen that death or serious injury was a "natural consequence" of their actions. On appeal, the House of Lords rejected this and held that death or serious injury had to be a probable as well as a natural consequence. The jury, therefore, ought to have been told that intent could be inferred where death or serious injury was a "natural and probable" consequence and also that the higher the probability, the more likely it was that the accused had intended the result.
- In *R. v Nedrick* [1986] 3 All E.R. 1, the Court of Appeal modified the test again. The facts of this case were similar to those of *Hyam*, and the jury

was directed that the accused could be convicted if he was aware that it was "highly probable" that his actions would result in someone's death. The Court of Appeal held that the jury would be entitled to infer an intention to kill or seriously injure where the defendant recognised that death or serious injury, as a result of his actions, was a "virtual certainty".

- Finally, in *R. v Woolin* [1999] 1 A.C. 82, the House of Lords held that where a result was virtually certain, it could be viewed as being the intended result. The leading Irish case is *DPP v Douglas and Hayes* [1985] I.L.R.M. 25. In that case, the defendants were appealing against their convictions for shooting with intent to kill, an offence contained in the Offences against the Person Act 1861, on the basis that there had been no intention to kill. The Court of Criminal Appeal followed the decision of the House of Lords in *Hyam* and held that where there was evidence that a reasonable person would have foreseen that the natural and probable consequences of the defendants' conduct was that death would result, and that where it could be established that the defendants had acted recklessly, the jury was entitled to infer from that that the defendant had intended to cause death by his actions, subject to the requirement that both these facts be established beyond reasonable doubt. In *Clifford v DPP* [2008] IEHC 322, Charleton J. explained oblique intention in the following way:

> "A person may intend to blow up a plane in flight and so kill the passengers. That is direct intention. A person may claim to intend only to blow up a suitcase in a plane in flight but hope, that through some miracle, all the passengers in the plane will survive. It might usefully be noted, on the relevant case law, that the closer the impugned conduct comes to inevitably causing the consequence charged, as for instance in that example intending the death of the plane passengers, the more readily a court may feel able to infer that intention, in the example given of causing death, against the accused. The more obscure the consequence, the less readily can the inference of an intention in that regard be made. In no instance, whether of direct or oblique intention, is the inference that the accused intended either an act or its consequences automatically to be inferred from particular behaviour. In each instance, it is a matter of judgment for the court."

The presumption of intent

Section 4(2) of the Criminal Justice Act 1964 provides that "the accused person shall be presumed to have intended the natural and probable consequences of his conduct; but this presumption may be rebutted." This section applies to the mens rea required for murder, but the presumption of intent applies to all offences in Irish law. In *DPP v McBride* [1997] I.L.R.M. 233, the Court of Criminal Appeal held that the presumption of intent did not affect the presumption of innocence since it was "only a presumption and could be rebutted". In *DPP v Hull*, unreported, Court of Criminal Appeal, 8 July 1996, the court held that the presumption of intent should be regarded by the jury as being a two-step process, the first step being the determination of what the natural and probable consequences of the defendant's conduct were. If the jury accepted that the natural and probable consequence of the defendant's conduct was the death of the victim, the jury was entitled to conclude that the defendant had intended that consequence. The jury would then have to deal with the second step, which was to decide whether the presumption had been rebutted and that the direction of the trial judge to this effect had been correct.

Recklessness

This is a lesser form of mens rea than intention and arises where the accused has taken an unjustifiable risk. Recklessness can be objective or subjective. Subjective recklessness occurs where the accused was aware of the risk but decided to take it anyway. The leading English case on subjective recklessness is *R. v Cunningham* [1957] 2 All E.R. 412, in which the court held that the test to be applied was whether the risk was in the mind of the accused. If the accused was aware of the risk and decided to take it, he was subjectively reckless in doing so. Objective recklessness occurs where the accused did not allude to the possibility that there was a risk which would have been obvious to the reasonable man. The test for objective recklessness was laid down in *Metropolitan Police Commissioner v Caldwell* [1981] 1 All E.R. 901, where the House of Lords held that the word "reckless" should be given its ordinary meaning and that where there was an "obvious risk", albeit one which was unknown to the accused, which the reasonably prudent person would have known about, the accused acted recklessly where he failed to appreciate it. The ruling in *Caldwell* was subsequently affirmed by the House of Lords in *R. v Lawrence* [1981] 1 All E.R. 974. The main problem with objective recklessness, as defined in *Caldwell*, was that it did not cover situations in which the accused may have considered whether or not a risk existed but decided that there was none. Equally, the application of an objective test for recklessness under *Caldwell* meant that an accused was being judged against the standard of the reasonable man even where it was manifestly unjust to the accused to do so. It was also argued that having two different forms of recklessness, each judged according to different standards, was in breach of art.6 of the European Convention on Human Rights, which provides that anyone charged with a criminal offence is entitled to a "fair and public hearing within a reasonable time by an independent and impartial tribunal established by law." In *Elliott v C. (A Minor)* [1983] 2 All E.R. 1005, the Court of Appeal upheld the conviction of a mildly mentally disabled child who had set fire to a shed, on the basis that the risk attached to such conduct would have been obvious to the "reasonably prudent person". The effect of the so-called "*Caldwell* loophole" was that no distinction was drawn between the accused who had knowingly taken a risk and the accused who had not considered whether there was a risk at all. The House of Lords finally overruled *Caldwell* in *R. v G. and R.* [2003] 4 All E.R. 765, where it was held that a person acts recklessly when he takes an unreasonable risk in circumstances where the risk is known to him, knowing that a certain outcome is likely. The English courts have, therefore, reverted to a subjective test.

The position in Irish law, however, is not altogether clear. The decisions of the House of Lords are of persuasive authority only in this jurisdiction, but it is arguable that the Irish judiciary are more flexible in their approach to various tests (see, for example, the rules on insanity). There also appears to be a greater preference for subjective tests in the Irish courts. The leading case in this jurisdiction on recklessness is *DPP v Murray* [1977] I.R. 360, where the two accused were charged with capital murder and argued that they did not have the necessary mens rea for that offence. The question for the court was whether Mrs Murray, who had fired the fatal shot, had acted recklessly by so doing. An essential component of the offence was knowledge or recklessness on the part of the accused as to whether the victim was a member of the Gardaí. In rejecting objective recklessness, the Supreme Court (per Walsh J.) stated that, "in this context objective recklessness is really constructive knowledge; and constructive knowledge has no place in our criminal system in establishing intent".

The decision in *Murray* raises questions as to the application of subjective recklessness in cases other than capital murder. In that case, Henchy J. stated that the mens rea for capital murder is subjective, without stating what the position was in relation to other offences. The same could be said of the judgments of Parke and Kenny JJ. More recent cases like *DPP v Cagney*, *DPP v McGrath* [2008] 2 I.R. 111 and *Clifford v DPP* [2013] IESC 43 also demonstrate that recklessness is to be determined subjectively by the Irish courts.

Criminal negligence

This form of mens rea applies to manslaughter only and is of a higher standard than the principles of negligence under the law of tort. In *People (Attorney General) v Dunleavy* [1948] I.R. 95, it was held on appeal that to establish negligence sufficiently grave to sustain a conviction for manslaughter, the level of negligence would have to be considerably greater than would suffice in a civil action. Criminal negligence, being a more grave form of negligence, is judged objectively.

Negligence, as a form of mens rea, really only arises where the offence in question requires that the accused failed to carry out some duty or acted in a way that breaches a duty. The duty in question is usually a statutory duty, such as is imposed under the Road Traffic Acts, and negligence in this context is more akin to the concept of negligence in tort.

Strict liability/absolute liability

These terms are sometimes used interchangeably, although they are not identical. In *R. v City of Sault Ste Marie* [1978] 2 S.C.R.1229, the Supreme Court of Canada discussed both terms, holding that the two types of offences should be regarded as distinct and that the law should continue to view them as such. Offences of absolute liability will result in conviction on the basis that the accused engaged in the prohibited conduct regardless of whether he was at fault. In some situations, an offence of strict liability may have a defence of reasonable belief/mistake. In *C.C. v Ireland* [2006] 4 I.R. 1, the Supreme Court struck down as unconstitutional s.1(1) of the Criminal Law Amendment Act 1935 because it failed to provide for a defence of mistake. The section contained the offence known as statutory rape, and was drafted in such a way as to impose liability regardless of the possibility that the defendant may have been honestly mistaken as to the girl's age. In both cases, only the actus reus need be established, and the mens rea is not relevant. Offences of strict or absolute liability are usually created by statute and tend to focus on conduct that is deemed risky or which ought to be discouraged.

Coincidence of Actus Reus and Mens Rea

In order to convict someone of a criminal offence, the prosecution must not only establish the elements of that offence (actus reus and mens rea) *and* disprove any/all defences raised on behalf of the accused, but it must also show that:

(a) the actus reus and mens rea coincided; and
(b) the defendant's intentional and voluntary act *caused* the result. This does not arise in the case of a conduct offence, the result of which is irrelevant to the imposition of liability.

The actus reus and mens rea must coincide

Fundamentally, this means that the accused must have the mens rea to commit the offence in question when he is committing the actus reus element of the offence. Where the two do not coincide and cannot be shown to be a part of a continuing transaction, the accused will not be found guilty. A number of approaches have been formulated to deal with situations in which this problem arises.

(1) Continuing act

A number of acts, separate in themselves, can nonetheless be viewed as one continuing act. In *Fagan v Metropolitan Police Commissioner* [1968] 3 All E.R. 442, the accused accidentally parked his car on a policeman's foot. When asked to remove it, he refused. He argued that mens rea and actus reus did not coincide, and that consequently he could not be guilty of assault. The court held that the entire incident was a continuing act, the actus reus was already in place when the accused formed the mens rea for the offence by refusing to move the vehicle. A similar approach was adopted in *Kaitamaki v R.* [1985] 2 All E.R. 435. In this case, the court held that rape was a continuing act beginning with penetration and ending at withdrawal. The accused had realised after penetration that there was no consent on the part of the woman but carried on. At that point, he formed the mens rea for rape and, as the actus reus was already in place, his conviction for rape was upheld.

(2) Duty

This approach was employed by the House of Lords in *R. v Miller* [1983] 1 All E.R. 978. In this case, the accused had accidentally started a fire but did nothing to extinguish it. The Court of Appeal had upheld the conviction on the basis that it was a continuing act, having also looked at the duty approach. This approach imposes a duty on an individual to do something to mitigate the results of their conduct. Liability can then be imposed where the individual breaches that duty. The House of Lords stated that the duty approach was the better of the two in this case, on the basis that a jury would find it easier to understand.

(3) The "supposed corpse" rule

The clearest example of this approach is to be seen in *Thabo Meli v R.* [1954] 1 All E.R. 373. The accused, believing that he had killed someone whom he had assaulted, threw the "body" over a cliff. The victim died as a result of exposure rather than from the injury caused by the initial assault. In this case, the conviction for murder was upheld on the basis that both acts were part of the one transaction. A similar decision was given in *R. v Church* [1965] 2 All E.R. 72, where the Court of Appeal held that where different actions are part of the one plan, a conviction could be sustained. Clearly, when the second act is an attempt to cover up the first act, a conviction is likely.

Causation

In result offences, a causal link must be established between the actions of the accused and the result of those actions. In *R. v White* [1910] All E.R. 340, the accused had administered poison to his mother but the actual cause of her death had been heart failure. In this case, the accused was convicted of attempted murder.

Whether or not a link exists between the actions of the accused and the outcome of those actions can be inferred from the surrounding circumstances. In *R. v Cato* [1976] 1 All E.R. 260, the accused was convicted of manslaughter where his friend had died of an overdose of heroin. Both men were taking the drug and each man had handed the syringes to the other in order to inject the substance. Both men overdosed but the accused was saved. The Court of Appeal held that where the accused had injected the deceased and the deceased then died from the effects of the drug, a causal link had been established.

Novus Actus Interveniens

This concept arises in tort as well as in criminal law and in both situations may break the chain of causation, with the result that the accused may be absolved of liability. It is essential that, in order for liability to be imposed, the causal link between the actions of the accused and the result of those actions is not broken. Where an act by either a third party or the accused intervenes, the chain of causation may be broken. In the case of a novus actus by a third party, there is the requirement that the action is voluntary. In *R. v Pagett* [1983] Crim. L.R. 394, the deceased had been placed against her will, by the accused, in the line of bullets fired by the police who had been trying to arrest the accused. He appealed his conviction for murder arguing that the actions of the police amounted to a novus actus interveniens. This argument was rejected and the Court of Appeal also pointed out that the deceased had been placed in the situation, involuntarily, by the accused. If the actions of the third party are calculated to protect him from the actions of the accused, and are foreseeable by the accused, no novus actus interveniens will arise.

In addition, the actions of the third party must be unconnected to those of the accused and must amount to a new cause in order for a novus actus interveniens to arise. In *R. v Jordan* (1956) 40 Cr. App. Rep. 152, a conviction for murder was quashed. The accused had stabbed the victim, causing him to be hospitalised. The victim's wound had actually almost healed but he died from pneumonia which was caused by a series of negligent acts carried out by doctors in the course of his treatment. The Court of Appeal held that the medical treatment had been "palpably wrong" and effectively held it to have been the cause of death. In *R. v Smith* [1959] 2 All E.R. 193, the Court of Appeal held that where the original wound was an operating and substantial cause of death, the chain of causation would not be broken. In *R. v Malcherek and R. v Steel* [1981] 1 W.L.R. 690, the Court of Appeal held that where a life-support system is switched off due to a diagnosis of brain stem death, the cause of death is attributable to the actions of the accused. In *R. v Cheshire* [1991] 3 All E.R. 670, the Court of Appeal held that only treatment which could be described as extraordinary and unusual would amount to a novus actus interveniens, and even then, it would have to be something that completely overshadowed the original wound. This issue also arose in *Dunne v DPP* [2016] 2 I.L.R.M. 169 where the Supreme Court held that an intervention by a third party does not preclude a conviction for murder. In *Dunne* the accused had pleaded guilty to a charge of attempted murder and was sentenced for that offence. Some two years later, the victim, who had been in a vegetative state as a direct result of being shot by the accused, died in hospital from pneumonia, a decision having been made by doctors and the victim's family not to embark on further medical treatment. As such, it was not a case which involved the withdrawal of medical treatment per se. Drawing on the case law of the English courts and the decision of the Supreme Court in *Re A Ward of Court (Withholding Medical Treatment (No.2)* [1996] 2 I.R. 79, the Supreme Court identified the following principles which apply in the context of causation and novus actus interveniens:

(1) Exceptionally negligent medical treatment may break the chain of causation but conventional treatment, even if it is not the best treatment available, will not. The chain is also not broken in circumstances where the victim decided to refuse appropriate treatment.
(2) A lawful and ethically proper decision to withdraw life-support in cases of brain stem death does not displace the original injury as the operational cause of death.
(3) The right to life, protected by Bunreacht na hÉireann, encapsulates the right to die a natural death and, in appropriate cases, the discontinuation of treatment that serves no curative purpose does not become the cause of death. The original injury remains the cause of death unless there is a "true novus actus interveniens".

(4) A novus actus interveniens must be so independent of the actions of the accused that it must be viewed in law as being the cause of death.

The Supreme Court went on to say:

> "In any of these situations, which may arise in any case where the assault does not result in immediate death, the actual date of death will be influenced by factors beyond the actions of the accused. In the absence of a true novus actus interveniens that does not mean that the chain of causation is broken."

The Eggshell Skull Rule

In tort, a plaintiff must take steps to mitigate his loss, and his failure to do so will result in a smaller award of damages. This is not the case in criminal law. The accused is not entitled to expect his victim to take any steps which would lessen the effects of the accused's conduct. Equally, the accused must take his victim as he finds him and will not be able to rely on the fact that his victim suffered from some condition that renders him more susceptible to injury. In *R. v Blaue* [1975] 3 All E.R. 446, the Court of Appeal refused to quash a conviction where the victim was a Jehovah's Witness and had refused a necessary blood transfusion following an attack on her by the accused. The defendant had argued that the victim would not have died had she accepted the blood transfusion. The Court of Appeal held that the victim's injuries had been caused by the defendant and that he could not then argue that her religious beliefs were unreasonably held in order to be absolved of liability.

Key Cases

Woolmington v DPP [1935] All E.R. 1—Prosecution bears the burden of proof.

Miller v Minister for Pensions [1947] 2 All E.R. 372—"Beyond reasonable doubt" does not mean "beyond all doubt".

People (Attorney General) v Byrne [1974] I.R. 1—Accused entitled to acquittal where benign interpretation of the evidence is available.

R. v Deller (1952) 36 Cr. App. Rep. 184—No offence where actus reus has not been committed.

R. v Dytham [1979] 3 All E.R. 641—Criminal liability where contractual/statutory duty not fulfilled.

KEY CASES

R. v Miller [1983] 1 All E.R. 978—Liability where accused failed to mitigate effects of his actions.

R. v Stone [1977] 2 All E.R. 341—Liability imposed where accused breached voluntarily assumed duty.

Hyam v DPP [1974] 2 All E.R. 41; *R. v Moloney* [1985] 1 All E.R. 1025; *R. v Nedrick* [1986] 3 All E.R. 1; *R. v Woolin* [1999] 1 A.C. 82; *DPP v Douglas and Hayes* [1985] I.L.R.M. 25—Oblique intention.

R. v Cunningham [1957] 2 All E.R. 412—Subjective "*Cunningham*" recklessness.

Metropolitan Police Commissioner v Caldwell [1981] 1 All E.R. 901—Objective "*Caldwell*" recklessness.

R. v G. and R. [2003] 4 All E.R. 765—Objective/*Caldwell* test for recklessness rejected. Subjective/*Cunningham* test affirmed by English courts.

Dunne v DPP [2016] IESC 24—Principles governing causation/novus actus interveniens.

Criminal Liability and Secondary Participation

Criminal liability is imposed where the prosecution discharges the burden of proving that the accused committed the actus reus of the offence with which he is charged and that he did so having formed the necessary mens rea. If the prosecution goes on to disprove any defences put forward by the defence, the accused will be fixed with criminal liability in respect of the offence with which he has been charged.

Transferred Malice

There are situations where liability may be imposed even where the actual victim of the defendant's action is not his intended target. In these situations, the defendant's malice towards his intended victim is deemed to have been transferred to his actual victim. In this context, the term "malice" means "intent". In *R. v Latimer* (1886) 16 Cox C.C. 70, the defendant had intended to hit one person but missed, hitting and injuring another person instead. He appealed his conviction on the basis that he had not meant to injure the actual victim. His conviction was upheld on the grounds that his malicious intent had been transferred from his intended target to the injured party.

The doctrine does *not* apply in situations where there is no similarity between the mens rea for the intended offence and that which is required for the actual offence with which the defendant is charged. For example, in *R. v Pembliton* (1874) 12 Cox C.C. 607, the accused had been charged with an offence of intentionally causing damage to property. He had thrown a stone with the intention of hitting another person but instead broke a nearby window.

The doctrine of transferred malice is also provided for in some statutory provisions. For example, s.4(1) of the Criminal Justice Act 1964 provides that, "where a person kills another unlawfully the killing shall not be murder unless the accused intended to kill, or cause serious injury to, *some person, whether the person actually killed or not*" (emphasis added). Similar provisions are to be found in s.6 of the Non-Fatal Offences against the Person Act 1997 in relation to syringe offences.

Liability of Children for Criminal Offences

Until 2006, the defence of infancy provided an absolute defence to children younger than seven years of age against criminal prosecution. The defence was based on the common law doctrine of doli incapax, which regarded children under a certain age as being incapable of forming mens rea. The phrase "doli incapax" simply means "incapable of crime". In this jurisdiction, children were categorised into different age groups for the purposes of criminal liability.

The enactment of the Children Act 2001 (the "2001 Act") heralded a major departure from the existing statutory and common law framework for dealing with children who committed criminal offences. The provisions of the 2001 Act, which would have raised the age of criminal responsibility from seven years of age to 12 years, were never commenced, and those sections have since been amended by the Criminal Justice Act 2006, which repealed the defence in respect of children aged between seven and 14 years of age and provides a general commitment not to prosecute children under 12 years of age for most criminal offences. For comparative purposes, the rules pertaining to the criminal liability of children prior to the commencement of Pt V of the 2001 Act (as amended) are set out below.

- A child under the age of seven years was conclusively presumed to be doli incapax. This presumption could be not be rebutted, regardless of the actual understanding of the child or the circumstances in which the alleged offence takes place. The effect of the presumption was to prohibit the prosecution of children under the age of seven years in any circumstances.
- Children between seven and 14 years of age were presumed to be doli incapax. The difference between this group and those in the younger age group was that if the child was older than seven and younger than 14 years of age, the presumption of doli incapax could be rebutted where there was evidence of a "mischievous discretion". The standard required to rebut the presumption was quite high and required that the child knew that his conduct went beyond mere mischief. The test was whether the child appreciated the seriousness of his actions. In *R. v Gorrie* (1919) 83 J.P. 136, the court held that the child had to know that his conduct was gravely or very seriously wrong. This test was followed in this jurisdiction in *K.M. v DPP* [1994] 1 I.R. 514.

Until the passing of the Criminal Law (Rape) (Amendment) Act 1990, a boy younger than 14 years of age was conclusively presumed to be incapable of committing rape. This presumption applied to the offence of rape only, and did not preclude the prosecution of a boy under the age of 14 for other forms of sexual assault. This presumption was abolished by s.6 of the Criminal Law (Rape) (Amendment) Act 1990, with the result that, provided the presumption of doli incapax was rebutted, a boy aged between seven and 14 years of age could be charged with rape.

Prior to the amendments effected by the Criminal Justice Act 2006, Pt V of the 2001 Act sought to raise the age of criminal responsibility to 12 and stated that "it shall be conclusively presumed that no child under the age of 12 years is capable of committing an offence." Section 52(2) provided that "there is a rebuttable presumption that a child who is not less than 12 but under 14 years of age is incapable of committing an offence because the child did not have the capacity to know that the act or omission was wrong." These provisions would have had the effect of widening the group of children who were conclusively presumed to be doli incapax and narrowing the group of children to whom a rebuttable presumption applied. The section was never commenced and has since been amended significantly by s.129 of the Criminal Justice Act 2006.

The Criminal Justice Act 2006

The current position regarding the liability of children for criminal offences is set out in s.52 of the 2001 Act, as substituted by s.129 of the Criminal Justice Act 2006. The substituted section provides as follows:

(i) Children under the age of 12 shall not be charged with a criminal offence. This is a general prohibition against prosecuting children. The general rule is subject to the exception that a child aged 10 or 11 may be charged with murder, manslaughter, rape, aggravated sexual assault or rape under s.4 of the Criminal Law (Rape) (Amendment) Act 1990. The reference to the capacity of the child to commit an offence has been removed.
(ii) The common law doctrine of doli incapax, insofar as it pertained to children between the ages of seven and 14, is abolished.
(iii) A child under the age of 14 years may only be prosecuted by or with the consent of the DPP.

In addition, s.53 of the 2001 Act (as amended) provides that where a member of An Garda Síochána believes on reasonable grounds that a child who is younger than 12 years of age has committed an offence other than murder, manslaughter, rape, aggravated sexual assault or rape contrary to s.4 of the Criminal Law (Rape) (Amendment) Act 1990, the member must endeavour to bring the child to his/her parent(s) or guardian(s).

CRIMINAL LIABILITY OF CORPORATIONS

At common law, corporations could not be held criminally liable, notwithstanding the fact that they are viewed as persons by the law. Practical considerations also applied—not all penal sanctions could be imposed on a corporation. It need hardly be said that there are certain crimes which are incapable of being committed by a company, for example, bigamy, but there are numerous regulatory offences for which companies can be held liable. Section 8 of the Environmental Protection Agency Act 1992 and s.11 of the Air Pollution Act 1987 and offences under the Companies Acts are some examples of statutory provisions that impose criminal liability on companies for offences under those Acts. Corporations may also be prosecuted for offences which require proof of mens rea. Examples of these may be found in the Criminal Justice (Theft and Fraud Offences) Act 2001 and the Competition Act 2002.

However, it is possible to impose criminal liability on a corporate entity in some situations. To determine corporate liability for criminal acts, the question to be answered is whether the act was carried out by someone who had control within the company, such as would enable him to direct the activities of the company. The so-called "controlling mind" test was set out by Denning L.J. in *HL Bolton (Engineering) Co Ltd v TJ Graham and Sons* [1956] 3 All E.R. 624:

> "A company may in many ways be likened to a human body. They have a brain and nerve centre which controls what they do. They too have hands which hold the tools and act in accordance with directions from the centre. Some of the people in the company are mere servants and agents who are nothing more than hands to do the work and cannot be said to represent the directing mind or will. Others are directors and managers who represent the directing mind and will of the company, and control what they do. The state of mind of these managers is the state of mind of the company and is treated by the law as such."

In *Tesco Supermarkets v Nattrass* [1972] A.C. 153, the House of Lords held that a regional manager employed by the plaintiff company could not be regarded as senior enough within the company to enable him to direct the mind and will of the company. In *Vehicle Operator Services Agency v FM Conway Ltd* [2012] EWHC 2930 (Admin), the court held that an asset manager who worked for the defendant and who was authorised by the company to act on its behalf could not be regarded as being the controlling mind of the company since he was neither a director nor the company secretary.

Imposition of criminal liability on a corporate entity, particularly one with many employees, for crimes such as manslaughter is problematic, not least because of the difficulties posed by the requirement to prove mens rea. The controlling mind test is met only by very high-ranking personnel within the company. On the other hand, it is unlikely that such a person would be personally involved in the circumstances giving rise to the prosecution. This issue arose in *R. v P & O Ferries* (1991) 93 Cr. App. R. 72 where the prosecution sought, unsuccessfully, to link the actions of various employees so that, taken together, they would add up to the level of culpability required to secure a conviction. In *Attorney General's Reference (No. 2 of 1999)* [2000] 3 All E.R. 182, two questions were referred to the Court of Appeal of England and Wales arising from the trial, on seven counts of manslaughter, of a train driver and a train company. Various problems had been identified which amounted to negligence and the questions for the Court of Appeal were, first, whether a defendant could be convicted of manslaughter by gross negligence in the absence of any evidence as to his state of mind, and secondly, whether it was possible to convict a company of manslaughter by gross negligence where there was no evidence to establish the guilt of a human defendant for the same crime. On the first question, the Court of Appeal held that the mens rea for manslaughter by gross negligence had been set out by the House of Lords in *R. v Adomako* [1994] 3 All E.R. 79 and was entirely objective. Following *Adomako*, evidence of the defendant's state of mind was not a prerequisite to a conviction for manslaughter by gross negligence. On the second issue, the court held that it was not possible for a non-human defendant to be convicted of manslaughter by gross negligence if there was no evidence to establish the guilt of a human defendant for the same crime. In its 2005 *Report on Corporate Killing* (LRC 77-2005), the Law Reform Commission recommended that an offence of corporate killing be created in order to provide clarification on liability under Irish law but, to date, no legislation has been enacted. The matter is governed in England and Wales by the Corporate Manslaughter and Corporate Homicide Act 2007.

A corporation cannot be held liable for the fraudulent acts of employees where the fraud is perpetrated against the company itself. This was held in *Canadian Dredge and Dock Co v R.* [1985] 1 S.C.R. 662.

Secondary Participation

There are occasions when liability is imposed on individuals other than the person who actually committed the offence on the basis of what is called "secondary participation". Secondary participation is the term used to describe any assistance given to the perpetrator/principal before, during or after the offence that is of such a degree as to warrant the imposition of criminal liability.

Traditionally, there were four categories of participation recognised by the common law and by the Accessories and Abettors Act 1861:

(1) Principal in the first degree—the person who actually committed the offence;
(2) Principal in the second degree—a person who aided or abetted the commission of an offence or who was present at the time of the commission;
(3) Accessory before the fact—a person who provided assistance prior to the commission of the offence;
(4) Accessory after the fact—a person who provided assistance to the person who committed a felony after the offence had been committed and "knowing that" a felony had been committed.

Section 8 of the Accessories and Abettors Act 1861 provided that any person who aided, abetted, counselled or procured the commission of a misdemeanour was liable to be prosecuted as a principal offender.

The Criminal Law Act 1997 (the "1997 Act") repealed the older legislation, and the relevant provisions are now contained in ss.7 and 8 of the 1997 Act. Section 7(1) provides that, "any person who aids, abets, counsels or procures the commission of an indictable offence shall be liable to be indicted, tried and punished as a principal offender." In the case of summary offences, a similar provision to that contained in s.7(1) of the 1997 Act is to be found in s.22 of the Petty Sessions (Ireland) Act 1851.

In order to be "indicted, tried and punished" as a principal offender, an offence must actually be committed. This is also the case in respect of persons charged with summary offences. This differs from the situation in which a person is charged with an inchoate offence. An inchoate offence (attempt, conspiracy or incitement) is an offence in itself.

Both Acts refer to a person who "aids, abets, counsels or procures".

Aiding

To aid someone in the commission of an offence is to knowingly provide assistance in its commission. It is not required that the person providing such assistance is present at the scene of the crime.

In *Gillick v West Norfolk and Wisbech Area Health Authority* [1985] 3 All E.R. 402, it had been argued that a doctor who prescribed contraceptives for an under-age girl would be aiding and abetting the commission of an offence. The House of Lords held that this might be the case depending on the intention of the doctor, and was not dependent upon the doctor's presence at the time/location of the actual offence. Similarly, in *People (DPP) v O'Reilly*

[1991] 1 I.R. 77, it was held that the provision of a vehicle for the purpose of a burglary could lead to a conviction for aiding that offence, even though the accused had not actually taken part in the burglary itself. The Court of Criminal Appeal reached a similar conclusion in *DPP v Egan* [1989] I.R. 681.

Abetting

This term is more often than not used in conjunction with the term "aiding" and for all intents and purposes, appears to mean the same thing.

Counselling

This term refers to encouragement or advice given prior to the commission of the offence. The encouragement need not have been the cause of the offence. In *R. v Calhaem* [1985] 2 All E.R. 266, the defendant told a man to kill a woman whom the accused regarded as being a "love-rival". The accused appealed against her conviction and argued that there had been no causal link between what she had said and the death of the victim. The Court of Appeal held that no causal link was required; where there had been some form of contact between the accused and the killer, this would suffice. In *R. v Giannetto* [1996] Crim. L.R. 722, the trial judge stated:

> "Supposing somebody came up to [the defendant] and said 'I am going to kill your wife', if he played any part, either in encouragement, as little as patting him on the back, nodding, saying 'oh goody', that would be sufficient to involve him in the murder, to make him guilty, because he is encouraging the murder."

Procuring

This occurs where the desired outcome is achieved through some effort on the part of the accused. In *Attorney General's Reference (No.1 of 1975)* [1975] 2 All E.R. 684, it was held that there did not have to be any agreement between the parties nor any encouragement on the part of the accused: "You procure a thing by setting out to see that it happens and taking the appropriate steps to produce that happening" (per Widgery L.J.).

Unlike the other forms of secondary participation, the prosecution must establish causation in the case of procuring. There is also a further distinction between the different forms of secondary participation in that aiding, abetting and counselling all require some form of "meeting of minds" between the principal offender(s) and the secondary participants. This is not the case with procuring.

Actus Reus of Secondary Participation

There must be some evidence that actual assistance was provided to the principal offender. The level of assistance need not be very high, as can be seen from *Giannetto*, but there will be no secondary liability imposed where a person merely happens to be at the scene of a crime or fails to stop the commission of a crime. The exception to this general rule is where there is a duty to intervene and that duty is not fulfilled, as occurred in *R. v Dytham* [1979] 3 All E.R. 641. Another exception exists where the perpetrators of the offence derive some encouragement from the presence at the scene of the crime of the accused. In *R. v Clarkson* [1971] 3 All E.R. 344, it was held that for liability to be imposed in such a situation, the fact that the perpetrators of the offence were encouraged by the presence of the accused was not enough in itself. The court held that the prosecution would have to prove that the accused had intended to encourage the commission of the offence. In *People (Attorney General) v Ryan* [1966] 1 Frewen 304, the Court of Criminal Appeal adopted the same position, and in *DPP v Rose*, unreported, Court of Criminal Appeal, 21 February 2002, a murder conviction was overturned on the basis that words uttered by the appellant could not be shown to have encouraged the commission of the offence.

Mens Rea of Secondary Participation

It must be shown that the accessory to the offence intended to assist the principal offender *and* that the accessory knew that an offence was being committed by the principal offender. Intention in this context relates to encouragement or assistance in the commission of the offence. Knowledge that an offence is to be committed appears to be enough. In *DPP v Madden* [1977] I.R. 336, a conviction was upheld where the accused provided a vehicle knowing that the vehicle was to be used in a violent crime. Similarly, in *DPP v Egan* [1989] I.R. 681, a conviction for robbery was upheld even though the accused did not know that an armed robbery had been planned. Liability was imposed on the basis that he had provided the robbers with a place to store a vehicle that had been used in the commission of the offence, knowing that a "small stroke" was to take place.

A victim of an offence will not be convicted as an accessory despite the fact that she could be said to "facilitate" or encourage its commission. An example would be where a man is charged with incest under the Punishment of Incest Act 1908, as amended by the Criminal Law (Incest Proceedings) Act 1995. The female in that situation will not be deemed to be an accomplice, particularly in view of the fact that the 1908 Act seeks to protect people from being victims of the offence.

Section 7(2) of the Criminal Law Act 1997 provides that where a person, knowing that an arrestable offence has been committed, acts with the intention of preventing the arrest of a guilty party, he is guilty of an offence.

The Doctrine of Common Design (Joint Enterprise)

Although there are similarities between the doctrine of common design and secondary participation, the main difference is that under the doctrine of common design, where two or more agree to commit an offence, each party is a principal offender, whereas secondary participants are complicit in offences carried out by principals. In the former, all parties *are* principal offenders, whereas in the latter the parties are dealt with *as though they were* principal offenders.

This, however, would appear to be becoming more of an academic or theoretical distinction rather than a practical one. Dicta from various judgments of the Court of Criminal Appeal suggest that the judiciary regard the two concepts as overlapping. For example, in *DPP v Doohan* [2002] 4 I.R. 463, the accused had hired another man to carry out a punishment beating but told him not to shoot the victim. The victim died from shotgun wounds to the leg. Arguably, these facts point towards the offence of procuring the commission of an indictable offence under s.7 of the Criminal Law Act 1997. The defence argued that the joint enterprise went no further than the punishment beating and that the use of the shotgun had been outside the scope of the original agreement. The court applied *R. v Anderson and Morris* [1996] 2 All E.R. 644 and concluded that there had been a common design and that it had been agreed that the victim would suffer serious injury. That being enough to prove murder, the use of the gun, even though it had not been sanctioned, was not outside the scope of common design.

In *R. v Anderson and Morris* [1996] 2 All E.R. 644, the Court of Appeal held:

> "Where two persons embark on a joint enterprise, each is liable for the acts done in pursuance of that joint enterprise, that includes unusual consequences if they arise from the execution of the agreed joint enterprise but ... if one of the adventurers goes beyond what has been tacitly agreed as part of the common enterprise, his co-adventurer is not liable for the consequences of that unauthorised act."

The main point to be taken from that definition is that where there is an agreement to carry out an offence, all parties to that agreement are liable. But where one party goes further than what was agreed and does something else that was not foreseeable to the other parties, then they are not liable for this unsanctioned activity.

This is so even where it would have to be established that the actual killer must have had the required mens rea for murder. In *DPP v Murray* [1977] I.R. 360, the defendants, a married couple, were involved in a bank robbery. They were pursued by Gardaí and Mrs Murray shot and killed a Garda. Both were convicted of capital murder. On appeal, the Supreme Court held that there had been a common design in relation to the robbery and to the use of violence and also with regard to murder, but that there was no common design with regard to capital murder because there was no evidence to suggest that there had been an agreement on the use of violence against the Gardaí.

However, in both *DPP v Pringle* [1981] 2 Frewen 57 and *DPP v Eccles*, unreported, Court of Criminal Appeal, 10 February 1986, the Court of Criminal Appeal found that there had been a common design in respect of capital murder. The difference between these cases and the *Murray* case is that in *Pringle* and *Eccles*, there had been some evidence of the intention to overcome the Gardaí using whatever force was necessary, whereas no such evidence existed in *Murray*.

The approach of the English courts to the issue of foresight had been different to that taken by the Irish courts. Until recently, the matter had been subject to the principle set out in *Chan Wing-Siu v R.* [1985] A.C. 168, where the three accused, armed with knives, set about committing a robbery, during which a person was stabbed and later died as a result. The accused were each charged with murder and their defence was that although they had brought knives along in order to carry out the robbery, there had been no intention to use them. Their argument was that the knives had been used in self-defence and that neither accused had foreseen the actual use of the knives. The trial judge directed the jury that if the defendants had foreseen serious bodily harm or death as a possibility, this would be enough to convict them, even where they did not intend the eventual outcome. On appeal, it was held that the trial judge's direction had been correct and that where the prosecution could show that the use of the weapon was foreseen by the defendants as being a real possibility, this would suffice for a conviction for murder arising from a joint enterprise. This remained the law in England and Wales until it was overturned by the UK Supreme Court in joined cases *R. v Jogee, Ruddock v The Queen* [2016] UKSC 8, where the court held that the law had taken a "wrong turn" in *Chan Wing-Siu*. The court further held:

"The error was to equate foresight with intent to assist, as a matter of law; the correct approach is to treat it as evidence of intent. The long-standing pre *Chan Wing-Siu* practice of inferring intent to assist from a common criminal purpose which includes the further crime, if the occasion for it were to arise, was always a legitimate one; what was illegitimate was to treat foresight as an inevitable yardstick of common purpose."

Withdrawal from Complicity

If an accessory calls off the arrangement before the crime is committed, he will not be liable for any offences carried out after he has withdrawn. The withdrawal should be communicated to the other participants. In *R. v Jensen and Ward* [1980] V.R. 1904, it was held that withdrawal should either be communicated or that some positive step should be taken, such as calling the police.

KEY CASES AND LEGISLATION

Section 52 of the Children Act 2001, as substituted by s.129 of the Criminal Justice Act 2006—Criminal liability of children.

HL Bolton (Engineering) Co Ltd v TJ Graham and Sons [1956] 3 All E.R. 624—"Controlling mind" test.

R. v Jogee, Ruddock v The Queen [2016] UKSC 8—Ruling on the law on common design in England and Wales.

9 Homicide

The term "homicide" denotes the unlawful killing of a human being. The circumstances of any particular case, coupled with the level of mens rea on the part of the accused, will determine whether the homicide is murder, manslaughter or infanticide.

MURDER

Murder has always been an offence at common law. The most frequently quoted common law definition of murder is that of Coke C.J.:

> "Murder is when a man of sound memory, and at the age of discretion, unlawfully killeth within any country of the realm any reasonable creature *in rerum natura* under the King's peace with malice aforethought either expressed by the party or implied by law, so as the party wounded, or hurt, etc. die of the wound, or hurt, etc. within a year and a day of the same."

The common law definition still holds true but with a number of modifications. First, the mens rea for murder is now contained in s.4(1) of the Criminal Justice Act 1964, which provides: "Where a person kills another unlawfully the killing shall not be murder unless the accused intended to kill, or cause serious injury to, some person, whether the person actually killed or not." Section 4(2) provides: "The accused person shall be presumed to have intended the natural and probable consequences of his conduct, but this presumption may be rebutted."

Secondly, it is no longer the case that the death has to occur within a year and a day of the injury. The so-called "year and a day rule" was abolished by s.38 of the Criminal Justice Act 1999.

Thirdly, the common law definition requires that the accused be "of sound memory, and of the age of discretion". This simply means that the accused must be sane and over the age of criminal responsibility, which, since the enactment of the Criminal Justice Act 2006, is currently 10 years of age in this jurisdiction where the accused is charged with murder or manslaughter.

Finally, the requirement at common law that the victim be "any reasonable creature *in rerum natura*" means that the victim must have been a human being, born alive and with an existence independent of its mother.

Causation

Murder is a result offence and therefore it must be shown that the accused caused the unlawful death. Where the link between the accused's conduct and the victim's death is broken by a novus actus interveniens, the accused will not be liable. In the event that the evidence does not support a conviction for murder, s.9(2) of the Criminal Law Act 1997 provides that a jury may alternatively find the accused guilty of manslaughter, attempted murder, causing serious harm, or aiding/abetting/counselling/procuring suicide. A verdict of manslaughter will also be recorded against an accused who successfully pleads the defence of provocation or excessive self-defence.

Attempted murder

In order to prove the charge of attempted murder, the prosecution must show that the accused carried out the actus reus with the *intention to kill*. In *DPP v Douglas and Hayes* [1985] I.L.R.M. 25, the Court of Criminal Appeal held that the accused cannot be convicted of attempted murder if the mens rea was the intention to cause serious injury.

Penalty on conviction

Murder is an indictable offence and carries a mandatory sentence of life imprisonment. The term "life" means life, although it is commonly and wrongly believed that the term is of a specific duration. The imposition of a sentence is a judicial function. The administration of that sentence is a matter for the Executive. Consequently, an offender sentenced to life imprisonment may be released on licence after a substantial amount of time has been served. The licence will set out the conditions to be imposed and breach of any of these will result in the revocation of the licence and the re-committal of the offender. Article 13.6 of Bunreacht na hÉireann provides that the President has the right to pardon an offender or commute a sanction imposed by a court. Section 23 of the Criminal Justice Act 1951 (as amended) provides that the Government may commute or remit criminal sanctions, including terms of imprisonment, subject to any conditions which they think proper. This power does not apply to aggravated murder. The Government may delegate this power to the Minister for Justice and Equality.

Aggravated murder

The offence of aggravated murder is contained in s.3 of the Criminal Justice Act 1990 (the "1990 Act"). The aggravating factor is the identity of the victim or where the killing is carried out in the course of the commission of certain offences under the Offences against the State Act 1939. The unlawful killing of any of the following people will amount to aggravated murder:

(1) A member of An Garda Síochána acting in the course of his duty;
(2) A prison officer acting in the course of his duty;
(3) The Head of a foreign State, a member of the Government of a foreign State, or a foreign diplomat, where the murder is committed within this State in furtherance of a political objective.

Section 3 of the 1990 Act also applies to attempts to carry out any such murders.

This offence replaces the offence of capital murder which was an offence punishable by death. The death penalty was abolished by s.1 of the 1990 Act, and s.4 of that Act provides that the penalty for aggravated murder is a mandatory life sentence, with the specification that a minimum term of 40 years be served. In the case of attempted aggravated murder, the minimum term of imprisonment is 20 years.

Manslaughter

Manslaughter is a common law offence and arises in two ways: voluntary and involuntary.

Voluntary manslaughter

Where the accused has committed the actus reus for murder and has the mens rea for that offence, but successfully pleads either provocation, excessive self-defence or diminished responsibility, he will be acquitted of murder but convicted of manslaughter. This is because these defences are partial defences which reduce the offence from murder to manslaughter. An acquittal will never be justified since, by definition, the accused has committed the actus reus of murder with the necessary mens rea. The justification for the reduction of the offence to manslaughter is that the mens rea was caused by the action(s) of the deceased. From the point of view of the accused, the main benefit of this reduction is that the mandatory life sentence is avoided, leaving the penalty, which can be anything up to life imprisonment, to be decided by the judge.

INVOLUNTARY MANSLAUGHTER

Involuntary manslaughter occurs where the accused does not have the mens rea for murder, but where the victim dies as a result of the actions or sometimes the omissions of the accused. There is, therefore, no mens rea for manslaughter per se; the offence occurs where, but for the availability of either provocation or excessive self-defence (voluntary manslaughter), the accused would be convicted of murder or, alternatively, where the actions of the accused led to the unintended death of the victim (involuntary manslaughter). Liability for involuntary manslaughter can arise in any one of a number of ways.

(1) A criminal and dangerous act

N.B

The leading case on this type of manslaughter in this jurisdiction is *People (Attorney General) v Crosbie and Meehan* [1966] I.R. 490, where the Court of Criminal Appeal held that in order to sustain a conviction for manslaughter, the act causing the death of the victim had to be unlawful and dangerous. In *DPP v Hendley*, unreported, Court of Criminal Appeal, 11 June 1993, the Court of Criminal Appeal held that in addition to the requirement that the act causing death be unlawful and dangerous, it is also necessary to show that it had been deliberate. The issue of whether an act is dangerous is for the jury to decide but the test is an objective one. In *DPP v Horgan* [2007] 3 I.R. 568, Kearns J. explained that in Irish law, a conviction for manslaughter arising from a criminal and dangerous act requires that:

(a) The act causing the victim's death must be a recognised criminal offence and poses the risk of bodily harm to another;
(b) The act is one which would be considered by an ordinary reasonable person to be dangerous. This refers to an act that is likely to cause bodily harm;
(c) What is "dangerous" is to be judged by objective standards.

(2) Criminal negligence

This occurs where an otherwise lawful act is performed with such a high level of negligence that any reasonable person would have been aware that it carried a substantial risk of serious injury. In *R. v Adomako* [1994] 3 All E.R. 79, the House of Lords held that in order to decide whether the accused had been criminally negligent, the jury had to ask the following questions:

(i) Was there negligence as that term is understood in the context of civil law?

(ii) Was the victim's death caused by the negligence of the accused?
(iii) In acting as he did, had the accused deviated considerably from the standard of care which would have been expected of him?

Where these questions were answered in the affirmative, the accused could be convicted of manslaughter.

In *People (Attorney General) v Dunleavy* [1948] I.R. 95, the Court of Criminal Appeal held that the jury should be told that a very high degree of negligence has to be established in the case of manslaughter. The test is objective and the accused's subjective belief in the reasonableness of his actions is irrelevant. Similarly, in *DPP v Cullagh*, unreported, Court of Criminal Appeal, 15 March 1999, it was stated that the negligence of the accused has to be shown to be "gross negligence" and that the ordinary standard of negligence in civil cases is not enough to sustain a conviction for manslaughter.

(3) Breach of duty

Where the accused refuses or neglects to fulfil a duty that is imposed on him by virtue of a contract, a statute, his relationship with the victim, his office or by his own assumption of a duty to care for the victim, a conviction for manslaughter may result where the victim dies as a result of that breach of duty by the accused. In *R. v Instan* (1893) 17 Cox C.C. 602, the accused refused to provide food or medical assistance to an elderly relative with whom she lived. This refusal led to the death of the victim and the accused was convicted of manslaughter. Similarly, in *R. v Stone* [1977] 2 All E.R. 341, convictions for manslaughter were returned where the two accused had failed to provide medical help for a dependent relative who lived with them. The court held that in the case of the first defendant, the duty had arisen from his blood relationship to the deceased, and in the case of the second defendant, the duty had arisen because she had taken it upon herself to carry out certain tasks for the deceased. Once this responsibility had been accepted, a duty had been assumed by the second defendant and that breach of duty resulted in a conviction for manslaughter. Further examples of convictions arising from breach of duty can be seen in *R. v Senior* (1899) 19 Cox C.C. 219 and *R. v Taktak* (1988) 34 A. Crim. R. 334.

Penalty on conviction

The penalty is at the discretion of the court.

Infanticide

The term "infanticide" is used in two ways in Irish law and is somewhat of a curiosity in that it operates as both an offence and a defence.

The offence of infanticide is a very narrowly defined one and is provided for by the Infanticide Act 1949 (the "1949 Act") (as amended). Section 1 of the 1949 Act creates the offence which is the killing of an infant (under one year of age), through an act or omission that would otherwise be murder, by the mother of the infant who, at the time of the offence, was suffering from the effects of pregnancy and childbirth or from a mental disorder as set out in the Criminal Law (Insanity) Act 2006 (the "2006 Act"). The offence is based on the recognition that a woman may well be suffering from physical and emotional/psychological ill-effects of pregnancy and childbirth, but is illogical in the sense that the offence only applies to the killing of a child under the age of one year.

The wording of the amended s.1 of the 1949 Act raises the question of whether a man suffering from a mental disorder, as defined in the 2006 Act, could also rely on infanticide as a defence. The issue was discussed briefly in *M.D. (A Minor) v Ireland* [2010] 2 I.L.R.M. 491 where the court stated:

> "That particular provision clearly does not apply to men. However it is a provision which on the face of it could be said to discriminate in favour of women but it is a discrimination which is clearly founded on the physical differences between men and women and the effect of childbirth on women."

Penalty on conviction

Section 6(3) of the 2006 Act provides that "a woman found guilty of infanticide may be dealt with in accordance with subsection (1)." Section 6 of the 2006 Act provides for diminished responsibility. The 2006 Act is dealt with in the chapter on insanity. Prior to the enactment of the 2006 Act, the penalty for a woman convicted of infanticide was left to the discretion of the court and was dealt with as manslaughter.

Euthanasia/Assisted Suicide

Euthanasia is the intentional killing of another human being and is also known as "mercy killing". It is a deliberate act, carried out in order to prevent or end suffering. Nonetheless, any person who intentionally kills another is guilty of murder, and his motivation for doing so, however well-intentioned, is irrelevant, as is the "consent" of the victim. A deliberate act, coupled with the intention to kill or seriously injure, is murder, and a benign motive is irrelevant in Irish law.

It is not unlawful to withdraw or withhold medical treatment even where to do so will result in death. Where a patient refuses medical treatment or requests that it be discontinued and the patient is of sufficient capacity to make that decision, such a request must be acceded to. In *Re a Ward of Court (Withdrawal of Medical Treatment) (No. 2)* [1996] 2 I.R. 79, the Supreme Court held that the so-called "right to die" is regarded as being a corollary of the constitutionally protected right to life and an expression of the unenumerated right of bodily integrity, which was recognised in *Ryan v Attorney General* [1965] I.R. 294, and privacy, recognised in *McGee v Attorney General* [1974] I.R. 284 and *Kennedy v Ireland* [1987] I.R. 587.

Suicide is no longer a criminal offence in this jurisdiction, having been abolished by s.2(1) of the Criminal Law (Suicide) Act 1993 (the "1993 Act"). Aiding and abetting the suicide of another person is, however, an offence under s.2(2) of that Act. A challenge to the constitutionality of s.2 was rejected by a Divisional High Court in *Fleming v Ireland* [2013] 2 I.L.R.M. 9. The applicant in this case challenged the constitutionality of the statutory prohibition on assisted suicide and also sought a declaration of incompatibility with the European Convention on Human Rights. The applicant suffered from advanced multiple sclerosis and would have required assistance to end her life. The court held that whilst it was within the rights of a competent adult to refuse medical treatment, "if this Court were to unravel a thread of this law by even the most limited constitutional adjudication in her favour, it would—or, at least, might—open a Pandora's Box which thereafter would be impossible to close". The decision of the High Court was appealed unsuccessfully to the Supreme Court ([2013] 2 I.R. 417) which held:

> "[T]here is no constitutional right to commit suicide or to arrange for the determination of one's life at a time of one's choosing. Thus, the appellant has no right which may be interfered with by any disability. As there is no right to commit suicide so issues, such as discrimination, do not arise; nor do values such as dignity, equality, or any other principle under the Constitution, apply to the situation ... The Court rejects the submission that there exists a constitutional right for a limited class of persons, which would include the appellant. While it is clear that the appellant is in a most tragic situation, the Court has to find constitutional rights anchored in the Constitution. The appellant has relied on her very distressing situation on a fact based argument that the blanket ban affects her adversely. That is not a basis upon which a

constitutional right may be identified. It has not been the jurisprudence of the Constitution that rights may be identified for a limited group of persons."

In 2015, the first prosecution for the offence of aiding, abetting, counselling or procuring a suicide under s.2(2) of the 1993 Act resulted in the acquittal of the accused.

Abortion

Termination of pregnancy had been an offence under the Offences against the Person Act 1861 and it carried a maximum sentence of life imprisonment. Following the referendum on the Eighth Amendment to Bunreacht na hÉireann, the right to life of the unborn was granted explicit protection by Art.40.3.3° of the Constitution. The decision of the Supreme Court in *Attorney General v X.* [1992] 1 I.R. 1 established that abortion could lawfully be obtained in Ireland in circumstances where there was a risk to the woman's life, including the risk of suicide. Two further referendums were subsequently held, resulting in the 13th and 14th Amendments to Bunreacht na hÉireann. These guaranteed the right to travel to avail of abortion services abroad and the right to obtain or make available information on abortion services in other states. In *A., B. and C. v Ireland* (2011) 53 E.H.R.R. 13, the European Court of Human Rights held that by failing to provide a statutory framework within which a woman could obtain an abortion in accordance with the law, Ireland had breached the European Convention on Human Rights in respect of one of the applicants. In the wake of this ruling and public outcry over the death of Savita Halappanavar, the Oireachtas passed the Protection of Life During Pregnancy Act 2013 (the "2013 Act"). Arguably more restrictive than the decision of the Supreme Court in the *X* case, the 2013 Act refers to medical procedures "in the course of which, or as a result of which, an unborn human life is ended". Unlike the wording of the Abortion Act 1967 which governs the issue in England and Wales, the wording of the 2013 Act is more akin to the doctrine of double effect which permits a course of action to be taken even in circumstances where it is foreseeable that another negative side-effect will or probably will ensue.

The main points of the 2013 Act are as follows:

- Section 5 of the 2013 Act repeals ss.58 and 59 of the Offences against the Person Act 1861 (the "1861 Act"). Under s.58 of the 1861 Act, it was an offence to administer drugs or use an implement to procure an abortion. Procuring drugs to cause an abortion had been an offence under s.59 of the 1861 Act.

- Section 22 of the 2013 Act creates the offence of intentional destruction of unborn human life. A prosecution under s.22 can only be brought by/with the consent of the DPP and the maximum penalty on conviction is a fine and/or 14 years' imprisonment.
- Section 7 provides that a medical procedure, during which or as a result of which a pregnancy is terminated, is lawful if two medical practitioners certify that there is a real and substantial risk to the woman's life from physical illness and that the risk can only be averted by performing an abortion. In this instance, the medical procedure must be carried out at an appropriate institution, as defined in the 2013 Act.
- Section 8 of the 2013 Act deals with circumstances in which the risk to the woman's life arises in an emergency situation. In this instance, only one medical practitioner is required to certify that there is an *immediate risk* to the woman's life from physical illness and that the medical practitioner has formed the reasonable opinion that the procedure is *immediately necessary* to save the woman's life.
- Section 9 of the 2013 Act deals with situations where the risk to the woman's life comes from a threat of suicide. In this case, three medical practitioners, two of whom must be psychiatrists, must jointly certify that there is a real and substantial risk to the life of the woman by way of suicide and that the risk can only be averted by carrying out the medical procedure.
- Section 10 of the 2013 Act provides that the opinion of a medical practitioner under s.7 or s.9 may be reviewed on the application of the woman or someone on her behalf. Subsequent parts of the 2013 Act set out the framework and timelines within with reviews must be completed.

KEY CASES AND LEGISLATION

DPP v Douglas and Hayes [1985] I.L.R.M. 25—Mens rea for attempted murder is the intention to kill. Intention to cause serious injury is insufficient.

People (Attorney General) v Crosbie and Meehan [1966] I.R. 490—Leading case on manslaughter by a criminal and dangerous act.

DPP v Horgan [2007] 3 I.R. 568—What must be established in order to secure conviction for manslaughter by a criminal and dangerous act.

Fleming v Ireland [2013] 2 I.R. 417—Constitutionality of prohibition on assisted suicide upheld.

KEY CASES AND LEGISLATION

Attorney General v X. [1992] 1 I.R. 1—Supreme Court decision which held that abortion is permitted where there is a real and substantial risk, including from suicide, to a woman's life.

A., B. and C. v Ireland (2011) 53 E.H.R.R. 13—Ireland held to be in breach of the European Convention on Human Rights by not providing a statutory framework to provide for abortion lawful under the *X* case.

Protection of Life During Pregnancy Act 2013—This Act sets out the circumstances in which an abortion may lawfully be carried out in Ireland.

10 Sexual Offences

The law pertaining to sexual offences has traditionally condemned three types of sexual conduct: sexual activity carried out in the absence of the consent of one of the parties; sexual conduct carried out where one of the parties lacks capacity to give legal consent; and that which, although engaged in consensually, was deemed to be inherently wrong on the basis that it was repugnant to traditional moral standards.

Rape is the clearest example of the first of these categories, but despite the moral and legal condemnation it attracted, a man could not be convicted for raping his wife until the "marital rape exemption" was abolished by the Criminal Law (Rape) (Amendment) Act 1990. Additionally, the law did not recognise male rape until the passing of that Act.

The law in relation to the second type of sexual conduct has also undergone a radical change following the Supreme Court decision in *C.C. v Ireland* [2006] 4 I.R. 1, which struck down as unconstitutional s.1(1) of the Criminal Law Amendment Act 1935 on the basis that a man charged with unlawful carnal knowledge of a girl under the age of 15 years did not have a defence of reasonable mistake available to him. In *A. v Governor of Arbour Hill Prison* [2006] 4 I.R. 88, the applicant, who had been charged, tried and convicted of the offence which had been struck down by the Supreme Court in *C.C. v Ireland*, challenged the legality of his continued detention in respect of the offence. His application was granted by the High Court and he was duly released from custody. This decision was subsequently overruled by the Supreme Court and the applicant was then rearrested. The Criminal Law (Sexual Offences) Act 2006 was rushed through the Oireachtas in the wake of the case of "Mr A" and the offences contained within it are applicable to both sexes.

Finally, the law has traditionally also criminalised activity which, even when carried out by consenting adults, was deemed sufficiently harmful to the moral fabric of society to warrant criminal sanction. The most obvious example of this category of offence was the offence of buggery, which had been covered by ss.61 and 62 of the Offences against the Person Act 1861. This offence was abolished by s.2 of the Criminal Law (Sexual Offences) Act 1993.

This chapter looks at the main offences of a sexual nature covered by Irish law.

Rape

Section 2(1) of the Criminal Law (Rape) Act 1981 (the "1981 Act") provides the statutory definition of what is still referred to as "common law rape". Rape is committed where a man has sexual intercourse with a woman, who at the time of the intercourse does not consent, and where the man either knows that the woman does not consent, or is reckless as to whether or not she consents.

The actus reus of rape is having sexual intercourse with a woman who does not consent. The mens rea is knowledge of, or recklessness as to, the absence of the woman's consent.

Rape, under the 1981 Act, is a gender-specific offence which can only be carried out by a man against a woman. Until the passing of the Criminal Law (Rape) (Amendment) Act 1990 (the "1990 Act"), a man could not be convicted of raping his wife due to the requirement at common law that in order to convict for rape, sexual intercourse had to be "unlawful", and since this meant outside marriage, husbands were granted a "marital rape exemption". Section 5 of the 1990 Act abolished this requirement, although the consent of the DPP is still required before a prosecution for rape within marriage can be brought. Another exemption existed in respect of boys under the age of 14, who were conclusively presumed to be incapable of rape. This presumption was abolished by s.6 of the 1990 Act and, consequently, a boy under the age of 14 (but older than seven) could be prosecuted, provided that the presumption of doli incapax had been rebutted. This position has changed as a result of the enactment of the Criminal Justice Act 2006 and, currently, a boy of 10 may be charged with rape, provided that the consent of the DPP is granted.

For the purposes of s.2(1) of the 1981 Act, sexual intercourse means vaginal intercourse only. The offence is complete upon penetration, which must be proven. In *People (Attorney General) v Dermody* [1956] I.R. 307, it was held that the slightest penetration would suffice.

Consent

Absence of the woman's consent is an essential part of the actus reus and this must be established. The following comment by Charleton J. in *DPP v C.O'R.* [2016] 2 I.L.R.M. 465 provides a clear statement on the issue of consent in the context of rape: "The border between rape and sexual intercourse is consent."

In *DPP v C.O'R.*, the accused had been convicted of raping his mother and sentenced to 15 years' imprisonment, with a portion of the sentence suspended. The conviction was appealed to the Court of Appeal on various grounds, including that the trial judge had inadequately instructed the jury as to the elements of the offence of rape. The appeal was dismissed and the accused obtained leave to bring the appeal to the Supreme Court pursuant to Art.34.5.3°, where a ruling was sought on two issues:

(1) Whether the mens reas for rape allows for a situation where an accused genuinely believes, even on unreasonable and irrational grounds, that a woman has consented to sexual intercourse, when in fact, she has not;
(2) Must a man ascertain, prior to sexual intercourse, that a woman is capable of consenting and that she has, in fact, consented.

The court held that belief that the woman *might* be consenting to sexual intercourse is not a defence. However, in cases where the accused genuinely believed, even unreasonably, that the woman was consenting, he must be acquitted. A jury should be told by the trial judge that they are not obliged to believe a story that is obviously false and that they are entrusted "using shrewdness and common sense" to judge the claim of mistaken belief by reference to their view of what an ordinary or reasonable person would have realised in the same circumstances as the accused.

Consent must be freely given, and where consent is subsequently withdrawn, the man must desist or he will be liable to a charge of rape. The same applies where the man realises that there is no consent on the part of the woman. In *Kaitamaki v R.* [1984] 2 All E.R. 435, it was held that rape was a continuing act and that the accused was guilty of the offence when he continued having intercourse after he had become aware that the woman did not consent.

Vitiating factors

Consent may be vitiated where it is induced by fraud. In *R. v Flattery* (1877) 13 Cox C.C. 388 and *R. v Williams* [1922] All E.R. 433, convictions for rape were returned where the consent of the complainants had been induced by fraudulent misrepresentations as to the nature of the act. The complainant in the first case had been told that she was having a surgical procedure carried out, and the complainant in the second case had been told that she was undergoing a procedure that would improve her singing voice. The fraudulent misrepresentation must be in relation to the nature of the act of sexual intercourse. In *R. v Linekar* [1995] 3 All E.R. 69, the accused was acquitted of raping a prostitute. She had agreed to have intercourse with him in return for a specified sum of money which was then not paid. There was evidence indicating that the accused had no intention of paying. This, however, did not amount to fraud for the purpose of gaining consent to sexual intercourse. The complainant had agreed to have intercourse with the accused, and the fact that he made off without paying her did not have any relevance to the issue of consent.

A question arises as to whether consent to sexual intercourse is vitiated in cases of impersonation. In *DPP v C.* [2001] 3 I.R. 345, the Court of Criminal Appeal stated:

> "Knowledge or understanding of facts material to the act being consented to is necessary for the consent to be voluntary or constitute acquiescence. In stating that a person who has sex with one person believing it to be another person, that person is not consenting to sexual intercourse with the former, the court is satisfied that the trial judge made a correct statement of the law".

In such a case, following the ruling in *DPP v C.O'R.*, the man's genuine belief as to the woman's consent and the presence or absence of objectively reasonable grounds for that belief will be a matter for the jury.

The woman must be capable of giving consent. In *R. v Mayers* (1872) 12 Cox C.C. 311 and in *DPP v X.*, unreported, Central Criminal Court, Budd J., 20 May 1995, it was held that a sleeping woman was incapable of giving consent. Similarly, consent may be vitiated where it is induced by intoxication. In *R. v Camplin* (1845) 1 Cox C.C. 220, the accused was convicted of rape where he had caused the complainant to become intoxicated and then had sexual intercourse with her. In *R. v Lang* (1975) 62 Cr. App. Rep. 50, the Court of Appeal held that it is the effect of the intoxicant on the complainant and not the fact that she consumed it that is relevant, and that where a woman is incapable of exercising judgement due to intoxication, consent will not be valid.

Submission and failure to resist

Failure to resist is not the same as consent. Section 9 of the 1990 Act provides that failure to offer resistance does not of itself constitute consent. The jury is entitled to take this matter into account and may infer consent where no evidence of resistance is adduced.

Submission to sexual intercourse is not the same as consenting to it. Where the complainant submits to intercourse due to fear or intimidation, consent is not freely given. In *R. v Olugboja* [1981] 3 All E.R. 443, it had been argued by the defence that the complainant had been "persuaded" to have sexual intercourse with the accused. The Court of Appeal held that a jury in a rape trial should be told that consent and submission are not the same and that, while consent involves submission, the reverse is not always true. The threat does not have to be one of force and the jury should take the complainant's state of mind and the surrounding facts into account when deciding whether the submission to sexual intercourse amounted to consent.

Mens rea

As previously stated, the mens rea for rape, as with most sexual offences, is the man's knowledge of the woman's absence of consent or his recklessness to that fact. It is set out in s.2(1)(b) of the 1981 Act. In the situation where a man believes that the woman is consenting, the question as to whether a genuine belief that the woman is consenting is enough, or whether it must also be reasonable, was answered by the Supreme Court in *DPP v C.O'R*. Section 2(2) of the 1981 Act states that where this issue is raised, the jury is to have regard to the presence or absence of reasonable grounds for the defendant's belief. The test has both subjective and objective elements; the defendant's genuine belief is relevant, but the jury must then determine whether the defendant had any reasonable grounds upon which to base his belief. This approach was eventually adopted in England following the decision of the House of Lords in *DPP v Morgan* [1975] 2 All E.R. 347. In that case, the House of Lords held that an honest belief, however unreasonably held, meant that an accused could not be convicted of rape. In this jurisdiction, the jury in a rape trial need only be directed as to the provisions of s.2(2) if the accused claims that he believed that the woman was consenting. This is clear from the wording of the provision itself and was held to be the case by the Supreme Court in *DPP v McDonagh* [1996] 1 I.R. 565.

Recklessness

The test for recklessness is likely to be subjective. In *DPP v Creighton* [1994] 1 I.L.R.M. 551, the Court of Criminal Appeal stated that recklessness is the same as heedless conduct. The test in English law is subjective. In *R. v Satnam* [1988] Crim. L.R. 236, the Court of Appeal held that where the defendant had continued having intercourse regardless of the woman's consent, the jury was entitled to conclude that he had acted recklessly.

Penalty on conviction

Rape is an indictable offence and is punishable by a maximum sentence of life imprisonment.

Rape under s.4 of the Criminal Law (Rape) (Amendment) Act 1990

This section deals with offences of a penetrative nature other than those covered by s.2 of the 1981 Act. Unlike rape under the 1981 Act, the offences covered by s.4 of the 1990 Act are drafted in gender-neutral terms. There are two elements to the actus reus:

(a) Penetration of the anus or mouth by the penis; or
(b) Penetration of the vagina by any object held or manipulated by another person.

Clearly, the offence contained in the first category may only be committed by a male and it may be committed against a male or a female. The offence in the second category may be committed by a male or a female but only against a female.

The mens rea is not stated in the section itself, but given that an offence under s.4 is one of sexual assault, albeit one which involves penetration, it makes sense to regard the mens rea for sexual assault or rape as being applicable, with the same being the case in relation to the issue of consent.

Penalty on conviction

Rape under s.4 of the 1990 Act is an indictable offence and is punishable by a maximum sentence of life imprisonment.

Sexual Assault

Section 2 of the 1990 Act gives statutory expression to the common law offences of indecent assault upon a male person and indecent assault upon a female person. Both offences are now combined in a gender-neutral form in the section. In *DPP v E.F.*, unreported, Supreme Court, 24 January 1994, the court held that the common law offence of indecent assault remained an offence at common law but that it was possible to re-name it and set out the appropriate penalty in legislation. At common law the offence of indecent assault consists of two elements: (a) an assault, and (b) circumstances of indecency, both of which must be established in order to secure a conviction. It had been the case that the actus reus of sexual assault was considered to be the same as that for the offence of assault under s.2 of the Non-Fatal Offences against the Person Act 1997 (the "1997 Act"), with the additional requirement that it be carried out in circumstances of indecency. A number of decisions of the High and Supreme Courts have, however, cast doubt on this. In *Minister for Justice and Equality v Dolny* [2009] IESC 48, the Supreme Court upheld a decision of the High Court which had held that the offence of assault under s.2 and that of assault causing harm under s.3 of the 1997 Act were free-standing offences and that s.2 was not intended to define assault for all purposes of the 1997 Act.

In *Doolan v DPP* [1993] I.L.R.M. 387, indecent assault was defined by O'Hanlon J. as the "use of unlawful force, threatened or perpetrated against another person." This approach was affirmed by the Supreme Court in *DPP v E.F.* In *S.O'C. v Governor of Curragh Prison* [2002] 1 I.R. 66, the Supreme Court held that unlike other common law offences such as assault and battery, the offence of indecent assault had not been abolished by the 1997 Act.

The second element of the actus reus is that the assault must take place in circumstances which are indecent. What amounts to indecency will depend on the facts of each case but where there is uncertainty, the guidelines laid down by the House of Lords in *R. v Court* [1988] 2 All E.R. 221 may be of some assistance. In that case, the House of Lords categorised different types of conduct under three headings:

(i) Acts which are not inherently indecent. An example might be where the accused removes someone's coat. This is not an inherently indecent act and the fact that the accused derives some form of gratification from doing it will not suffice to render it an indecent act.
(ii) Acts which are inherently indecent, regardless of the motive of the accused. These will suffice for the purpose of establishing circumstances of indecency.
(iii) Acts which may be indecent depending on the circumstances. In determining whether these acts are indecent, the jury should have regard to how they might be viewed by right-minded people, taking the relationship between the parties and the reason for the accused's actions into consideration.

Consent may be a defence to a charge of sexual assault, provided, of course, that consent is freely given by a person with the capacity to give it and that the conduct in question is capable of being consented to.

Penalty on conviction

Section 2 of the 1990 Act, as amended by s.37 of the Sex Offenders Act 2001, provides that the maximum penalty for the offence of sexual assault is a term of 10 years' imprisonment. If the offence is committed against a person younger than 17 years of age, the maximum penalty is a term of 14 years' imprisonment.

Aggravated Sexual Assault

Section 3 of the 1990 Act deals with the offence of aggravated sexual assault. Essentially, this is a more serious form of the offence under s.2 of the 1990 Act, and comprises sexual assault coupled with the use or threat of serious violence, grave humiliation, degradation or injury.

The actus reus has two elements: the intentional assault in circumstances of indecency, and the use or threat of serious violence, grave humiliation, degradation or injury. There are two parts to the mens rea also: the intention to commit an indecent assault, and the intention to use or threaten to use serious violence, grave humiliation, degradation or injury.

Consent may not be a defence to an offence under s.3 of the 1990 Act. The section envisages activity of a much graver nature than that which is contemplated by s.2. An analogy might be drawn with s.4 of the 1997 Act, which creates the offence of "causing serious harm". Consent is not a defence to that offence and it seems reasonable to suppose that given the nature of the offence under s.3 of the 1990 Act, as reflected by the potential penalty attracted by it, consent would not be a defence to a charge of aggravated sexual assault either.

In *R. v Brown* [1993] 2 All E.R. 75, the House of Lords refused to allow a defence of consent to charges of assault causing actual bodily harm. The case involved a group of sado-masochists who had inflicted injuries, some of which required hospitalisation, on each other. The defendants argued that they had participated in the conduct consensually and that their convictions should be overturned. When the House of Lords ruled against them, they brought a case before the European Court of Human Rights, arguing that their rights under the European Convention on Human Rights had been breached. In *Laskey, Jaggard and Brown v UK* (1997) 24 E.H.R.R. 39, the European Court of Human Rights held against the applicants, stating that the respondent had the right and the duty to protect vulnerable sectors within society and that this did not breach any right asserted by the applicants under the Convention.

Penalty on conviction

Aggravated sexual assault is an indictable offence and carries a maximum sentence of life imprisonment.

Defilement of a Child

A girl who is under the age of consent (17 years) cannot, by definition, give consent to sexual intercourse. Therefore, regardless of the girl's willingness to engage in sexual intercourse, no defence of consent can avail an accused.

The legislation governing this issue had been the Criminal Law Amendment Act 1935 (the "1935 Act"), s.1(1) of which provided that unlawful carnal knowledge of a girl who is under the age of 15 was an offence, regardless of any purported consent on the part of the girl and regardless of the belief on the part of the man that the girl was older than 15. Section 2 of the 1935 Act provided that the unlawful carnal knowledge of a girl between the ages of 15 and 17 was also an offence, albeit a less serious one.

Consent on the part of the girl was irrelevant, as was the belief on the part of the man that the girl was older than 17. In effect, these offences, commonly referred to as "statutory rape", were offences of absolute liability; all that had to be established was the age of the girl and that sexual intercourse had taken place. Section 1(1) of the 1935 Act was struck down by the Supreme Court as being repugnant to the terms of Bunreacht na hÉireann in *CC v Ireland* [2006] 4 I.R. 1 on the basis that an accused did not have any defence of honest mistake available to him.

Honest mistake

In response to the Supreme Court's ruling, the Oireachtas passed the Criminal Law (Sexual Offences) Act 2006 (the "2006 Act"). Section 2 of the 2006 Act replaces s.1(1) of the 1935 Act with a similar provision, but provides in s.2(3) that:

> "It shall be a defence to proceedings for an offence under this section for the defendant to prove that he or she honestly believed that, at the time of the alleged commission of the offence, the child against whom the offence was alleged to have been committed had attained the age of 15 years."

Where the accused relies on the defence of honest mistake, the 2006 Act provides that the court shall have regard to the presence or absence of reasonable grounds for such belief. Although the only provision struck down as being repugnant to the terms of Bunreacht na hÉireann in *CC* was s.1(1) of the 1935 Act, s.1(2), which provided for the attempted defilement of a girl under the age of 15, and s.2, which provided for similar offences in respect of girls between 15 and 17, were repealed by s.8 of the 2006 Act. The new offences are drafted in gender-neutral terms and, consequently, apply to offences against males as well as females. The defence of honest mistake is similarly available to these offences. Section 2 of the 1935 Act was ultimately struck down as unconstitutional by the Supreme Court in *Z.S. v DPP* [2013] 3 I.R. 626.

Defilement of a Child under the Age of 15 Years

Section 2 of the 2006 Act provides that it is an offence for any person to engage in a sexual act with a child who is younger than 15 years of age or to attempt to do so. The 2006 Act defines "sexual act" as an act consisting of sexual intercourse or buggery between persons who are not married to each other or an act described in s.3(1) or s.4(1) of the 1990 Act. Where the accused raises the defence of honest mistake as to the age of the child, the court must consider whether there were reasonable grounds for the belief of the accused. Consent by the child is not a defence. The offence under s.2 carries a maximum penalty of life imprisonment.

Defilement of a Child under the Age of 17 Years

The offence created by s.3 of the 2006 Act is committed in the same way as the offence under s.2. The difference between the two offences is the age of the child against whom the offence is committed. The penalty for this offence is a maximum term of five years' imprisonment or, if the accused is a person in a position of authority in relation to the child, to a term of up to 10 years' imprisonment. In the case of an inchoate offence under s.3, the penalty is a maximum term of imprisonment of five years, and in the case of a person in a position of authority, a maximum of 10 years' imprisonment, in accordance with s.5 of the Criminal Law (Sexual Offences) (Amendment) Act 2007. The section provides that in the case of a subsequent commission of the offence, longer terms of imprisonment may be imposed. The defence of honest belief is available to the accused and, if raised, the court will have regard to the presence or absence of reasonable grounds for the belief.

An offence under s.2 or s.3 of the 2006 Act may be tried summarily if:

(i) the court is of the opinion that the facts alleged constitute a minor offence capable of being tried summarily;

(ii) the accused, having been informed of his right to trial by jury, does not object to the summary disposal of the case; and
(iii) the DPP consents to the summary trial of the offence.

If tried summarily, the 2006 Act provides for the imposition of lesser penalties. Somewhat curiously, the 2006 Act provides that a female child under the age of 17 will not be found guilty of an offence under the 2006 Act by reason only of having engaged in sexual intercourse. This provides a positive defence to females which is denied to males and, accordingly, has been identified by many commentators as being discriminatory having regard to the equality provisions of Bunreacht na hÉireann. The constitutionality of s.5 was upheld by the Supreme Court in *M.D. (A Minor) v Ireland* [2012] 1 I.R. 697 where Denham C.J. stated:

> "The danger of pregnancy for the teenage girl was an objective to which the Oireachtas was entitled to regard as relating to 'differences of capacity, physical and moral and of social function', as provided for in Article 40.1 of the Constitution."

The Supreme Court in *M.D.* also stated that the DPP had discretion in her choice of prosecuting under s.2 or s.3 of the 2006 Act.

Under s.6 of the Criminal Law (Sexual Offences) Act 1993 (the "1993 Act"), as amended by the Criminal Law (Sexual Offences) (Amendment) Act 2007, it is an offence for any person to solicit or importune a child for the purpose of committing an act that contravenes s.2 of the 1990 Act, s.5 of the 1993 Act, or s.2 or s.3 of the 2006 Act.

Repeal of certain offences by the Criminal Law (Sexual Offences) Act 2006

Following the decision of the European Court of Human Rights in *Norris v Ireland* (1991) 13 E.H.R.R. 186, the Oireachtas passed the 1993 Act. Under the provisions of the 1993 Act, the offence of buggery as contained in s.61 of the Offences against the Person Act 1861 was abolished, thereby decriminalising this form of sexual activity between consenting male adults. Section 3 of the 1993 Act contained offences of buggery against males under the age of 15, and between 15 and 17 respectively. This section was replaced by ss.2 and 3 of the Criminal Law (Sexual Offences) Act 2006 (the "2006 Act").

Section 11 of the Criminal Law Amendment Act 1885 (the "1885 Act") provided that it was an offence to commit or attempt to commit any act of gross indecency, whether in public or in private. The 1885 Act provided no definition for "gross indecency", but essentially, the offence amounted to sexual activity between males excluding buggery. Section 11 of the 1885 Act had been repealed by s.4 of the 1993 Act, which provided that it was an offence to commit or attempt to commit acts of gross indecency with males under 15 years of age or with males between 15 and 17. This too was replaced by ss.2 and 3 of the 2006 Act.

Sexual Offences against Mentally Ill Persons

Section 5 of the 1993 Act created the offences of:

(1) intercourse with a mentally impaired person or an attempt to have intercourse with a mentally impaired person;
(2) buggery or attempted buggery of a mentally impaired person;
(3) acts or attempted acts of gross indecency by a male against a male who is mentally impaired.

Mental impairment is defined in s.5 as "suffering from a disorder of the mind, whether through mental handicap or mental illness which is of such a nature or degree as to render a person incapable of living an independent life or of guarding against serious exploitation". Where the accused did not know and had no reason to suspect that the person was mentally impaired, the accused will have a defence on this basis. Whilst the object of s.5 of the 1993 Act is to protect mentally impaired people from sexual exploitation, it has been criticised for adopting an overly paternalistic approach to sexual activity involving mentally impaired persons. It might also be criticised on the basis that it does not criminalise sexual activity other than sexual intercourse and buggery which might involve an equal level of exploitation and abuse, leaving this to be prosecuted under the 1990 Act. Nor does it envisage that unmarried people, who may be mentally impaired, may nonetheless have capacity to consent to sexual activity. Section 5 also appears to presume consent in the case of marriage and the absence of consent in the case of unmarried people.

The jury must have regard to the accused's state of mental health also, and where the accused is of limited intelligence, this factor should be borne in the minds of the jury.

INCEST

The Punishment of Incest Act 1908 (the "1908 Act") makes it an offence to engage in sexual intercourse with someone who is closely related by blood. The offence does not include sexual intercourse between persons of the same sex. For the purposes of the offence of incest, sexual intercourse is vaginal intercourse only. Consequently, any other sexual activity is excluded from the scope of the 1908 Act. Consent is not a defence to a charge of incest. Where there is no ostensible or purported "consent", a prosecution under the Criminal Law (Rape) Act 1981 or under s.4 of the Criminal Law (Rape)(Amendment) Act 1990 may be brought instead since the absence of consent is a key component of both offences. A prosecution under s.2 or s.3 of the Criminal Law (Sexual Offences) Act 2006 may also be appropriate if either/both of the parties is/are under 17 years of age; by definition, a female younger than 17 cannot be convicted of incest under s.2 of the 1908 Act. It would also be possible to charge one party as a principal offender and the other as an accomplice. The terms "brother" and "sister" include half-siblings.

INCEST BY A MALE

Section 1 of the 1908 Act, as amended by the Criminal Law (Incest Proceedings) Act 1995, provides that incest by a male is committed where a man has sexual intercourse with a woman who is to his knowledge his mother, sister, half-sister, daughter or granddaughter. The offence is not committed if there is no blood relationship between the accused and the woman and the age of the parties is irrelevant. The accused must also be acquitted if the prosecution fails to prove that he knew of the blood relationship between him and the woman. Recklessness will not suffice. The offence is triable on indictment and, on conviction, carries a maximum penalty of life imprisonment.

INCEST BY A FEMALE

Incest by a female is an offence under s.2 of the 1908 Act. It is committed where a woman over the age of 17 permits her father, grandfather, brother, half-brother or son to have sexual intercourse with her, knowing that they are related by blood. This offence carries a maximum term of seven years' imprisonment.

SEXUAL EXPLOITATION

The Child Trafficking and Pornography Act 1998 (the "1998 Act") was enacted with the objective of combating international paedophile rings who rely on the availability of children. The 1998 Act has been amended by the Criminal Law (Sexual Offences) (Amendment) Act 2007, the Criminal Law (Human Trafficking) Act 2008 (the "2008 Act"), and the Criminal Law (Human Trafficking) (Amendment) Act 2013 (the "2013 Act"). The 1998 Act seeks to achieve this objective by setting out a number of offences. Section 3 of the 1998 Act provides that it is an offence to organise or knowingly facilitate the entry into, or exit from, the State of a child for the purpose of the sexual exploitation of the child. It is also an offence to provide accommodation for a child for the purpose of sexual exploitation. This offence is clearly directed at those who are involved in paedophile rings and is committed regardless of whether the accused sexually abuses the child or not. Where a person takes, detains or restricts the liberty of a child for the purpose of sexual exploitation or uses the child for this purpose, he will be liable on conviction to a term of imprisonment for life. Sexual exploitation is broadly defined in the 1998 Act and includes the use of the child for prostitution or pornographic purposes. As amended by the 2013 Act, where an offence under s.3(1) of the 1998 Act is committed by a public official during the performance of his duties, the court must regard this as an aggravating factor. When imposing sentence, other than a life sentence, the court must, unless there are exceptional circumstances for not doing so, impose a sentence that is greater than would have been imposed in the absence of the aggravating factor.

The 2008 Act, as amended by the 2013 Act, is concerned with the trafficking of adults and children for the purpose of exploitation. Exploitation is defined in the 2008 Act as labour exploitation, sexual exploitation, exploitation consisting of the removal of one or more organs of the person, or forcing a person to engage in criminal activity for the purpose of financial gain.

The making or possession of child pornography is also an offence under s.4 of the 1998 Act. The offence is committed where any person who has custody, charge, or care of a child permits the child to be used for the purpose of child pornography. This is an indictable offence and it is punishable by a maximum fine of €31,743 [£25,000] and/or up to 14 years' imprisonment.

Section 5 of the 1998 Act effectively criminalises any conduct that relates to child pornography that is not covered by s.4, whether or not for profit. This offence may be tried summarily or on indictment. On summary conviction, the maximum penalty is a fine of €2,500 and/or 12 months' imprisonment. On indictment, the maximum penalty is an unlimited fine and/or 14 years' imprisonment.

Section 6 of the 1998 Act provides that a person who knowingly has possession of child pornography commits an offence. This offence carries a maximum penalty on summary conviction of a fine of €2,500 and/or 12 months' imprisonment. On indictment, the maximum penalty is a fine of €6,348.69 (£5,000) and/or five years' imprisonment.

Section 6 also exempts people from liability for possession of child pornography if it is in their possession in the exercise of various statutory functions or for the investigation of offences under the 1998 Act. A person who can prove that he had possession of child pornography for the purposes of bona fide research will have a defence.

The Sex Offenders Act 2001

The Sex Offenders Act 2001 (the "2001 Act") contains a number of provisions which impose certain obligations on individuals convicted of any of the sexual offences to which the 2001 Act applies. The relevant offences are contained in the Schedule to the 2001 Act, and where further offences have been created since the enactment of the 2001 Act, these may also be subject to the requirements of the 2001 Act. The obligations imposed by the 2001 Act exist alongside any penal sanction imposed by the court in respect of such offences, and the 2001 Act provides for the length of time for which these obligations are effective. Part 2 of the 2001 Act imposes obligations on sex offenders to provide the Gardaí with certain information concerning their name, home address or any other address used by them. This is commonly referred to as the "sex offenders register", although no such register exists. Sex offenders convicted in another jurisdiction are also amenable to the provisions of the 2001 Act. Part 3 of the 2001 Act provides for Sex Offenders Orders, which are granted on the application of a member of the Gardaí not below the rank of Chief Superintendent where the court is satisfied that the order should be granted in order to protect the public. The order prohibits the person named within it from carrying out certain types of conduct specified in the order.

The Criminal Law (Sexual Offences) Act 2017

The Criminal Law (Sexual Offences) Act 2017 (the "2017 Act") was signed by the President on 22 February 2017 but at the time of writing was awaiting commencement. The stated purpose of the 2017 Act is to give effect to Directive 2011/93/EU on combating the sexual abuse and sexual exploitation of children and to replace Council Framework Decision 2004/68/JHA. The 2017 Act amends various pieces of legislation, notably, the 1998 Act, the 1908 Act, and the Criminal Law (Sexual Offences) Act 2006. These Acts remain in force until such time as the relevant amending provisions in the 2017 Act come into force. The 2017 Act introduces a number of new offences into Irish law. These include:

- Child grooming offences and offences involving online predators;
- Public indecency;
- The purchase of sexual services.

The 2017 Act also amends and expands the existing offences relating to the sexual exploitation of children and child pornography.

Sexual Exploitation of Children

Part 2 of the 2017 Act contains a range of offences of sexual exploitation of children. Section 3 of the 2017 Act makes it an offence to obtain or provide a child, defined for the purposes of s.3 as a person younger than 18 years of age, for the purposes of sexual exploitation. The offence is committed by anyone who pays, or offers to pay, money or any other form of remuneration/ consideration or who promises to do so in order to obtain a child or who accepts or agrees to accept a child either for himself or for another person, for the purposes of sexual exploitation. The penalty for this offence on summary conviction is a class A fine and/or up to 12 months' imprisonment. On indictment, the maximum penalty is an unlimited fine and/or 10 years' imprisonment.

Under s.4, any person who, for sexual purposes, invites, induces, counsels, or incites a child of under 15 years of age to touch, with a part of the child's body or an object, the body of any person, commits an offence. This offence is punishable by a maximum term of up to 14 years' imprisonment.

Section 5 of the 2017 Act creates the offence of sexual activity in the presence of a child younger than 17 years of age. Any person who intentionally engages in sexual activity in front of a child, for the purposes of obtaining sexual gratification from the presence of a child or from corrupting/depraving a child, is guilty of this offence. The sexual activity need not involve another participant. For the purposes of s.5, the offence is committed due to the child's presence or where the child is in a place where the sexual activity can be observed by the child and the person knows or believes that the child knows that sexual activity is taking place, or intending that the child should be aware of it. The offence under s.5 is an indictable offence which carries a maximum term of imprisonment of 10 years. Section 6 of the 2017 Act contains a related offence which is committed by a person who causes a child, younger than 17 years of age, to watch another person engaging in sexual activity or to look at images of sexual activity. The maximum penalty for this offence is a term of imprisonment of 10 years.

Section 7 of the 2017 Act creates the offence of meeting a child for the purpose of sexual exploitation. A person who intentionally meets or travels to any place with the intention of meeting a child, younger than 17 years of age, for the purpose of sexual exploitation, commits an offence. The person is also guilty of the offence if he makes arrangements to meet a child or to have the child travel to meet with him, having first communicated on at least one occasion with the child. This offence is triable on indictment and carries a maximum penalty of 14 years' imprisonment.

Section 8 of the 2017 Act provides that it is an offence to use information and communication technology to facilitate the sexual exploitation of a child. The maximum penalty for this offence is a term of imprisonment of 14 years. A further offence of sending sexually explicit images or words to a child is contained in s.8(2). A child, for the purposes of s.8, is a person younger than 17 years of age. The penalty on summary conviction for the offence under s.8(2) is a class A fine and/or up to 12 months' imprisonment. On indictment, the maximum penalty is a term of five years' imprisonment. The offence under s.8(2) encompasses situations where sexually explicit material is shared by phone or on the internet by under-age children, commonly referred to as "sexting". A person under the age of 17 may only be prosecuted under s.8 with the consent of the DPP.

Section 11 of the 2017 Act sets out offences involving any activity concerned with organising child prostitution or child pornography. This encompasses a wide range of conduct, namely:

- Controlling or directing the activities of a child for prostitution or the production of child pornography;
- Organising child prostitution or the production of child pornography;
- Compelling, coercing, or recruitment of children to engage in prostitution or child pornography;
- Knowingly making a gain from child prostitution or child pornography;
- Inciting or causing a child to become involved in prostitution or pornography.

The maximum penalty for an offence under s.4A of the 1998 Act, as inserted by s.11 of the 2017 Act, is an unlimited fine and/or 14 years' imprisonment.

Section 12 of the 2017 Act deals with the production or distribution of child pornography. This offence can be committed in many different ways and provides that a person commits an offence if he:

- knowingly produces, distributes, transmits, disseminates, prints, or publishes any child pornography;
- knowingly imports, exports, sells, or shows any child pornography;
- knowingly supplies or makes child pornography available to any other person;

- knowingly publishes, distributes, transmits, or disseminates an advertisement likely to convey that the advertiser or any other person produces, distributes, transmits, disseminates, prints, publishes, imports, exports, sells, shows, supplies, or makes available any child pornography;
- encourages, knowingly causes, or facilitates any of the above activities; or
- knowingly possesses any child pornography for the purposes of supplying it by any means.

The penalty on summary conviction is a class A fine and/or a term of up to 12 months' imprisonment. On indictment, the maximum penalty is an unlimited fine and/or 14 years' imprisonment.

Section 13 of the 2017 Act criminalises any conduct which causes a child to participate in a pornographic performance. It provides that any person who:

- causes, incites, compels or coerces, or
- recruits, invites, or induces

a child to take part in a pornographic performance, or who makes a gain from the child's participation, will be guilty of an offence. The maximum penalty for this indictable offence is a term of imprisonment of 10 years. It is also an offence under s.5A of the 1998 Act, as inserted by s.13 of the 2017 Act, to knowingly attend at a pornographic performance involving a child. A pornographic performance, for the purposes of s.5A, includes a live performance aimed at an audience, including by means of information or communication technology depicting a child engaged in real or simulated sexual activity or the sexually explicit exhibition of the child.

On summary conviction, this offence carries a penalty of a class A fine and/or up to 12 months' imprisonment. On indictment, the maximum penalty is an unlimited fine and/or 10 years' imprisonment.

Offences related to the possession of child pornography are set out in s.14 of the 2017 Act. This offence can be committed in two ways: first, where a person knowingly acquires or possesses child pornography, or secondly, where a person knowingly obtains access to child pornography, using information and communication technology. The penalty for possession of child pornography on summary conviction is a class A fine and/or up to 12 months' imprisonment. On indictment, the maximum penalty is an unlimited fine and/or five years' imprisonment. Section 14 of the 2017 Act exempts people from liability for possession of child pornography if it is in their possession in the exercise of various statutory functions or for the investigation of offences under the 2017 Act. A person who can prove that he has possession of child pornography for the purposes of bona fide research will have a defence.

Sections 16 and 17 of the 2017 Act amend ss.2 and 3 of the Criminal Law (Sexual Offences) Act 2006 (the "2006 Act") respectively. The wording of s.2 of the 2006 Act is substituted by a newly worded provision, the effect of which is that a person who engages or attempts to engage in a sexual act with a child under 15 years of age is guilty of an offence. The maximum penalty on indictment is life imprisonment. The defence of reasonable mistake may be raised by the defence who must, on the civil standard of proof, discharge the onus of proving it. If the defence is raised, the court must consider whether, in all the circumstances of the case, a reasonable person would have believed that the child was over 15 years of age. The purported consent of the child is not a defence except where the offence is committed by children between the ages of 15 and 17 years and the defendant is younger or less than two years older than the other child and was not, at the time of the commission of the alleged offence, a person in authority in respect of the child or in a relationship with the child that was intimidatory or exploitative.

Section 17 of the 2017 Act contains a similar offence to the one contained in s.16 and applies in circumstances where a person engages or attempts to engage in a sexual act with a child younger than 17 years of age. This offence carries a maximum penalty of seven years' imprisonment on indictment. If the accused is a person in authority, the maximum penalty is 15 years' imprisonment. The defence of reasonable mistake may be raised by the defence who must, on the civil standard of proof, discharge the onus of proving it. If the defence is raised, the court must consider whether, in all the circumstances of the case, a reasonable person would have believed that the child was over 17 years of age. The purported consent of the child is not a defence. A prosecution under s.17 requires the consent of the DPP.

Sexual Acts with Protected Persons

Part 3 criminalises the commission of sexual acts with vulnerable people, referred to in s.21 of the 2017 Act as "protected persons". For the purposes of the 2017 Act, a protected person is a person who lacks the capacity to consent to a sexual act as they have a mental or intellectual disability or mental illness which renders them incapable of:

- understanding the nature of the act or what might be reasonably foreseeable as a consequence of it;
- evaluating relevant information for the purposes of deciding whether they should engage in the act; or
- communicating their consent to the act by speech, sign language or by some other means.

Section 21 of the 2017 Act defines "sexual act" as sexual intercourse (as that term is understood in the Criminal Law (Rape) Act 1981), buggery, an act described in s.3 or s.4 of the Criminal Law (Rape) (Amendment) Act 1990, or any act which would amount to sexual assault if it was carried out in the absence of consent.

Under s.21(1) of the 2017 Act, a person who engages in a sexual act with a protected person knowing them to be a protected person, or reckless as to that fact, commits an offence. The penalty for the offence under s.21 depends on the nature of the act engaged in. If the sexual act is one of sexual intercourse, buggery, or an act described in s.3 or s.4 of the 1990 Act, the maximum penalty is life imprisonment. In the case of a sexual act which would amount to sexual assault, the maximum penalty is a term of 14 years' imprisonment. Under s.21(2) of the 2017 Act, it is an offence for a person to invite, induce, counsel, or incite a protected person to engage in a sexual act, knowing that the person is a protected person or being reckless as to this fact. It appears that the offence under s.21(2) can be committed in circumstances where the protected person is invited, induced, counselled, or incited to engage in a sexual act with someone other than the accused. Section 21(3) provides for a rebuttable presumption that the accused knew or was reckless as to whether the victim of either offence was a protected person.

The maximum penalty for the offence under s.21(2) is a term of 10 years' imprisonment.

Section 22 of the 2017 Act deals with another category of sexual offence against a person who is vulnerable, referred to in s.22 as a "relevant person". A relevant person is one who suffers from a mental or intellectual disability or a mental illness which restricts the person's ability to protect themselves against serious exploitation. The offence under s.22 is committed by a "person in authority", defined as any person who is employed under a contract of service or under a contract for services, and who is responsible for the education, supervision, training, treatment, care or welfare of the relevant person. A person in authority who engages in a sexual act with a relevant person commits an offence under s.22(1), and one who invites, induces, counsels, or incites a relevant person to engage in a sexual act commits an offence under s.22(2). A defence of reasonable mistake is available to the accused who must show, on the civil standard of proof, that at the time of the commission of the alleged offence, he was reasonably mistaken as to whether the person was a "relevant person" for the purposes of the 2017 Act. The purported consent of the relevant person is not a defence. As with the offences set out in s.21, the penalties for the offence under s.22 depend on the nature of the act engaged in. Where the sexual act is one of sexual intercourse, buggery, or an act described in s.3 or s.4 of the 1990 Act, the maximum penalty is 10 years' imprisonment. In the case of a sexual act which would amount to sexual assault, or an offence under s.22(2), the maximum penalty is five years' imprisonment.

Prosecutions for offences under s.21 or s.22 of the 2017 Act require the consent of the DPP.

Purchase of Sexual Services

The purchase of sexual services is an offence under Pt 4 of the 2017 Act, which amends the Criminal Law (Sexual Offences) Act 1993 (the "1993 Act") and the Criminal Law (Human Trafficking) Act 2008 (the "2008 Act"). The 1993 Act is amended by s.25 of the 2017 Act, which provides that a person who pays, offers or promises to pay any person, including a prostitute, money or any other form of consideration for the purpose of engaging in sexual activity with a prostitute commits an offence. This is a summary offence which carries a penalty of a class E fine for a first offence and a class D fine in the case of all subsequent offences. Sexual activity is not defined in terms of any specific act but rather by what a reasonable person would consider to be of a sexual nature given the surrounding circumstances.

The 2008 Act is amended by s.26 of the 2017 Act which provides that a person who pays, gives, offers or promises to pay or give a person, including a trafficked person, money or any other form of consideration for the purposes of the prostitution of a trafficked person commits an offence. The penalty for this offence on summary conviction is a fine of up to €5,000 and/or a term of up to 12 months' imprisonment. On indictment, the maximum penalty is an unlimited fine and/or five years' imprisonment.

Incest

Part 5 of the 2017 Act deals with incest offences and repeals the Criminal Law (Incest Proceedings) Act 1995.

Section 28 of the 2017 Act amends the Punishment of Incest Act 1908 (the "1908 Act") by the substitution of a newly worded s.1, which provides that any male person who has carnal knowledge with a woman whom he knows is his grand-daughter, daughter, sister, or mother commits an indictable offence. The maximum penalty for this offence is life imprisonment. Consent by the female is not a defence.

Section 29 of the 2017 Act provides that proceedings under the 1908 Act are to be heard in camera with only officers of the court, persons directly concerned in the proceedings, bona fide members of the press and such other persons as the court may permit, being allowed to remain in the courtroom. Section 30 of the 2017 Act deals with the anonymity of the accused and the person to whom the offence relates. The section permits restricted reporting of the facts and verdict but nothing that might identify the accused or the person to whom the offence relates may be reported. Breach of s.30 is an offence carrying a penalty of a class B fine and/or up to 12 months' imprisonment on summary conviction, and an unlimited fine and/or up to three years' imprisonment on indictment. A person charged with an offence under s.30 will have a defence if he can show that, at the time of the alleged offence, he did not know or suspect or have any reason to suspect that the matter was subject to restrictions under s.30.

KEY CASES AND LEGISLATION

Criminal Law (Sexual Offences) Act 2017—Enacted but not in force until commencement.

People (Attorney General) v Dermody [1956] I.R. 307—Offence complete upon penetration, however slight.

Kaitamaki v R. [1984] 2 All E.R. 435—Rape is a continuing act.

R. v Flattery (1877) 13 Cox C.C. 388 and *R. v Williams* [1922] All E.R. 433—Consent vitiated by fraud.

R. v Olugboja [1981] 3 All E.R. 443—Consent must be freely given and submission does not equate with consent.

C.C. v Ireland [2006] 4 I.R. 1—Failure to provide for defence of honest mistake in cases of "statutory rape" in the Criminal Law Amendment Act 1935 held to be unconstitutional. Defence now contained in ss.2 and 3 of the Criminal Law (Sexual Offences) Act 2006.

11 Non-Fatal Offences against the Person

Prior to the enactment of the Non-Fatal Offences against the Person Act 1997 (the "1997 Act"), the law in relation to non-fatal offences was contained primarily in the Offences against the Person Act 1861 (the "1861 Act"). The 1861 Act, which contained many specifically defined offences, was often criticised for being overly technical and was amended on many occasions. The 1997 Act modernised the law in relation to these types of offences and also created certain new offences.

Assault

The offence of assault is contained in s.2(1) of the 1997 Act. Section 2(1) provides that an assault is committed where the defendant, without lawful excuse and without consent, intentionally or recklessly:

(a) directly or indirectly applies force to or causes an impact upon the body of another, or
(b) causes another to believe on reasonable grounds that he or she is likely to be immediately subjected to the direct or indirect application of such force or impact.

Section 2 therefore encompasses the common law offence of assault which is now contained in s.2(1)(b), and battery which is provided for by s.2(1)(a). The common law offences of assault and battery were abolished by the 1997 Act. The actus reus of assault is the direct or indirect application of force, or causing an impact on the body of another, or causing the other person to believe, on objectively reasonable grounds, that the application of such force or the causing of such impact is imminent. The absence of the victim's consent is also a part of the actus reus. The mens rea is intention or subjective recklessness.

Consent

Consent may be either express or implied. No offence under s.2 will be committed where the force occurs in circumstances which are no more than what is to be expected as part of everyday life, was not intended to cause injury and was unlikely to do so, and where the defendant does not know or believe that the impact is unacceptable to the other person.

Words as a form of assault

Section 2 of the 1997 Act is silent on the issue of whether mere words can amount to an assault. Clearly, words would not suffice for s.2(1)(a). At common law, words were not capable of constituting an offence unless they were accompanied by some threatening gesture. In *Tuberville v Savage* (1669) 1 Mod. Rep. 3, words were held to negative an assault where the accused had put his hand on his sword and told the victim that "if it were not assize time, I would not take such language". In effect, the accused had told the victim that he was not going to assault him. The common law rule appears to have been abolished by s.2, which provides that an assault is committed where the accused "causes another to believe on reasonable grounds" that the application of force is imminent.

Force

Section 2(2) of the 1997 Act defines "force" and provides that force includes the application of heat, light, electric current, noise or any other form of energy or the application of matter in any form.

Immediacy

For the purposes of s.2(1)(a), there is no requirement that the victim have any apprehension of the immediate application of force. In the case of the form of assault under s.2(1)(b), however, the victim must believe that the direct or indirect application of force will be immediately forthcoming.

Punishment on conviction

Assault under s.2 of the 1997 Act is a summary offence only and is punishable by a maximum sentence of six months' imprisonment and/or a fine of up to €2,500.

Assault Causing Harm

Section 3 of the 1997 Act provides that "a person who assaults another, causing him or her harm shall be guilty of an offence". Harm is defined in s.1 of the 1997 Act as being "harm to the body or mind and includes pain and unconsciousness".

The actus reus of an offence under s.3 has two components, both of which must be established. It must be shown that the accused has committed an assault and that harm, as defined in s.1, has resulted. It had been assumed, in theory and in practice, that assault for the purposes of s.3 of the 1997 Act was the same as for s.2 of the 1997 Act, with the added requirement of proving harm. The Irish courts have, on a number of occasions, ruled that this is not the case. In *Minister for Justice, Equality and Law Reform v Dolny* [2008] IEHC 326, the High Court ruled as follows:

> "The offences created respectively by s.2 and s.3 of the 1997 Act, are distinct and different offences ... it is not the case that s.2 is intended to define the concept of 'assault' for all purposes of the Act."

The High Court in *Dolny* went on to hold that the definition of "assault" contained in the *Concise Oxford English Dictionary* was to be given to the word "assault" for the purposes of s.3 of the 1997 Act. The approach of the High Court was affirmed on appeal to the Supreme Court in *Minister for Justice, Equality and Law Reform v Dolny* [2009] IESC 48. More recently, in *DPP v Brown* [2016] IECA 405, the Court of Appeal stated:

> "The drafting of these related sections, (to the extent that they both refer to assault), creates confusion as is evident from this and other cases and might have been the subject of more careful drafting. It is nevertheless appropriate that the offences described in ss. 2 and 3, respectively, should be treated as separate and distinct offences."

Section 3 of the 1997 Act is silent on the issue of mens rea and no question of consent arises, unlike s.2 of the 1997 Act. Whether by accident or design, the wording of s.3 appears to create an offence of strict liability.

Punishment on conviction

An offence under s.3 of the 1997 Act may be tried summarily or on indictment. On summary conviction, the penalty is a maximum term of imprisonment of 12 months and/or a fine of up to €2,500. On conviction on indictment, the penalty is a maximum term of imprisonment of five years and/or an unlimited fine.

Causing Serious Harm

Section 4 of the 1997 Act provides that "a person who intentionally or recklessly causes serious harm to another shall be guilty of an offence". "Serious harm" is defined in s.1 as being "an injury which creates a substantial risk of death or which causes serious disfigurement or substantial impairment of the mobility of the body as a whole or of the function of any particular bodily member or organ".

The actus reus of this offence is causing serious harm. It is not necessary to prove the elements of an assault for the purposes of s.4, although the harm inflicted must come within the definition set out in s.1 of the 1997 Act. In many cases, the level and nature of the injury sustained will imply an assault, but it is important to note that assault is not a part of the actus reus of an offence under s.4.

The mens rea is intention or subjective recklessness. The accused must have mens rea with regard to the dangerous conduct and to the likelihood that serious harm would be caused by it.

Consent

Absence of consent is an integral part of the actus reus of an offence under s.2 but, following *Dolny*, not for s.3, although there are circumstances in which consent will provide a defence. Since it is not necessary to show that an assault has taken place to establish the actus reus of an offence under s.4, the question arises as to whether consent may be a defence to such an offence.

It would appear that consent is not generally a defence to serious harm, but there may be exceptional circumstances in which it might amount to a defence. The issue arises in the context of otherwise lawful activities, such as medical treatment and sport. The Court of Appeal of England and Wales has held that only conduct which is "sufficiently grave to be properly characterised as criminal" should lead to a prosecution. In *R. v Barnes* [2005] 1 W.L.R. 910, the accused was charged with unlawfully and maliciously inflicting grievous bodily harm contrary to the Offences against the Person Act 1861. The incident occurred in the course of a football match where the accused was said to have injured the victim with a "crushing, late, unnecessary, reckless and high" tackle from behind. In addition to stating the required gravity of the conduct, the Court of Appeal said that unless the conduct complained of went beyond what a player could reasonably be regarded as having accepted by participating in the sport, he will be regarded as having implicitly consented to the injury.

The case of *R. v Brown* [1993] 2 All E.R. 75 has already been discussed in the context of sexual offences, but is also relevant to a discussion of consent in the context of serious harm.

The difference between the judgments of the respective courts in *Brown* and *Barnes* does not readily permit of a logical explanation. Both involved the voluntary participation of consenting adults. In *Attorney General's Reference (No.6 of 1980)* [1981] 2 All E.R. 1057, the House of Lords accepted that consent provided a defence in certain circumstances, such as properly conducted games and sports, and stated that "[t]hese apparent exceptions can be justified as ... needed in the public interest".

The House of Lords also stated that "[i]t is not in the public interest that people should try to cause or should cause each other actual bodily harm for no good reason".

It seems, therefore, that where the conduct in question is deemed to be beneficial to the public interest, consent will provide a defence. The social benefit derived from sporting activities appears to be what differentiates it from the type of conduct engaged in in *Brown*. The case law thus suggests that public policy considerations will take precedence over the individual's consent even in the context of conduct carried out privately. This will not be the case where the conduct giving rise to the harm is itself unlawful.

Punishment on conviction

An offence under s.4 of the 1997 Act is triable on indictment and carries a maximum penalty of an unlimited fine and/or life imprisonment.

Threats to Kill or Cause Serious Harm

Section 5 of the 1997 Act provides as follows:

> "A person who, without lawful excuse, makes to another a threat, by any means intending the other to believe it will be carried out, to kill or cause serious harm to that other or a third person shall be guilty of an offence."

The actus reus of this offence is making a threat to kill or cause serious harm. The method of making such a threat is irrelevant. The mens rea is the intention to make the threat coupled with the intention that the victim believes that the threat will be carried out.

There are both similarities and differences between this offence and that of assault. If a threat is made that is capable of being immediately carried out, an offence under both sections has been committed, provided that the threat is to kill or cause serious injury. One difference between the two offences is that whereas an assault centres around the immediacy of the threat, an offence under s.5 of the 1997 Act does not. Another difference is that for an assault to take place, the victim must believe that the application of force is imminent, whereas an offence under s.5 is committed regardless of the actual belief of the victim. What matters is that the accused *intended* the victim to believe that the threat will be carried out.

Punishment on conviction

An offence under s.5 of the 1997 Act may be tried summarily or on indictment. On summary conviction, the penalty is a maximum term of imprisonment of 12 months and/or a fine of up to €2,500. On conviction on indictment, the penalty is a maximum term of imprisonment of 10 years and/or an unlimited fine.

Syringe Offences

Sections 6, 7 and 8 of the 1997 Act create various offences involving the use of syringes. It is arguable that the inclusion of syringe offences in an Act originally intended to streamline the existing legislation defeats that purpose somewhat, since the conduct prohibited by these provisions criminalises the modus operandi of carrying out activities that were not lawful to begin with. A comparison might be made with the various offences relating to the criminal damage to property contained in the Criminal Damage Act 1991, s.14(1) of which provides that where any of the offences contained in s.2 of that Act are committed by means of fire, this will be an aggravating factor which will attract a higher penalty. Arguably, the same could have been done in the 1997 Act in respect of offences carried out using syringes.

Section 1 of the 1997 Act provides definitions relevant to the offences contained in the 1997 Act. "Syringe" is defined as including "any part of a syringe or a needle or any sharp instrument capable of piercing skin and passing onto or into a person blood or any fluid or substance resembling blood". "Contaminated blood" and "contaminated fluid" are also defined, and a "contaminated syringe" is one which has "in it or on it contaminated blood or contaminated fluid".

Syringe Attacks

Section 6(1) provides that it is an offence to injure another by piercing the skin of that other person with a syringe or threatening to do so, intending the victim to believe that it is likely that he may become infected with a disease. There is no requirement under s.6(1) that the syringe contain any fluid, contaminated or otherwise.

The actus reus is piercing the victim's skin with a syringe or threatening to do so. The mens rea is intention or subjective recklessness in relation to the piercing or the threat thereof, coupled with intention or objective recklessness in relation to causing the victim to believe that he has been infected with a disease.

Spraying blood or a blood-like substance

Section 6(2) provides that it is an offence to pour, put or spray blood, or a blood-like substance, on to another person or to threaten to do so, intending the victim to believe that he may become infected with a disease.

The actus reus is spraying, putting or pouring blood, or a blood-like substance, on to the victim or threatening to do so. The mens rea for this offence is intention or recklessness in relation to the spraying, putting or pouring of blood, or a blood-like substance, onto the victim, coupled with the intention of causing the victim to believe that he may become infected or being objectively reckless as to whether the victim will so believe.

Transferred intent

Section 6(3) provides that where, in the course of committing an offence under either of the two previous sections, the actual victim is a third party, the doctrine of transferred intent will apply and the accused, if convicted, will be liable to the penalties provided for by the relevant sections.

Punishment on conviction

The offences contained in s.6(1), (2) and (3) may be tried summarily or on indictment. On summary conviction, the maximum penalty is a prison sentence of 12 months and/or a fine of €2,500. On conviction on indictment, the maximum penalty is a term of imprisonment of 10 years and/or an unlimited fine.

Stabbing with a contaminated syringe

The offences contained in s.6(5) of the 1997 Act are aggravated forms of syringe offences. Section 6(5)(a) creates the offence of intentionally injuring another person by piercing his skin with a contaminated syringe.

The actus reus of the offence is stabbing with a contaminated syringe. The mens rea is the intention to pierce the skin with a syringe and knowledge of the fact that the syringe is contaminated.

Section 6(5)(b) makes it an offence to spray, put or pour contaminated blood onto another person. The actus reus is spraying, putting or pouring contaminated blood onto another person. It would appear, therefore, that to spray, pour or put contaminated fluid other than blood onto another person is an offence under s.6(2) but not under s.6(5). The mens rea is intention. Section 6(5)(c) provides for liability for the above offences arising out of transferred intent.

Punishment on Conviction

The offences under s.6(5) are tried on indictment and the maximum penalty is life imprisonment.

Possession and Abandonment of Syringes

Section 7 of the 1997 Act makes it an offence to possess a syringe or any blood in a container in any place with the intention of using it unlawfully to threaten or injure or intimidate another person. The section gives the Gardaí the power to stop, question and, if necessary, search a person where they have reasonable grounds for believing that the person is in possession of the relevant articles with the intention of using them to injure, threaten or intimidate. Failure to co-operate with the Gardaí or obstruction of a Garda is an offence under the section. It will be a defence to show that the syringe or container is in the possession of the accused for a valid reason.

Section 8(1) of the 1997 Act deals with the placement or abandonment of syringes in any place where it is likely that injury will be caused and is caused, or where it is likely to frighten another person. It will be a defence to show that the person in possession of the syringe has a valid reason for such possession. Where the syringe is found in the defendant's normal place of residence and the defendant did not intentionally leave it in such a place or in a manner that was likely to cause or did cause injury, this will also amount to a defence. A more serious offence is set out in s.8(2) which provides that it is an offence to intentionally place a contaminated syringe in any place and in such a manner that it injures another person.

Punishment on Conviction

The punishment for the substantive offence of possession under s.7 of the 1997 Act, on summary conviction, is a maximum term of imprisonment of 12 months and/or a fine of up to €2,500. On indictment, the maximum penalty is a sentence of seven years and/or an unlimited fine. The offence of failing to co-operate with or obstructing a Garda under s.7 of the 1997 Act carries a maximum penalty of a term of imprisonment of six months and/or a fine of €2,500.

On summary conviction, the maximum penalty for an offence under s.8(1) is a term of 12 months' imprisonment and/or a fine of €2,500. On indictment, the maximum penalty is a term of seven years' imprisonment and/or an unlimited fine. Where the accused is convicted on indictment of an offence under s.8(2), which is the intentional placement of a contaminated syringe in such a manner that it injures another, the maximum penalty is life imprisonment.

Coercion

Section 9 of the 1997 Act makes it an offence to engage in conduct with the objective of compelling the victim to do or to abstain from doing that which the victim is lawfully entitled to do or abstain from doing. The prohibited conduct includes violence, intimidation, damage to property, watching or besetting certain places frequented by the victim and following the victim.

Punishment on conviction

On summary conviction, the maximum penalty is a term of 12 months' imprisonment and/or a fine of €2,500. On conviction on indictment, the maximum penalty is a term of five years' imprisonment and/or an unlimited fine.

Harassment

The offence of harassment is provided for by s.10 of the 1997 Act and occurs where the accused persistently follows, watches, besets or communicates with the victim. The type of behaviour envisaged by the section is that which is commonly referred to as "stalking". The offence is committed where the accused "by his or her acts intentionally or recklessly, seriously interferes with the other's peace or privacy and causes alarm, distress or harm to the other". The accused's actions may be intentional or reckless, but the essence of the offence is the effect that those acts have on the victim. To this end, the actions must be "such that a reasonable person would realise that the acts would seriously interfere with the other's peace and privacy, or cause alarm, distress or harm". Although arguably broad enough to cover instances of "cyberstalking", the Law Reform Commission has published its *Report on Harmful Communications and Digital Safety* (LRC 116-2016) in which it recommends a number of amendments to close any potential loopholes in this area of law.

Punishment on conviction

On summary conviction, the maximum penalty is a term of 12 months' imprisonment and/or a fine of €2,500. On conviction on indictment, the maximum penalty is a term of seven years' imprisonment and/or an unlimited fine.

In addition, the court may impose a "non-contact" order. Section 10(3) permits the court to make such an order which is similar to an injunction in its effects. The order may prohibit certain conduct by the accused and failure to comply with the order is an offence in itself. The court, under s.10(5), is permitted to make such an order even where the accused has not been convicted of the offence, if it is satisfied that to do so would be in the interests of justice. In *DPP v Ramachandran* [2000] 2 I.R. 307, the accused had successfully appealed his conviction for harassment. Despite this, the court granted a "non-contact" order against him on the basis that his victims were in need of the court's protection.

Demands for Payment

Under s.11 of the 1997 Act, it is an offence to make demands for payment of a debt by methods which amount to misrepresentation, fraud, or where the demands are intended to cause distress, alarm or humiliation to the victim by virtue of their frequency.

Punishment on conviction

This is a summary offence in respect of which a fine of up to €2,500 may be imposed.

Poisoning

Section 12 of the 1997 Act provides as follows:

> "A person shall be guilty of an offence if, knowing that the other does not consent to what is being done, he or she intentionally or recklessly administers to or causes to be taken by another a substance which he or she knows to be capable of interfering substantially with the other's bodily functions."

This includes a substance which could cause sleep or unconsciousness. The offence is committed either by directly administering a substance or causing the victim to take it in the knowledge that the victim does not consent. The offence therefore encompasses the "spiking" of drinks.

Punishment on conviction

On summary conviction, the maximum penalty is a term of 12 months' imprisonment and/or a fine of €2,500. On conviction on indictment, the maximum penalty is a term of three years' imprisonment and/or an unlimited fine.

Endangerment

Section 13 of the 1997 Act provides that it is an offence for a person to intentionally or recklessly engage in conduct which creates a substantial risk of death or serious harm to another. In *DPP v McGrath* and *DPP v Cagney*, both unreported, Court of Criminal Appeal, 27 May 2004, convictions for endangerment were upheld. In *McGrath*, the conduct in question was running after the victim and threatening him, and in *Cagney*, the defendant had struck the victim, causing him to fall and sustain injury. A separate offence of endangering traffic is contained in s.14. This offence is committed by intentionally placing any dangerous obstruction on a road, railway, street, etc. and being aware that injury to a person or damage to property may be caused by doing so or being reckless as to that fact.

Punishment on conviction

Both offences can be tried summarily or on indictment. On summary conviction, the maximum penalty is a term of 12 months' imprisonment and/or a fine of €2,500. On conviction on indictment, the maximum penalty is a term of seven years' imprisonment and/or an unlimited fine.

False Imprisonment

The offence of false imprisonment is contained in s.15 of the 1997 Act, which abolishes the common law offences of kidnapping and false imprisonment. Section 15(1) provides that a person shall be guilty of false imprisonment if he:

- (a) takes or detains; or
- (b) causes to be taken or detained; or
- (c) otherwise restricts the personal liberty of another person.

The absence of consent on the part of the victim is a part of the actus reus of the offence. Section 15(2) provides that where the consent of the victim has been obtained by force, threat of force or deception, causing the victim to believe that he is legally obliged to consent, this will not amount to consent on the part of the victim.

Punishment on conviction

On summary conviction, the maximum penalty is a term of 12 months' imprisonment and/or a fine of €2,500. The maximum penalty on indictment is life imprisonment.

Child Abduction

The issue of child abduction is covered by ss.16 and 17 of the 1997 Act. Section 16 makes it an offence for a parent or guardian to remove a child from the jurisdiction in violation of a court order or without the consent of the other parent or guardian(s). The accused will have a defence if he was unable to obtain the consent of any other parties whose consent should have been obtained, but acted in the belief that such consent would have been forthcoming. The accused can also rely on the defence that it was not his intention to deprive the other parent or guardian(s) of their rights.

Section 17 deals with the abduction of children by anyone other than the categories of persons covered by s.16. In this case, there is no requirement that the child be removed from the jurisdiction. The essence of the offence is the intention to take or detain, or cause to be taken or detained, a child younger than 16 years of age, so that the child is removed from the custody of the person(s) who has or have control of the child. The accused will have a defence if he believes that the child is over the age of 16 years.

Punishment on conviction

Both offences can be tried summarily or on indictment, but the DPP must consent to proceedings being taken in respect of the offence contained in s.16. On summary conviction, the maximum penalty is a term of 12 months' imprisonment and/or a fine of €2,500. On conviction on indictment, the maximum penalty is a term of seven years' imprisonment and/or an unlimited fine.

Female Genital Mutilation

The Criminal Justice (Female Genital Mutilation) Act 2012 (the "2012 Act") creates a number of offences arising from the practice of female genital mutilation (FGM). Although it was always possible to prosecute this conduct under the 1997 Act where the act(s) of FGM took place within the State, the 1997 Act has no extra-territorial effect and it does not address the issue of removal from the State for the purpose of carrying out FGM elsewhere. The 2012 Act was passed in order to provide specifically for this class of offence.

Section 1 of the 2012 Act provides a statutory definition of FGM which is:

> "Any act the purpose of which, or the effect of which, is the excision, infibulation or other mutilation of the whole or any part of the labia majora, labia minora, prepuce of the clitoris, clitoris or vagina of a woman or girl."

Section 2 of the 2012 Act provides that to carry out or to attempt to carry out an act of FGM is an offence. An act or attempted act of FGM carried out on board an Irish-registered vessel or aircraft is also covered by the extra-territorial effect of the 2012 Act. This is provided for in s.4, which also applies to acts carried out by an Irish citizen or a person who is ordinarily resident in the State if the act is an offence in the place in which it is carried out or attempted. Section 2 provides a number of exemptions from liability. These are:

- A surgical operation which is carried out by a registered medical practitioner and which is necessary to protect the physical or mental health of the woman/girl;
- A surgical operation performed by a registered medical practitioner, midwife, or trainee midwife, in connection with labour/childbirth;
- Where the act is carried out by the woman/girl herself; and
- Where the act is done to a woman older than 18 years and there is no resultant permanent bodily harm.

In addition to the offence of FGM in s.2, it is also an offence under s.3 of the 2012 Act to remove a girl or woman from the State for the purpose of carrying out FGM. For the purposes of this offence, removal from the State includes:

> (a) arranging any part of her travel outside the State;
> (b) accompanying her for any portion of that travel;
> (c) arranging that she be met when her travel out of the State has terminated; or
> (d) doing any other act that could facilitate her travel out of the State.

The 2012 Act does not specify the precise mens rea for the offence and it is not altogether clear what level of knowledge (if any) is required in order to be guilty of the offence under s.3. Section 3(3) provides that where the accused removed the girl or woman from the State in circumstances which give rise to the reasonable inference that she was being removed for the purpose of FGM, and that an act of FGM had actually been inflicted on the girl or woman during her absence from the State, it will be presumed that she was removed for the purpose of FGM. The defence bears the burden of rebutting this presumption.

A defendant who carries out acts of FGM in circumstances of medical necessity or in the course of labour or childbirth will have a defence, provided that he is suitably qualified to carry out such procedures in the jurisdiction in which they are carried out. It is also a defence to show that the woman was over the age of 18 and that no resultant permanent bodily harm was caused.

Specifically excluded as a defence is any argument that FGM is consented to by the woman or girl concerned or by parents/guardians. Also excluded as a defence is the belief that FGM is required or permitted for reasons of custom or ritual.

The consent of the DPP is required for prosecutions under the 2012 Act. A person who has been prosecuted outside the State and has either been acquitted or convicted as the case may be, is protected by the rule on double jeopardy which is set out in s.7 of the 2012 Act.

Punishment on conviction

On summary conviction, the offender is liable to a class A fine, as set out in the Fines Act 2010, and/or up to 12 months' imprisonment. On conviction on indictment, the maximum penalty is an unlimited fine and/or 14 years' imprisonment.

12 Offences against Property

This chapter looks at offences relating to criminal damage to property and offences of dishonesty. The former are governed by the provisions of the Criminal Damage Act 1991 and the latter by those of the Criminal Justice (Theft and Fraud Offences) Act 2001.

The Criminal Damage Act 1991

The Criminal Damage Act 1991 (the "1991 Act") repealed most of the pre-existing common law and statutory rules in relation to criminal damage to property. Section 2 of the 1991 Act created three distinct offences: damaging another person's property; damaging property with the intent to endanger life; and damaging property with intent to defraud. Offences involving threats to damage property, possession of anything with the intent to damage property, and unauthorised accessing of data are also contained in ss.3–5 of the 1991 Act.

For the purposes of the 1991 Act, "property" is defined in s.1 as being either tangible or in the form of data. "Damage" is also defined in s.1 and includes destruction, defacing, rendering inoperable and also altering, corrupting and doing any act contributing to such alteration of data.

Lawful excuse

Section 6 of the 1991 Act provides for the defence of lawful excuse where the defendant honestly believed that the owner of the property had or would have consented to the damage or where the defendant believed that causing damage to property was necessary in order to protect himself or another person or property from immediate harm, and where the defendant believed that such action on his part was reasonable. This second application of the defence has been amended by s.21 of the Non-Fatal Offences against the Person Act 1997, which requires that the actions of the defendant in damaging property have to be objectively reasonable in the circumstances.

Damaging Property

Section 2(1) of the 1991 Act provides that, "[a] person who without lawful excuse damages any property belonging to another intending to damage any such property or being reckless as to whether any such property would be damaged shall be guilty of an offence." Section 1 of the 1991 Act sets out different definitions of damage according to whether the property is tangible or in the form of data.

The actus reus is causing damage to someone else's property in the absence of a lawful excuse for doing so. The mens rea is intention or recklessness as to whether damage is caused.

The actual owner of the property need not be identified and, further, s.7(2) provides that two presumptions arise in the context of damage to property. First, it is presumed that the property belongs to another person and, secondly, it is presumed that the owner of the property did not consent to the damage caused. Both presumptions are rebuttable. The first presumption may be rebutted by showing that, on the balance of probabilities, the property belongs to the defendant, and the second presumption may be rebutted, again on the balance of probabilities, by showing that the owner consented to the damage.

Damaging Property with Intent to Endanger Life

This offence is contained in s.2(2) of the 1991 Act and is an aggravated form of the offence contained in the previous section. The aggravating factor is the intent to endanger life. The offence is committed where a person, intentionally or recklessly, damages property and, by doing so, intends to endanger the life of another person or is reckless as to whether the life of another person would be endangered.

The actus reus is essentially the same as that required in s.2(1), but differs in respect of the question of ownership of property, which is irrelevant to the offence under s.2(2). The mens rea has two aspects. First, the accused must intend to damage the property or be subjectively reckless as to whether such damage is caused. Secondly, the accused must intend to endanger life or be subjectively reckless as to whether life is endangered by the damage.

Damaging Property with Intent to Defraud

This offence is contained in s.2(3) which provides that "[a] person who damages any property, whether belonging to himself or another with intent to defraud, is guilty of an offence."

The actus reus is damaging any property. In common with s.2(2), the issue of ownership of the property is irrelevant. The mens rea has two components. First, there must be the intent to damage the property. Secondly, the accused must intend by his actions to defraud others. Actual fraud need not be established.

For the purposes of all the offences under s.2, the relevant type of recklessness is subjective, with the caveat that the accused has foreseen the particular type of damage that was actually done. This is set out in s.2(6) of the 1991 Act. The common law offence of arson is abolished by s.14(1) of the 1991 Act and any statutory provisions which related to arson were repealed by s.15. Where damage under any offence contained in s.2 is caused by fire, such offence will be treated as arson, in accordance with s.2(4) of the 1991 Act.

Punishment on conviction

The offences contained in s.2 may be tried summarily or on indictment. On summary conviction, the maximum penalty is a fine of €2,500 and/or 12 months' imprisonment.

On indictment, the maximum penalty for an offence under s.2(1) or (3), regardless of whether arson is involved, is an unlimited fine and/or life imprisonment. In the case of the offence under s.2(2), the maximum penalty on indictment is a fine of €22,220 and/or life imprisonment. Again, this is regardless of whether arson was involved.

Threats to Damage Property

It is an offence under s.3 of the 1991 Act to threaten, without lawful excuse, to damage property owned by another person or to threaten to damage one's own property in circumstances where it would be likely to endanger the life of the person threatened or another person. The essence of the offence is the threat to damage property with the intention that the person to whom the threat is directed fears that it will be carried out. The threat might actually not be carried out, but if it is carried out, the matter will be dealt with under the appropriate part(s) of s.2.

Punishment on conviction

On summary conviction, the maximum penalty is a term of imprisonment of 12 months and/or a fine of €2,500. On conviction on indictment, the maximum penalty is a sentence of 10 years' imprisonment and/or a fine of €22,220.

Possession with Intent to Damage Property

Under s.4 of the 1991 Act, it is an offence to have in one's custody or under one's control, without lawful excuse, any implement that is intended to be used to:

- damage any property belonging to another person; or
- damage one's own or the intended user's property in a way which one knows is likely to endanger another person's life or with the intention of defrauding another person.

The offence also covers situations where the person causes or permits a third party to use the implement to commit an offence. Consequently, the prosecution must prove the possession element and the absence of any lawful excuse for the possession.

Punishment on conviction

On summary conviction, the maximum penalty is a term of imprisonment of 12 months and/or a fine of €2,500. On conviction on indictment, the maximum penalty is a sentence of 10 years' imprisonment and/or a fine of €22,220.

Unauthorised Accessing of Data

Section 5 of the 1991 Act creates the offence of unauthorised accessing of data. This offence relates to the activity commonly referred to as "hacking". The offence is committed where a person within this jurisdiction "hacks" into a computer which is either within the State or outside it. It is also an offence for someone outside the State to use a computer to access any data kept within the State. In both cases, the prosecution must prove the absence of "lawful excuse" as set out in s.6 of the 1991 Act. It appears that the potential scope of this provision is very broad. The offence is committed where a computer is used with the intent to access data; it is not committed when data is actually accessed. Potentially, therefore, an offence under s.5 is committed where the computer user even inadvertently types in the wrong password to access online material such as email.

Punishment on conviction

An offence under s.5 is a summary offence and carries a maximum penalty of three months' imprisonment and/or a fine of €1,000.

The Criminal Justice (Theft and Fraud Offences) Act 2001

The Criminal Justice (Theft and Fraud Offences) Act 2001 (the "2001 Act") repealed the Larceny Acts 1861, 1916 and 1990 and the Forgery Acts 1861 and 1913, which had previously governed the area of dishonesty. The 2001 Act consolidates and streamlines the offences contained in the older Acts and creates new offences relating to white-collar and computer crime.

Theft

Section 4 of the 2001 Act provides that, "[a] person is guilty of theft if he or she dishonestly appropriates property without the consent of its owner and with the intention of depriving its owner of it." The actus reus of theft is the appropriation of property without the consent of its owner. The mens rea is the intention to deprive the owner of the property.

Dishonesty

"Dishonesty" is defined in s.2(1) of the 2001 Act as being "without a claim of right made in good faith". The test here is subjective. In *People (DPP) v O'Loughlin* [1979] I.R. 85, the Court of Criminal Appeal held that where there was an honest belief on the part of the accused as to whether he had a right to take property belonging to someone else, such belief would amount to a claim of right even where the belief turned out to be mistaken.

Under s.4(4) of the 2001 Act, the jury should have regard to the presence or absence of reasonable grounds for the belief.

Appropriation

Section 4 differs significantly from the provision of the Larceny Act 1916 on the issue of appropriation. Whereas the 1916 Act required the accused to have taken and carried away the property, the 2001 Act provides that appropriation may occur even where the accused has possession of property belonging to another person. Appropriation, as defined in the 2001 Act, occurs where the accused engages in "usurping or adversely interfering with the proprietary rights of the owner".

It is not necessary, under s.4, to show that the accused intended to *permanently* deprive the owner of his property. This is another significant departure from the older legislation which required proof of an intention to permanently deprive.

Consent

Consent is a defence to a charge of theft. Section 4(2) of the 2001 Act provides that property is not appropriated without the consent of the owner in the following circumstances:

(i) Where the accused believes that he has, or would have, the consent of the owner, if the owner was aware of the appropriation of the property; or
(ii) Where the accused believes that the owner cannot be ascertained by taking reasonable steps to do so.

The belief on the part of the accused is to be viewed subjectively, but under s.4(4), the jury is to have regard to the presence or absence of reasonable grounds for his belief. The defence is lost if consent is obtained by intimidation or fraud.

Exceptions to Theft

Section 5 of the 2001 Act deals with situations involving appropriation of property. Section 5(1) provides that theft does not occur in circumstances where property rights are transferred to a purchaser who buys the property in good faith and a defect in the title to the property is subsequently discovered.

Generally, land cannot be stolen, and the term "land" includes anything that forms part of the land or anything that is affixed to the land.

Section 5(2) of the 2001 Act sets out the following three exceptions to the general rule that real property cannot be stolen:

(1) Where the defendant has a duty imposed upon him by virtue of his being a trustee, a personal representative, the liquidator of a company or someone with power of attorney and he appropriates land in breach of his duty; or
(2) Where the defendant appropriates anything that forms part of the land by severing it or causing it to be severed, while not being in possession of the land; or
(3) Where the defendant possesses the land under a tenancy agreement or a lease and appropriates any fixture or structure.

Appropriation in either of these circumstances amounts to theft under the 2001 Act.

Punishment on conviction

Theft is an indictable offence which carries a maximum sentence of 10 years and/or an unlimited fine. The offence is capable of being tried summarily by the District Court, in which case the penalty on conviction is a class A fine, as set out in the Fines Act 2010, and/or up to 12 months' imprisonment.

Making Gain or Causing Loss by Deception

Sections 6, 7 and 8 of the 2001 Act deal with the offences of making gain or causing loss by deception, obtaining services by deception and making off without payment, respectively.

In accordance with s.6 of the 2001 Act, a person will be guilty of the offence of "making gain or causing loss by deception" where he dishonestly, and with the intention of making a gain for himself or another person, *or* causing loss to the victim, uses deception to induce the victim to act or to refrain from acting in a particular way. It must be established that the deception induced the victim to act or refrain from acting in a particular way. The section does not require proof of actual gain to the accused or to another person. Nor does it require proof of actual loss to the victim.

The offence of "obtaining services by deception" is provided for by s.7 of the 2001 Act. This offence is substantially similar to the offence under s.6 in terms of the conduct of the accused. The difference between the two offences is the outcome. Under s.7, it must be shown that the accused obtained services as a result of his deceptive conduct. Section 7(2) provides that a person obtains services where the victim is induced to confer some form of benefit on someone on the understanding that the benefit has been or will be paid for. The offence is also committed where the service conferred is a loan, in accordance with s.7(3) of the 2001 Act.

Section 8 provides for the offence of "making off without payment". The offence is committed where the accused, knowing that immediate payment is required for any goods or services, dishonestly makes off without paying with the intention of avoiding payment. The goods/services must not be unlawful and payment must be legally enforceable.

Punishment on conviction

These are all indictable offences which are capable of being tried summarily before the District Court. On indictment, the offences under ss.6 and 7 are punishable by a maximum term of imprisonment of five years and/or an unlimited fine. Tried summarily, the penalty on conviction is a class A Fine, as set out in the Fines Act 2010, and/or up to 12 months' imprisonment. On indictment, the offence of making off without payment under s.8 carries a maximum sentence of two years and/or a fine of up to €4,000. If tried in the District Court, the penalty is a class A fine, as set out in the Fines Act 2010, and/or up to 12 months' imprisonment.

Unlawful Use of a Computer

This was a new offence created by s.9 of the 2001 Act. It amplifies the provisions of s.5 of the Criminal Damage Act 1991, which created the offence of unauthorised accessing of data, or "hacking". The type of action contemplated by s.9 is deemed to be more serious in nature than the "hacking" offence prohibited by s.5 of the 1991 Act, and requires evidence that the accused made unlawful use of a computer either within the State or outside the State with the intention of making a gain for himself or causing a loss to another.

Punishment on conviction

This is an indictable offence which may also be tried summarily before the District Court. On indictment, the maximum penalty is 10 years' imprisonment and/or an unlimited fine. If tried summarily, the penalty is a class A fine, as set out in the Fines Act 2010, and/or up to 12 months' imprisonment.

False Accounting

Section 10 of the 2001 Act deals with a wide range of activities that may occur in the context of accounting. Under s.10, a person who dishonestly, and with the intention of making a gain or causing a loss to another, does any of the following, commits an offence:

- Destroys, defaces, conceals, or falsifies any account or document made or required for any accounting purpose;
- Fails to make or complete any account or any document required for the purposes of accounting; or
- In providing information for any purpose, produces or makes use of any account or any required document which he knows is/may be misleading, false, or deceptive in a material particular.

For the purposes of s.10, an account/document is "falsified" if it contains an entry that is/may be misleading, false, or deceptive in a material particular or one from which a material particular has been omitted.

Punishment on conviction

False accounting is an indictable offence which may also be tried summarily before the District Court. On indictment, the maximum penalty on conviction is a term of 10 years' imprisonment and/or an unlimited fine. In the case of conviction before the District Court, the penalty is a class A fine, as set out in the Fines Act 2010, and/or up to 12 months' imprisonment.

Burglary

Section 12 provides that the offence of burglary is committed where a person enters a building as a trespasser with intent to commit an arrestable offence or, being present as a trespasser, commits or attempts to commit an arrestable offence. An arrestable offence is defined in s.12(4) as being an offence "for which a person of full age and not previously convicted may be punished by imprisonment for a term of five years or by a more severe penalty".

The actus reus of burglary is entry on to premises as a trespasser to commit an arrestable offence *or* being on the premises as a trespasser and committing or attempting to commit such an offence. There are two aspects to the mens rea; first, the accused must have the mens rea to enter the premises as a trespasser. It must be shown that he either intended to trespass or was subjectively reckless as to whether he was trespassing. Negligence on the part of the accused, which would lead to liability in tort, will not suffice for criminal liability. Secondly, the accused must have the mens rea for the arrestable offence.

Trespass

Trespass is the unauthorised entry on to the property of another. It can happen in a number of ways:

(i) Where the accused knowingly enters the premises without consent; or
(ii) Where the accused has permission to be on the premises but then acts in a way that is not compatible with that permission; or
(iii) Where the accused, having entered the premises innocently, subsequently realises that he is trespassing and fails to leave.

Entry

Section 12(2) provides the definition of "building" or "part of a building". For the purposes of the offence of burglary, entry does not necessarily have to mean full entry. In *R. v Brown* [1985] Crim. L.R. 212, it was held that where the accused had partially entered a shop through a broken window, this constituted a sufficient entry. The question of whether a person has entered a building or part thereof will depend on the facts of each case and is a matter for the jury to decide.

Punishment on conviction

Burglary is an indictable offence which may be tried summarily before the District Court. On conviction on indictment, the maximum penalty is a term of imprisonment of 14 years and/or an unlimited fine. If convicted following a District Court trial, the penalty is a class A fine, as set out in the Fines Act 2010, and/or up to 12 months' imprisonment.

Aggravated Burglary

This offence is covered by s.13 of the 2001 Act and occurs where the offence of burglary (s.12) is committed by the accused, who has with him or has at the time, a firearm, imitation firearm, any weapon of offence or an explosive.

Weapon

For the purposes of the 2001 Act, s.13(2) provides definitions of the types of weapons referred to in s.13(1).

A "firearm" is defined as including the following:

(a) a lethal firearm or other lethal weapon capable of discharging a shot, bullet or other missile;
(b) an airgun or any other weapon which incorporates a barrel and which is capable of firing metal or other slugs;
(c) a crossbow;
(d) any type of stun gun which emits energy and causes shock or other disablement.

An "imitation firearm" is anything that is not a firearm, but which resembles one. A "weapon of offence" is any article with a sharp blade or point, any other article made or adapted to cause injury or incapacitation, or any weapon of any description that is designed to emit any noxious substance.

The actus reus of aggravated burglary is essentially the same as with burglary, but includes the possession of a weapon at the material time. The mens rea is the same as for burglary, with the added requirement that the accused knew that he had a weapon.

Punishment on conviction

Aggravated burglary is an indictable offence which carries a maximum sentence of imprisonment for life. If the case is dealt with before the District Court, the penalty is a class A fine, in accordance with the Fines Act 2010, and/or up to 12 months' imprisonment.

Robbery

The offence of robbery is provided for by s.14 of the 2001 Act. A person commits robbery when he steals and, at the time or immediately before the stealing, and in order to do so, he uses force or puts or seeks to put any person in fear of being then and there subjected to force.

The actus reus of robbery has two separate components:

(i) stealing;
(ii) the use of force or threat of force at the time of the stealing or immediately prior to the stealing.

The use or threat of force need not be directed at the owner of the property. The use or threat of force must be immediately prior to or at the time of the stealing. It is not, therefore, robbery to take someone's property and *then* subject them to force or threaten to do so. In this instance, the appropriate charges are theft and assault. The essence of the offence of robbery is the use or threat of force in order to facilitate the stealing.

The mens rea also has two components: first, the accused must have the intention to steal, and secondly, the accused must intend to use force or threaten to use force in order to steal.

Punishment on conviction

Robbery is an indictable offence which carries a maximum sentence of imprisonment for life. If the case is dealt with before the District Court, the penalty is a class A fine, in accordance with the Fines Act 2010, and/or up to 12 months' imprisonment.

Handling

Section 17 provides that the broadly defined offence of handling is committed where a person, knowing that property is stolen, or reckless as to that fact, dishonestly receives it or undertakes to assist in its retention, removal, disposal or realisation.

The actus reus of handling is receiving stolen property and assisting in its removal, disposal or realisation. The mens rea is knowledge of or recklessness as to whether the property is stolen.

Recklessness is defined by s.16(2) of the 2001 Act and can be established where the accused has ignored or disregarded a substantial risk that the property is stolen.

Punishment on conviction

Handling stolen property is triable on indictment and carries a maximum prison sentence of 10 years and/or an unlimited fine. The penalty imposed will not exceed that which applies to the principal offence. If the case is dealt with before the District Court, the penalty is a class A fine, in accordance with the Fines Act 2010, and/or up to 12 months' imprisonment.

Possession of Stolen Property

Section 18 creates the offence of possession of stolen property. The offence is committed where a person, without lawful authority or excuse, possesses stolen property, knowing that the property has been stolen, or is reckless as to whether it has been stolen.

The actus reus is being in possession of stolen property. The mens rea is knowledge or recklessness as to whether the property is stolen.

Section 18(2) provides that where a person has in his possession stolen property in such circumstances that it is reasonable to conclude that the person knew the property to be stolen or was reckless as to the fact, it will be presumed that he knew it was stolen. This presumption will be rebutted where there is a reasonable doubt as regards such knowledge or recklessness on the part of the person who has possession of the property.

Punishment on conviction

Possession of stolen property is triable on indictment and carries a maximum prison sentence of five years and/or an unlimited fine. The penalty imposed will not exceed that which applies to the principal offence. If the case is dealt with before the District Court, the penalty is a class A fine, in accordance with the Fines Act 2010, and/or up to 12 months' imprisonment.

Money Laundering

Money laundering is a term that describes the various methods used in order to conceal the fact that assets or property are the proceeds of criminal activity. The offence is contained in Pt 2 of the Criminal Justice (Money Laundering and Terrorist Financing) Act 2010 (the "2010 Act"). The global nature of this activity has led to numerous initiatives with a view to co-ordinating an international response to money laundering. One of the purposes of the 2010 Act was to transpose the Third Money Laundering Directive (Directive 2005/60) into Irish law. The 2010 Act commenced in July 2010 and repealed the earlier statutory measures on money laundering contained in the Criminal Justice Act 1994. The 2010 Act has been amended by the Criminal Justice (Money Laundering and Terrorist Financing) Act 2013.

Section 7 of the 2010 Act provides that a person commits the offence of money laundering by:

(a) Concealing or disguising the true nature, source, location, disposition, movement or ownership of the property, or any rights relating to the property;
(b) Converting, transferring, handling, acquiring, possessing or using the property;
(c) Removing the property from, or bringing the property into, the State.

The accused must know or believe that the property has been obtained as a result of criminal activity or that it probably has been so obtained, or be reckless as to whether this is the case. A statutory test for recklessness, which is subjective in nature, is set out in s.7(5), which states:

> "[A] person is reckless as to whether or not the property is the proceeds of criminal conduct if the person disregards, in relation to the property, a risk of such a nature and degree that, considering the circumstances in which the person carries out any act referred to in [the preceding subsections], the disregard of that risk involves culpability of a high degree."

The offence in s.7 is carried out within the State. Section 8 provides that in some circumstances, the 2010 Act will have extra-territorial effect and in that event, a person whose conduct would constitute an offence under s.7 of the 2010 Act if it had been done in the State will have committed an offence if any of the following apply:

(a) The conduct in question takes place on board an Irish-registered ship or aircraft;
(b) The conduct is an offence in the place where it is carried out and the person is an Irish citizen or is ordinarily resident in the State, or is a body corporate registered under the Companies Acts;
(c) The surrender of the person had been sought under the Extradition Act 1965 and the request has been finally refused;
(d) The person had been the subject of a European Arrest Warrant but a determination had been made not to hand him over to the requesting authorities.

Where any of these circumstances apply, the person may be tried as if the offence had been committed within the State. The same penalties apply to ss.7 and 8. On summary conviction, the maximum penalty is a fine of €5,000 and/or 12 months' imprisonment. On conviction on indictment, the maximum penalty is an unlimited fine and/or 14 years' imprisonment. Any prosecutions in respect of offences committed outside the State require the consent of the DPP.

13 Public Order Offences

Offences against public order are set out in the Criminal Justice (Public Order) Acts 1994–2014. Until the enactment of the Criminal Justice (Public Order) Act 1994 (the "1994 Act"), the law governing this category of offence was contained in a number of different statutes, most of which had been enacted in the 19th century. The 1994 Act sought to centralise these offences within one statute by repealing and updating most of the common law offences against public order. Of critical importance for the successful prosecution of the offences under the 1994 Act is the requirement that the conduct with which the accused is charged occurs in a public place, as defined in the 1994 Act. This means that the location of the commission of the offence is part of what must be established by the prosecution. Where the prosecution fails or omits to discharge this element of the burden of proof, the accused must be acquitted.

A further issue to be considered is the potential vulnerability of certain sections of the 1994 Act to constitutional challenge. In particular, ss.5, 6 and 7 have been identified as potentially unconstitutional on the basis that they curtail a number of constitutionally protected rights, namely, freedom of assembly and freedom of expression.

Many of the offences created by the 1994 Act prohibit conduct carried out with the intention to cause breach of the peace or where the accused is reckless as to whether a breach of the peace will occur. Breach of the peace was described in *People (Attorney General) v Cunningham* [1932] I.R. 28 as an act which causes "reasonable alarm and apprehension to members of the public". More recently, the High Court was asked to determine whether a breach of the peace was a common law offence and, if so, whether it was capable of being prosecuted in the District Court. The decision of the High Court in *Thorpe v DPP* [2007] I.R. 502 was that a person could be arrested and charged with breach of the peace under the 1994 Act or, where the provisions of that Act do not apply, the person could be arrested and charged with breach of the peace at common law. The court also held that the term "breach of the peace" has two meanings at common law. The first of these is where the conduct of the accused causes reasonable alarm and apprehension to members of the public, and the second meaning refers to situations where breach of the peace is not an offence. These occur where judicial discretion pursuant to s.54 of the Courts (Supplemental Provisions) Act 1961 is exercised in favour of binding a person to keep the peace and be of good behaviour, and where a common law power of arrest is being exercised by An Garda Síochána.

The remainder of this chapter deals with the main offences created by the 1994 Act (as amended).

Intoxication in a Public Place

Section 4 of the 1994 Act makes it an offence for a person to be in a public place while intoxicated to such an extent as would give rise to a reasonable apprehension that he might endanger himself or some other person.

The actus reus of this offence is being intoxicated in a public place. The term "intoxicated" is defined in the 1994 Act as being under the intoxicating influence of any substance, and a "public place" is defined as including any highway, any outdoor place to which members of the public have access, a cemetery or churchyard, premises to which the public have access or a right of access on payment or otherwise, or any train, vessel or vehicle used as public transport.

The issue of mens rea does not really arise with this offence since it is committed by being in a public place whilst intoxicated to the extent that might give rise to the reasonable belief that a danger is posed to the defendant himself or to anyone else present. The "reasonable belief" requirement is an objective test. A prosecution under s.4 cannot be sustained if it is based solely on the fact that the accused was drunk in public. It must also be established that his behaviour gave rise to a reasonable fear that he was endangering himself or others.

Section 4(3) provides that if a Garda suspects, with reasonable cause, that an offence under s.4, 5 or 6 is being committed, the Garda may seize without warrant any bottle or container, and its contents, which is in the possession of the accused and which the Garda has reasonable cause to suspect contains an intoxicating substance.

Punishment on conviction

An offence under s.4 of the 1994 Act is a summary offence and the maximum penalty is a fine of €500. In addition to the confiscation powers of An Garda Síochána pursuant to s.4(3), s.3 of the Criminal Justice (Public Order) Act 2003 (the "2003 Act") empowers the District Court to grant an Exclusion Order prohibiting the accused from entering or being in the vicinity of certain premises for a specified period of time. A new s.23B was inserted into the 1994 Act by s.184 of the Criminal Justice Act 2006, which permits the imposition of a fixed charge fine in lieu of criminal proceedings under s.4.

Disorderly Conduct in a Public Place

Section 5 of the 1994 Act provides that it is an offence to engage in offensive conduct in a public place between the hours of 12am and 7am or at any other time after a Garda requests that the behaviour in question ceases. The actus reus is engaging in offensive conduct in a public place between the relevant hours or at any time after a Garda has asked that the conduct ceases. The mens rea is intention or objective recklessness.

Offensive conduct

Section 5(3) states that offensive conduct is any unreasonable behaviour which, having regard to all the circumstances, is likely to cause serious offence or annoyance to any person who is aware of such behaviour or who might reasonably be expected to be aware of it.

The purpose of s.5 is to outlaw behaviour that impacts adversely on the quality of life of others. The section is vaguely worded and it appears to create an offence of strict liability between the hours of 12am and 7am, whereas the same conduct will not attract criminal liability at any other time unless the accused has refused to desist having been requested to do so by a Garda.

Punishment on conviction

An offence under s.5 of the 1994 Act is a summary offence and the maximum penalty is a fine of €1,000. The District Court may also impose an Exclusion Order pursuant to s.3 of the 2003 Act. A new s.23A was inserted into the 1994 Act by s.184 of the Criminal Justice Act 2006 which permits the imposition of a fixed charge fine in lieu of criminal proceedings under s.5. For the purposes of s.23A, a member of An Garda Síochána may request that the person gives his name and address. If the person refuses or if the Garda is not satisfied with the information provided, the Garda may request the person to accompany him to the Garda station in order to confirm the person's name/address. An offence is committed by a person who fails to give his name/address, gives misleading details, or refuses to accompany the Garda to the station.

Threatening, Abusive or Insulting Behaviour

Section 6 of the 1994 Act provides that an offence is committed by a person who uses threatening, abusive or insulting words or behaviour in a public place, with intent to provoke a breach of the peace or being reckless as to whether a breach of the peace may be occasioned. The offence created by s.6 is effectively an aggravated form of the offence under s.5 of the 1994 Act.

The actus reus is being in a public place and using threatening, abusive or insulting words or behaving in a threatening, abusive or insulting manner. The mens rea is intention or subjective recklessness as regards the conduct in question and also as to whether a breach of the peace will occur. In *Clifford v DPP* [2008] IEHC 322, the High Court held that the trial court was entitled to infer an intention to commit breach of the peace or recklessness on the part of the accused as to whether a breach of the peace would be committed, if evidence regarding the accused's conduct supported such an inference.

Breach of the peace

A breach of the peace may occur where harm is caused to the person or property of an individual, or is likely to be caused, or where an individual is put in fear of suffering harm through violence or some form of public disturbance.

Punishment on conviction

This is also a summary offence which carries a maximum prison sentence of three months and/or a fine of €1,000. A conviction for this offence may also result in the imposition of an Exclusion Order in accordance with s.3 of the 2003 Act.

Obscene Displays

Section 7(1) of the 1994 Act makes it an offence to distribute or display in public any writing, sign or visible representation which is threatening, abusive, insulting or obscene, with intent to provoke a breach of the peace or being reckless as to whether a breach of the peace may occur. The actus reus is the distribution or display in public of anything that is threatening, abusive, insulting or obscene. The mens rea is intention or objective recklessness as regards the display or distribution of the material in question, coupled with intention or objective recklessness as to whether a breach of the peace may be occasioned.

Obscenity

The test used to determine whether something is obscene is whether the material in question tends to deprave and corrupt those whose minds are open to such immoral influences and into whose hands such a publication may fall. As a basis for imposing criminal liability, however, this is a test that could lead to arbitrariness, since what may be considered obscene by one person may well be regarded as an acceptable means of invoking the constitutionally protected right of freedom of expression by another. It is likely that the test to be applied is an objective one which would focus on what the reasonable person would consider to be obscene.

Punishment on conviction

An offence under s.7 is tried summarily and carries a maximum penalty of three months' imprisonment and/or a fine of €1,000 and may also result in the imposition of an Exclusion Order.

Wilful Obstruction

It is an offence under s.9 of the 1994 Act to wilfully prevent or interrupt the free movement of any person or vehicle, in a public place without lawful excuse. The actus reus is the prevention or interruption of the free movement of any person or vehicle in a public place, without lawful authority. The mens rea is intention or wilfulness.

Punishment on conviction

Wilful obstruction is a summary offence punishable by a fine not exceeding €500. An Exclusion Order may also be imposed.

Enforcement of the 1994 Act

Section 8 of the 1994 Act grants various powers of enforcement to the Gardaí, who may give an offender a direction either to desist from the conduct in question, to give his name/address, to hand over a bottle/container, or to immediately leave the vicinity in a peaceable and orderly manner. In order to invoke s.8, the Garda must have formed the reasonable belief that an offence under s.4, 5, 6, 7, or 9 has been committed or that the offender is loitering in a public place in circumstances which give rise to a reasonable apprehension that the safety of other people or property is under threat or that public peace may be disturbed. If the offender refuses or fails to comply with the direction of the Garda under s.8, without lawful excuse for so doing, an offence is thereby committed.

Punishment on conviction

An offence under s.8 of the 1994 Act is tried summarily and carries a maximum penalty of six months' imprisonment and/or a fine of €1,000. The court may also impose an Exclusion Order.

Entering a Building with Intent to Commit an Offence

Section 11 of the 1994 Act contains an offence which is quite similar to, yet drafted in much broader terms than, the offence of burglary. The offence is committed when a person enters any building or the curtilage of the building as a trespasser or is within the vicinity of any such building or curtilage of such building, for the purpose of trespassing "in circumstances giving rise to the reasonable inference that such entry or presence was with the intent to commit an offence or with the intent to unlawfully interfere with any property situate therein". A further offence of trespass is contained in s.13(1) of the 1994 Act. This offence is committed where a person trespasses on any building or curtilage of a building in a manner that causes or is likely to cause fear in a third party. Section 13(2) of the 1994 Act provides that a Garda may require a person whom he has reasonable cause to believe is committing/ has committed an offence under s.13(1) to desist and immediately leave the vicinity.

Punishment on Conviction

The offences under s.11 of the 1994 Act are summary offences and attract maximum penalties of a fine of €500 and/or 12 months' imprisonment. The penalty for an offence under s.13 of the 1994 Act is a maximum fine of €2,500 and/or a term of imprisonment of up to 12 months. Failure to comply with the direction of a Garda under s.13(2) is also an offence which is punishable on summary conviction by a fine of up to €1,000 and/or up to six months' imprisonment.

Riot

Section 14 of the 1994 Act abolishes the common law offence of riot and creates a new statutory offence of the same name. Riot is the most serious form of public disturbance and occurs where 12 or more persons who are present together in any place, public or private, use or threaten to use unlawful violence for a common purpose, and where the conduct of those persons taken together is such as would cause a person of reasonable firmness, whether present or not, to fear for his safety or for that of another person. Where this occurs, each of the group who *uses violence* shall be guilty of riot.

Section 14(2) provides that it is immaterial whether the group of 12 or more persons use or threaten to use unlawful violence simultaneously at any place. The section further provides that the common purpose of the group may be inferred from their conduct and that it is not necessary that a person of reasonable firmness actually be present or be likely to be present. The effect or likely effect of the conduct of the group on this hypothetical person of reasonable firmness is sometimes referred to as the "notional bystander test". It should be noted that a common purpose is not the same as a conspiracy, which is an agreement to carry out an unlawful act. No prior agreement is necessary to establish a common purpose.

The actus reus of riot is the use or threat of use of unlawful violence, in any place, for a common purpose, by a group of 12 or more people, present together, and the actual use of violence by one or more of the group and the imagined reaction of a reasonable person. The mens rea is intention or objective recklessness.

Punishment on conviction

Riot is an indictable offence which carries a maximum sentence of 10 years' imprisonment and/or an unlimited fine.

Violent Disorder

Section 15 of the 1994 Act creates the new offence of violent disorder. Section 15(5) states that references to the common law offence of riot, or to the common law offence of riot and to tumult in previous enactments, are to be construed as meaning violent disorder. Section 15(6) of the 1994 Act abolishes the common law offences of rout and unlawful assembly.

Essentially, the offence of violent disorder is a lesser species of riot and may be charged as an alternative offence. Section 15(1) provides that where three or more persons present together in any place, public or private, use or threaten to use unlawful violence, and the conduct of the group of three or more when taken together would cause a person of reasonable firmness to fear for his safety or that of another person, then each of the group using or threatening to use unlawful violence may be found guilty of violent disorder.

The actus reus of violent disorder is the use or threat of use of unlawful violence, in any place, by a group of three or more people, present together, and the imagined reaction of a reasonable person. The mens rea is intention or subjective recklessness. This can be seen from the wording of s.15(3), which provides that "a person shall not be convicted of the offence of violent disorder unless that person intends to use or threaten to use violence or is aware that his conduct may be violent or threaten violence".

Punishment on conviction

Violent disorder is tried on indictment and carries a maximum term of imprisonment of 10 years and/or an unlimited fine.

Affray

The common law offence of affray is abolished by s.16 of the 1994 Act, which creates a new statutory offence of the same name. This offence in effect criminalises public brawling. Section 16(1) provides that where two or more persons use or threaten to use unlawful violence against each other in a place that is public or private or both and their conduct, taken together, is such that a reasonable person would have cause to fear for his safety or for that of another person, each of the group will be guilty of affray.

The actus reus of affray is the use or threat of use of unlawful violence towards the other person(s) present in a place which is public, private or both and the reaction of a person of reasonable firmness to the conduct of the group, taken as a whole. The mens rea is intention or subjective recklessness. Section 16(3) provides that "[a] person shall not be convicted of the offence of affray unless that person intends to use or threaten to use violence or is aware that his conduct may be violent or threaten violence".

In *DPP v Reid and Kirwan* [2004] 1 I.R. 392, the Court of Criminal Appeal held that, "[u]nlike the offences of riot or violent disorder, the actual or threatened use of violence for the purpose of the new offence of affray must be violence 'towards each other'."

The facts of the case were that a group of people were fighting on a street and the Gardaí intervened in order to arrest them, whereupon the Gardaí were attacked. The first accused was charged with affray. There was no evidence adduced to show that he had been involved in the brawl, but rather that he had attacked the Gardaí. He was convicted of affray but the conviction was quashed on appeal on the basis that there was no evidence that he had used or threatened to use violence against any member of the group. The Court of Criminal Appeal held: "That being so, it follows that there was no prima facie case against the first accused on the charge of affray and that count should have been withdrawn from the jury."

For the purpose of affray, the threat of violence by words alone will not suffice; there must be some physical manifestation of the threat. It appears from the wording of the section that liability is imposed on each of the group, even where unlawful violence is only used or threatened by one person. This problem was discussed by the Court of Criminal Appeal in *Reid and Kirwan*, where Hardiman J. stated that "if that is the correct construction of the section, then, obviously, it raises questions of a far reaching nature".

Punishment on conviction

The offence of affray may be tried summarily or on indictment. The maximum penalty on conviction on indictment for the offence of affray is a term of imprisonment of five years and/or an unlimited fine. The maximum penalty on summary conviction is a fine of €1,000 and/or a term of imprisonment of 12 months.

Blackmail, Extortion, and Demanding Money with Menaces

Section 17 of the 1994 Act provides that any person who makes any unwarranted demand, with menaces, commits an offence. The person must be making the demand with a view to making a gain for himself or a third party or with the intention of causing a loss to the victim. For the purposes of s.17, a demand with menaces will be unwarranted unless the accused had reasonable grounds for making it and the use of menaces is a proper way of reinforcing the demand. A related offence is contained in s.15(1)(c) of the Criminal Justice (Theft and Fraud Offences) Act 2001 which provides that a person who has in his possession any article with the intention to use it for the purpose of committing an offence under s.19 of the 1994 Act commits an offence. The offence is not committed if the person is in his own place of residence. It is also an offence under s.15(1)(c) to be in possession of any article which has been made or modified for use in connection with an offence under s.17 unless the accused has lawful authority or a reasonable excuse for having the article in his possession.

Punishment on conviction

On summary conviction, an offence under s.17 of the 1994 Act carries a maximum penalty of a fine of €2,500 and/or 12 months' imprisonment. On indictment, the maximum penalty is an unlimited fine and/or 14 years' imprisonment.

Assault with Intent

Section 18 of the 1994 Act contains the offence of assault with intent to cause bodily harm or intent to commit an indictable offence. The offence is a species of aggravated assault. Given that the offence of common law assault was abolished by the Non-Fatal Offences against the Person Act 1997 (the "1997 Act") and that the 1994 Act does not provide a definition for assault for the purposes of s.18, it had been supposed that an assault under this section is the same as an assault under s.2 of the 1997 Act, since the latter Act does not appear to have repealed the assault offences contained in the 1994 Act. However, in *Minister for Justice, Equality and Law Reform v Dolny* [2008] IEHC 326, the High Court ruled:

> "The offences created respectively by s.2 and s.3 of the 1997 Act, are distinct and different offences ... it is not the case that s.2 is intended to define the concept of 'assault' for all purposes of the Act."

The High Court in *Dolny* went on to hold that the definition of "assault" contained in the *Concise Oxford English Dictionary* was to be given to the word "assault" for the purposes of s.3 of the 1997 Act. The approach of the High Court was affirmed on appeal to the Supreme Court in *Minister for Justice, Equality and Law Reform v Dolny* [2009] IESC 48. If, therefore, the definition of assault in s.2 of the 1997 Act pertains only to that offence and not to any other in the 1997 Act, it would seem logical that it would not be applicable to assault offences contained in other legislation but it remains to be seen whether this is a definitive statement on the issue as regards those other offences.

The actus reus is assault to commit bodily harm or to commit an arrestable offence. The mens rea is the intention to commit the assault and the intention to commit bodily harm or an arrestable offence. It appears that recklessness would not suffice for this offence.

Punishment on conviction

The maximum penalty that can be imposed for this offence on summary conviction is a fine of €2,500 and/or 12 months' imprisonment. On indictment, the maximum penalty is a fine and/or five years' imprisonment.

Assault or Obstruction of a Peace Officer

Section 38 of the Offences against the Person Act 1861 was repealed by s.19 of the 1994 Act, which creates a number of offences relating to obstruction of, and assaults on, a peace officer. The original definition of "peace officer", for the purposes of the section, was a member of An Garda Síochána, a member of the Defence Forces, or a prison officer. This definition has now been extended pursuant to s.185 of the Criminal Justice Act 2006 to include ambulance, fire brigade personnel and personnel working in hospital Accident and Emergency departments. The section also provides that an offence is committed where an assault is carried out against any person assisting a peace officer or where such person is obstructed whilst assisting a peace officer.

Section 19(1) provides that any person who does any of the following commits an offence:

> "(a) assaults a peace officer acting in the execution of the peace officer's duty, knowing that he is, or being reckless as to whether he is, a peace officer acting in the execution of his duty, or
> (b) assaults any other person acting in the aid of a peace officer, or
> (c) assaults any other person with intent to resist or prevent the lawful apprehension or detention of himself or any other person for any offence".

The actus reus for s.19(1)(a) is an assault on a peace officer acting in the execution of his duty. The mens rea is intention or subjective recklessness, as outlined in *DPP v Murray* [1977] I.R. 360.

The actus reus for s.19(1)(b) is assault on a person assisting a peace officer. The provision does not state that in this instance the peace officer must be acting "in the execution of his duty" but is more than likely intended to mean this. The mens rea for assault is intention or recklessness. The wording of the subsection is unclear as to the mens rea required for the rest of the actus reus. It would also seem that, following *Murray*, the accused must have some knowledge as to the fact that the victim is assisting a peace officer or be subjectively reckless in this regard and that the peace officer is acting, as per s.19(1)(a), "in the execution of his duty".

The actus reus of s.19(1)(c) is assault in order to prevent lawful apprehension or detention of the accused or any other person. The mens rea is intention or recklessness with regard to the assault. Additionally, there must be intention as regards the resistance to, or prevention of, lawful apprehension or detention. This appears to require knowledge on the part of the accused as regards the lawful apprehension or detention, which it appears does not necessarily have to be effected by a peace officer.

Section 19(3) provides that any person who resists or wilfully obstructs a peace officer in the execution of his duty, or a person assisting a peace officer in the execution of his duty, knowing or being reckless as to whether he is a peace officer acting in the execution of his duty, will have committed an offence by so doing. The actus reus is resisting or wilfully obstructing a peace officer or anyone assisting a peace officer in the execution of his duty.

The mens rea is intention or subjective recklessness. It might be argued that the vagueness inherent in s.19(1)(b) and (c) would have been largely avoided had those sections been drafted in similar terms.

Punishment on conviction

An offence under s.19(1) may be tried summarily at the election of the accused and in that instance carries a maximum penalty of 12 months' imprisonment and/or a fine of €5,000. If tried on indictment, the maximum penalty on conviction is a term of imprisonment of seven years and/or an unlimited fine. An offence under s.19(3) is tried summarily and carries a maximum penalty of six months' imprisonment and/or a fine of €2,500.

Begging

The Criminal Justice (Public Order) Act 2011 (the "2011 Act") creates a number of offences which occur in the context of begging. The 2011 Act does not outlaw begging per se, but rather, any activity that accompanies begging, such as harassment or other threatening conduct or the act of begging without the appropriate permit or licence. Prior to the passing of the 2011 Act, the offence of begging was contained in s.3 of the Vagrancy (Ireland) Act 1847 and it was punishable by a term of imprisonment. Section 3 of the 1847 Act was struck down as unconstitutional by the High Court in *Dillon v DPP* [2008] 1 I.R. 383, where the applicant successfully argued that s.3 amounted to an unconstitutional and disproportionate interference with his rights. The statutory definition of begging is set out in s.1(2) of the 2011 Act, which provides that a person is begging if:

> "(a) other than in accordance with a licence, permit or authorisation (howsoever described) granted by or under an enactment, he or she requests or solicits money or goods from another person or other persons, or
> (b) while in a private place without the consent of the owner or occupier of the private place, he or she requests or solicits money or goods from another person or other persons."

No offence is committed by a person who does no more than is set out in s.1(2)(a) and (b) above. An offence is committed by a person who, while begging in any place:

> "(a) harasses, intimidates, assaults or threatens another person or persons, or
> (b) obstructs the passage of persons or vehicles."

It is for the prosecution to prove that the defendant was begging without being in possession of a valid licence, permit or other authorising documentation. This was held by the High Court in *DPP v Rostas and Maughan* [2012] 1 I.R. 393.

The offence is summary in nature and attracts a maximum fine of €500 and/or imprisonment for one month.

Section 3 of the 2011 Act sets out the powers of An Garda Síochána in respect of beggars. Under s.3(1), a Garda may direct a beggar to move on to another vicinity. In order to use this power, the Garda must believe on reasonable grounds that the person is acting/has acted in such a way as to amount to an offence under s.2, or that his actions give rise to a reasonable apprehension for the safety of other people, property or the public peace.

A Garda may also, under s.3(2), direct a person to desist from begging at or near ATM machines, vending machines, night safes or at an entrance to a dwelling, and to leave the vicinity. No reasonable apprehension is required and it is not necessary that the beggar is doing anything other than being at/near any of these locations.

Section 3(3) provides that a person who is begging at/near the entrance to business premises, during opening hours, may be directed by a Garda to desist from begging and to move elsewhere. The Garda must have reasonable grounds for believing that members of the public are being, or are likely to be, deterred from entering the premises due to the person's behaviour or by the number of people begging there.

Section 3(4) permits a Garda to direct a person begging in a private place to desist from begging and to leave the place and vicinity in a peaceable manner.

The right of an owner or occupier of a private place to ask a beggar to desist from begging and to move elsewhere is not taken away by s.3, and a Garda must obtain the occupier's consent before any function under s.3 is performed in a dwelling.

A Garda must inform a person in clear language that failure to comply with a direction given under the 2011 Act is an offence and may arrest without warrant any person whom the Garda suspects, on reasonable grounds, to have committed an offence under s.2 or 3 of the 2011 Act. An offence under s.3 of the 2011 Act attracts a fine of up to €500. Failure to comply with a direction of a member of An Garda Síochána is an offence under s.8 of the 1994 Act. Section 8, however, requires the absence of lawful authority or reasonable excuse on the part of the accused. This form of words is absent from the offence under s.3 of the 2011 Act, with the result that the offence appears to be one of strict liability and is committed by mere failure to comply, as opposed to refusal to do so.

Further offences are set out in ss.5 and 6 of the 2011 Act. These are committed in the context of organised begging. Under s.5 it is an offence to:

(a) control or direct the actions of another person for the purposes of begging;
(b) organise or be materially involved in the organisation of begging by another person;
(c) force another person to beg; or
(d) otherwise cause another person to beg.

If tried summarily, an offence under s.5 attracts a maximum fine of €5,000 and/or a term of imprisonment of 12 months. The penalty on indictment is a maximum fine of €200,000 and/or a term of imprisonment of up to five years.

The offence under s.6 is linked with s.5 in that a further offence is committed by a person who lives off the proceeds of begging by another person. It does not seem that the offence under s.6 could be prosecuted on its own. The section reads:

> "A person who derives a living, in whole or in part, from the proceeds of begging by another person and who, in relation to that person, commits an offence under section 5 or aids and abets the commission of such an offence is guilty of an offence ...".

The offence under s.6 is tried summarily and the maximum penalty on conviction is a fine of €5,000 and/or a term of imprisonment of 12 months. The 2011 Act is silent on the question of mens rea in respect of the offences under ss.5 and 6.

KEY CASES AND LEGISLATION

Criminal Justice (Public Order) Act 2011—sets out offences related to begging and prohibits harassment of members of the public by anyone engaged in begging.

Dillon v DPP [2008] 1 I.R. 383—Section 3 of the Vagrancy (Ireland) Act 1847 held to be unconstitutional. Offences pertaining to begging now contained in Criminal Justice (Public Order) Act 2011.

14 Offences against the State

There are numerous pieces of legislation that deal with conduct which is deemed to be detrimental to the interests of the State, the gravest of which is treason. For the most part, offences of this nature are contained in the Offences against the State Act 1939, which has been amended on several occasions. Other offences are located in the Official Secrets Act 1963. This chapter deals with the most important of these statutory provisions.

TREASON

Article 39 of Bunreacht na hÉireann provides as follows:

> "Treason shall consist only in levying war against the State or assisting any state or person or inciting or conspiring with any person to levy war against the State, or attempting in force of arms or other violent means to overturn the organs of government established in this Constitution, or taking part or being concerned in or inciting or conspiring with any person to make or to take part or be concerned in any such attempt."

Article 39 is amplified by the provisions of the Treason Act 1939. Prior to the passing of the Criminal Justice Act 1990 (the "1990 Act"), the penalty for treason was death, although the sentence was usually commuted to life imprisonment by the President in accordance with Art.13.6 of Bunreacht na hÉireann. The death penalty was abolished by s.1 of the 1990 Act and a constitutional ban on the enactment of any law providing for the imposition of the death penalty was inserted into Art.15 of Bunreacht na hÉireann following the passing of the Twenty-First Amendment by referendum in 2001. All references to capital punishment, with the exception of the ban, were also removed from the text of the Constitution.

The Criminal Justice Act 1964 abolished the death penalty for most offences, with the exception of certain offences under the Offences against the State Act 1939, certain military law offences, capital murder and treason. Ireland's obligations under various Conventions and membership of the European Union required total abolition of the death penalty, and this came about with the enactment of the 1990 Act. Section 2 of the 1990 Act now provides that treason is an offence punishable by imprisonment for life. Section 4 of the 1990 Act provides that a minimum of 40 years be served, provided that the accused is an adult.

Sedition

Article 40.6.1° of Bunreacht na hÉireann grants protection to numerous rights, among which is freedom of expression. The Article also provides that this right may be subject to limitation on various grounds, among which are the protection of public order and the authority of the State. The Article goes on to declare that the publication or the utterance of seditious matter is an offence which shall be punishable by law. Sedition may be described as being conduct which goes beyond mere criticism of government and which is aimed at undermining the authority of the State, but falls short of treason. Sedition, therefore, can be seen as a lesser species of treason. Section 10(1)(c) of the Offences against the State Act 1939 provides that it is an offence to set up in type, print, send by post, distribute, sell or offer for sale any document which is or contains or includes a seditious document.

The Official Secrets Act 1963

The Official Secrets Act 1963 (the "1963 Act") contains three categories of offences. Part II of the 1963 Act deals with official information. Section 4 of the 1963 Act prohibits the disclosure of official information without authorisation to do so. Section 6 prohibits the retention of any official document or official information in the absence of any right or duty to do so. Part III of the 1963 Act deals with offences that involve the communication of information where to do so would be prejudicial to the safety or preservation of the State. Section 9 provides that a person shall not, in any manner prejudicial or contrary to the safety or preservation of the State, obtain, record, communicate or publish or have possession of any document or record of any of the following:

"(i) the number, description, armament, equipment, disposition, movement or condition of any of the Defence Forces or of any of the vessels or aircraft belonging to the State,

(ii) any operations or projected operations of any of the Defence Forces or of the Garda Síochána or of any of the vessels or aircraft belonging to the State,

(iii) any measures for the defence or fortification of any place on behalf of the State,

(iv) munitions of war, or
(v) any other matter whatsoever information as to which would or might be prejudicial to the safety or preservation of the State."

Exceptions to the application of s.9 are provided in the Freedom of Information Act 2014.

It will be a defence to show that the accused's conduct was authorised by the relevant Minister, someone acting on the Minister's behalf, or as pursuant to his duties as a holder of public office and under the Freedom of Information Act 2014. Section 10 of the 1963 Act provides that where the accused is charged with an offence under s.9 and he has been in communication with, or attempted to communicate with, whether inside or outside the State, a foreign agent or a member of an unlawful organisation, such communication will be evidence that his action was prejudicial to the interests of the State. Where the accused has visited the address of the foreign agent or a member of an unlawful organisation or has consorted or associated with such individuals, or where the address of such individuals is found in the possession of the accused, this will constitute evidence of communication between the accused and the foreign agent or member of an unlawful organisation. The onus of proof then shifts to the accused who must prove the contrary.

The provision further defines a "foreign agent" and a "member of an unlawful organisation" and includes people who are reasonably suspected to be such. Section 13 of the 1963 Act declares that a person who contravenes or attempts to contravene any of the provisions of the 1963 Act is liable on summary conviction to a maximum sentence of six months and/or a fine. Offences under s.9 and those contained in Pt II of the 1963 Act may be tried on indictment where, upon conviction, the maximum penalty is a term of imprisonment of seven years.

The Offences against the State Acts 1939–1998

The Offences against the State Act 1939 (the "1939 Act") is the principal piece of legislation dealing with offences against the State. The purpose of the 1939 Act, as originally enacted, was to suppress activity deemed to be subversive in nature and, to this end, the 1939 Act contains some fairly radical, if not utterly draconian, measures. The 1939 Act is divided into five parts, with only the first three being intended to be permanent. Part V of the 1939 Act provides for the establishment of the Special Criminal Court, the jurisdiction of which has already been discussed. Section 30 of the 1939 Act deals with the arrest and detention of suspected persons and is one of the few statutory measures that allow for detention for the purposes of questioning. The constitutionality of s.30 was upheld by the Supreme Court in *DPP v Quilligan* [1986] I.R. 495. In *Damache v DPP* [2012] 2 I.R. 266, the Supreme Court struck down s.29(1) of the 1939 Act on the basis that it had permitted a member of An Garda Síochána to issue a search warrant in circumstances where he had not been independent of the investigation. As a result, s.29 of the 1939 Act has been substituted by the Criminal Justice (Search Warrants) Act 2012, which provides that a warrant may be issued by a District Court judge if he is satisfied that relevant evidence is to be found at the location named. The evidence must come from a member of An Garda Síochána not below the rank of sergeant. A search warrant under the 1939 Act may be issued by a Garda whose rank is that of superintendent or higher, and it may only be issued to a Garda whose rank is that of sergeant or higher. The Garda issuing the warrant must be satisfied that it is necessary for the purposes of investigating the offence in question and that the urgency of the situation makes it impracticable to make an application before a District Court judge. The Garda issuing the warrant must also be unconnected with the investigation of the offence.

Although there are 59 sections in the 1939 Act in total, relatively few of these are used with any great frequency. What follows are the most commonly used.

Section 18

The purpose of s.18 of the 1939 Act is to provide justificatory grounds for the suppression of organisations which are deemed to be unlawful. An organisation may be deemed unlawful if it is one that:

> "(a) engages in, promotes, encourages, or advocates the commission of treason or any activity of a treasonable nature, or
> (b) advocates, encourages, or attempts the procuring by force, violence, or other unconstitutional means of an alteration of the Constitution, or
> (c) raises or maintains or attempts to raise or maintain a military or armed force in contravention of the Constitution or without constitutional authority, or
> (d) engages in, promotes, encourages, or advocates the commission of any criminal offence or the obstruction of or interference with the administration of justice or the enforcement of the law, or
> (e) engages in, promotes, encourages, or advocates the attainment of any particular object, lawful or unlawful, by violent, criminal, or other unlawful means, or

(f) promotes, encourages, or advocates the non-payment of moneys payable to the Central Fund or any other public fund or the non-payment of local taxation".

Section 19

The Government is not required to issue a declaration to the effect that a particular organisation is an unlawful one for the purposes of the 1939 Act. However, s.19 provides that the Government may make a suppression order with regard to any organisation where it is of the opinion that the organisation in question is an unlawful one. The suppression order is conclusive evidence that the organisation named within it is an unlawful organisation.

Section 20

A member of the organisation in respect of which the suppression order is made may, under s.20 of the 1939 Act, apply to either the High Court or the Attorney General for what is referred to in the 1939 Act as a "declaration of legality". This application must be made within 30 days of the making of the suppression order and an appeal from the decision lies to the Court of Appeal. If the declaration of legality is granted, the suppression order "shall forthwith become null and void". No action carried out pursuant to the suppression order prior to the granting of the declaration of legality will be affected by this. If the declaration is not granted, and an appeal against this decision to the Court of Appeal is not successful, neither the fact that the application was made nor any admissions or statements made by the applicant, whether orally or on affidavit, in the course of the application, may be used in evidence for the purposes of any subsequent prosecution of the applicant on charges of membership of the unlawful organisation.

Section 52

Section 52 of the 1939 Act provides that where a suspect is detained pursuant to s.30 of the 1939 Act, the Gardaí may demand that he gives a full account of his movements and actions within a specified period and all information in his possession regarding the commission or intended commission of any offence under the 1939 Act, or any scheduled offence, by another person. Section 52 was amended by s.13 of the Offences against the State (Amendment) Act 1998, with the result that s.52 will not have effect unless a suspect is told in ordinary language that the information is being sought under that section. He must also be informed of the consequences of failure/refusal to comply or for giving misleading information. Failure or refusal to give such an account or information as demanded is an offence under s.52(2) of the 1939 Act, which attracts a maximum penalty of six months' imprisonment. This provision has also been challenged on the grounds that it infringes the right to silence, a right protected by Bunreacht na hÉireann as being part and parcel of the right under Art.38 to a trial "in due course of law". In *Heaney v Ireland* [1996] 1 I.R. 580, the Supreme Court upheld the section on the basis that curtailment of the right to silence was a proportionate means of achieving the objective of the 1939 Act.

The Offences against the State (Amendment) Act 1972

The 1939 Act has been amended on a number of occasions, and one noteworthy example of such amendment is to be found in s.3 of the Offences against the State (Amendment) Act 1972 (the "1972 Act"), as amended by the Offences against the State (Amendment) Act 1998, which provides that any statements, made orally or in writing or otherwise, or any conduct by the accused, which implies or leads to the reasonable inference that he is a member of an unlawful organisation, shall be evidence of such membership.

"Conduct" includes movements, actions, activities, or associations on the part of the accused and an omission to deny published reports of such membership. The section provides that such failure to deny published reports of membership shall not, on its own, be conclusive evidence of membership. Section 3(2) of the 1972 Act further provides that where a member of the Garda Síochána, not below the rank of Chief Superintendent, states in evidence that he is of the belief that the accused is a member of an unlawful organisation, that statement shall be evidence of such membership.

Section 3(2) was challenged in *O'Leary v Attorney General* [1993] 1 I.R. 102 on the grounds that it was an infringement of the presumption of innocence. The accused was found in possession of Republican posters and was convicted of membership of an unlawful organisation, the posters being deemed to have been "incriminating documents".

The challenge failed on the basis that if the court agreed that the evidence did not establish the accused's guilt beyond reasonable doubt, he was entitled to be acquitted of the charge. In *DPP v Ferguson*, unreported, Court of Criminal Appeal, 27 October 1975, the Court of Criminal Appeal held that the statement of the Chief Superintendent as to his belief regarding the defendant's membership of an unlawful organisation was not conclusive, in and of itself, as regards the charge against the accused. O'Higgins C.J. stated that where the accused denied the charge on oath, "the value and cogency to be attached the expression of belief ... would be obviously very much diminished". In *DPP v Mulligan*, unreported, Court of Criminal Appeal, 17 May 2004, Keane C.J. stated that "the weight to be given to that evidence [the belief of the Chief Superintendent] was entirely a matter for the court of trial". More recently, the Supreme Court upheld s.3 in *DPP v Kelly* [2006] I.R. 115 notwithstanding the court's recognition of what it referred to as the "inherent limitation on cross-examination" contained in the section.

The Offences against the State (Amendment) Act 1998

Further amendments were made to the 1939 Act with the enactment, following the Omagh Bombing, of the Offences against the State (Amendment) Act 1998 (the "1998 Act"). The 1998 Act has itself been amended on a number of occasions. The most significant provisions of the 1998 Act are as follows:

Section 2

Section 2 provides that where evidence is given in the course of proceedings under s.21 of the 1939 Act, that the accused failed to answer any question material to the investigation of the offence, before or after being charged, the court is entitled to draw "such inferences from the failure as appear proper". Such failure may then be treated as corroborative of any other evidence, but this will not be sufficient, in and of itself, for the purposes of conviction.

Section 6

Section 6, as amended, creates the new offence of directing an unlawful organisation, an offence punishable by life imprisonment. The section provides that it is an offence to direct the activities of any unlawful organisation, at any level of that organisation's structure, which is the subject of a suppression order pursuant to s.19 of the 1939 Act.

Section 10

Section 10 provides for the extension of the maximum period of detention pursuant to s.30 of the 1939 Act. Since the passing of the 1998 Act, the maximum period of detention under s.30 is 72 hours.

KEY CASES

Damache v DPP [2012] 2 I.R. 266—Section 29(1) of the Offences against the State Act 1939 held to be unconstitutional. Replaced by the Criminal Justice (Search Warrants) Act 2012, which sets out rules on the granting of search warrants under the 1939 Act.

15 Organised Crime and Money Laundering

There are a number of significant legislative measures dealing with the issue of organised crime which, in popular perception, has become more prevalent in recent years. Among the relatively recent statutory initiatives introduced is the Criminal Justice (Terrorist Offences) (Amendment) Act 2015, which amends the Criminal Justice (Terrorist Offences) Act 2005 (the "2005 Act") by the creation of a number of new offences. The European arrest warrant, provided for under the European Arrest Warrant Act 2003, as amended, is applicable to offences under the 2005 Act, in accordance with Pt 8 of the 2005 Act. Part 7 of the 2005 Act had permitted the retention of data for up to three years for the purpose of the investigation of crime or for the security of the State, the Proceeds of Crime Acts 1996–2016, and the Criminal Assets Bureau Act 1996, to name but a few. Part 7 of the 2005 Act was repealed by the Communications (Retention of Data) Act 2011 (the "2011 Act") but a saver was provided in s.13(2) of the 2011 Act which provides that data which had been the subject of a data retention request under Pt 7 of the 2005 Act may still be adduced in evidence in proceedings taking place after the repeal of Pt 7. Further, s.3 of the 2011 Act requires that data be retained for a period of two years. Irish data retention laws had been based on EU Directives, in particular Directive 2006/24/EC (the Data Retention Directive) which was held to be invalid by the Court of Justice (ECJ) in the joined cases of *Digital Rights Ireland Ltd v Minister for Communications, Marine and Natural Resources* (C-293/12) and *Kärntner Landesregierung, Seitlinger, Tschohl and others* (C-594/12). The case brought by Digital Rights Ireland arose as a result of a High Court challenge to the validity of the Irish data retention framework. However, further amendments to Irish law to reflect the ruling of the ECJ have yet to be enacted. The Criminal Justice Act 2006 (the "2006 Act") provides for extended powers in the context of search warrants, seizure of goods and an extension of detention periods. Section 11 of the Criminal Justice Act 2007, which provided for a person released on bail to be electronically monitored, was not commenced and is to be replaced by a similar provision currently before the Houses of the Oireachtas as part of the Bail (Amendment) Bill 2016. In the context of organised or so-called "gangland" crime, two pieces of legislation are of significant importance and the remainder of this chapter deals with these.

Part 7 of the Criminal Justice Act 2006

Part 7 of the 2006 Act, as amended by the Criminal Justice (Amendment) Act 2009, deals with "organised crime". Section 70 of the 2006 Act sets out a number of definitions for the purposes of Pt 7. In particular, the term "criminal organisation" is defined as being a structured group of three or more people, acting in concert, which has been established over a period of time and which has, as its main objective, the commission or facilitation of one or more serious offences in order to obtain, directly or indirectly, a financial or other material benefit. A "serious offence", in the context of Pt 7 of the 2006 Act, is one which carries a potential sentence of four years' imprisonment. The group of three or more people must be a "structured group", defined in Pt 7 as one which is not randomly formed for the purpose of committing a single offence and which does not need to have formally defined roles for its members, continuity of membership or a developed structure.

Conspiracy

Section 71 of the 2006 Act creates the statutory offence of conspiracy in the context of organised crime. The offence, which may be committed within or outside the State, occurs where a person conspires with one or more persons to carry out an act, within the State or outside, that constitutes or would constitute a serious offence within the State. Any person found guilty of conspiracy is liable to the same penalty as the principal offender.

Organised Crime

Section 72, as substituted by the Criminal Justice (Amendment) Act 2009, provides that it is an offence for a person who has knowledge of the existence of a criminal organisation to participate in or contribute to any activity enhancing the ability of that criminal organisation or any of its members to commit a serious offence or facilitating the commission by the criminal organisation or any of its members of a serious offence, as defined in Pt 7 of the 2006 Act. The conduct of the accused need not itself be criminal in order to commit the offence of participation. This offence may be committed intentionally or recklessly. The penalty for the offence of conspiracy under s.72 of the 2006 Act is a term of imprisonment of up to 15 years and/or an unlimited fine.

Committing an Offence for a Criminal Organisation

Section 73 of the 2006 Act provides that a person who commits a serious offence for the benefit of, at the direction of, or in association with, a criminal organisation is guilty of an offence. The person need not be a member of the criminal organisation or even know any of its members. As amended by the Criminal Justice (Amendment) Act 2009, the penalty for this offence is a term of imprisonment of up to 15 years and/or an unlimited fine.

The Criminal Justice (Amendment) Act 2009

Significant amendments were made to Pt 7 of the 2006 Act with the enactment of the Criminal Justice (Amendment) Act 2009 (the "2009 Act"). The stated purpose of the 2009 Act is to, inter alia, provide for "additional measures with respect to combating organised crime and, in particular, with respect to countering the increased levels of violence towards, and intimidation of, members of the public perpetrated by criminal organisations". Prior to its enactment, a number of concerns were raised about the potential impact of the provisions of the Bill on constitutional rights. The Council of State was convened by the President in order to obtain advice on the potential referral of the Bill to the Supreme Court pursuant to Art.26 of Bunreacht na hÉireann, but ultimately the Bill was not referred and was signed into law. Thus, the 2009 Act enjoys the presumption of constitutionality.

Section 3 of the 2009 Act extends the definition of "criminal organisation" contained in the 2006 Act. For the purposes of the 2009 Act, and Pt 7 of the 2006 Act, a "criminal organisation" is now defined as "a structured group, however organised, that has as its main purpose or activity the commission of a serious offence."

A "structured group" is one which meets the following criteria:

(1) It must have three or more people;
(2) It must not have been randomly formed for the immediate commission of a single offence;
(3) The involvement of two or more of these individuals is with a view to their acting in concert.

The structured group need not have any formal rules or membership or any formal roles for any of its members. There need be no hierarchical or leadership structure and it is not necessary that all members of the group themselves directly participate in the commission of criminal offences.

Section 5 of the 2009 Act inserts a new s.71A into the 2006 Act. The newly inserted provision creates the offence of "directing a criminal organisation". The offence is committed where the accused directs the activities of a criminal organisation at any level. Pursuant to the 2009 Act, a person "directs" an organisation where he controls or supervises activities or gives an order, or issues guidance or a request with respect to the activities of the organisation. The maximum penalty on conviction for the offence under s.5 is life imprisonment. Further, the section provides that any statement or conduct by the accused which leads to a reasonable inference of his guilt is admissible as evidence of his guilt. The court may also have regard to a number of other factors in determining whether the accused has committed an offence under s.71A of the 2006 Act. These factors are set out in s.71A(4) and include any evidence of a pattern of behaviour by the accused which is consistent with the directing of a criminal organisation or the possession by the accused of any articles, documents or records which would give rise to a reasonable suspicion of guilt under s.71A.

A further offence of participating in, or contributing to, criminal activities is created by s.6 of the 2009 Act, which amends the 2006 Act by the substitution of a new s.72. The offence under s.72 of the 2006 Act is committed where the accused participates in or contributes to any activity with the intention of enhancing the capability of the criminal organisation or any of its members to commit a serious offence or to facilitate the commission of a serious criminal offence by the organisation or any of its members *or* being reckless as to whether his conduct could enhance the ability of the organisation to commit a serious offence or facilitate the commission of a serious offence by the organisation or its members. The activity engaged in by the accused need not be a criminal offence; in other words, the section criminalises any activity on the part of the accused which is carried out with the intention of assisting the criminal organisation to commit a serious offence. In order to convict the accused for an offence under s.72, it must be shown that he knew of the existence of the organisation when he participated in or contributed to its activities.

The prosecution need not prove that the criminal organisation, or any of its members, actually committed a serious offence within or outside the jurisdiction. Nor must the prosecution establish that the conduct of the accused actually enhanced the ability of the organisation to commit a serious offence or that it facilitated the commission of a serious offence by the criminal organisation. The penalty for an offence under s.72 of the 2006 Act is a term of imprisonment of up to 15 years and/or an unlimited fine. The court may consider any relevant factor, including whether the accused uses a name, word, symbol or other representation that identifies the criminal organisation or is associated with it. Section 72 of the 2006 Act also contains a Table of incriminating articles, including: balaclavas; boiler suits; any means of disguise or impersonation (including any article of Garda uniform or equipment); firearms; knives; any implement for burglary or gaining access to any premises; plans of premises; controlled drugs within the meaning of the Misuse of Drugs Act 1977; substantial amounts of cash or currency; false vehicle registration plates; or any other article which may be prescribed for the purposes of s.72. The significance of the Table of articles is that the possession by the accused of any of these articles can be a factor from which the intention of the accused, in relation to the offence, may be inferred.

Scheduled Offences

Section 8 of the 2009 Act declares that in respect of certain offences under the 2006 Act, as amended, the ordinary courts are "inadequate to secure the effective administration of justice and the preservation of public peace and order". Section 8 also provides that these offences are to be included in the list of offences scheduled to the Offences against the State Acts 1939–1998. These include the offences pertaining to criminal organisations contained in Pt 7 of the 2006 Act and those created by ss.5 and 6 of the 2009 Act. The effect of scheduling an offence to the Offences against the State Acts is that those offences are automatically sent for trial in the Special Criminal Court, which sits without a jury. To that end, s.8(1) provides:

> "It is hereby declared that the ordinary courts are inadequate to secure the effective administration of justice and the preservation of public peace and order in relation to ... [certain] ... provisions of Part 7 of the Act of 2006".

As noted previously, Art.38.5 of Bunreacht na hÉireann permits derogation from the general right to trial by jury for serious offences in certain, specified circumstances, one of which being where there is a declaration that the ordinary courts are inadequate to secure the administration of justice. Section 8 appears to forestall any challenge to the use of the Special Criminal Court for the trial of certain "gangland" offences. The wording of the relevant sections which create offences pertaining to criminal organisations has been the subject of much commentary, a lot of which centres around the vague wording of the offences. In that regard, the statement of the Supreme Court in *King v Attorney General* [1981] I.R. 233 is instructive. In that case, the Supreme Court held that a section of the Vagrancy Act 1824 was unconstitutional on grounds of vagueness, having been described by the Supreme Court as

> "so arbitrary, so vague, so difficult to rebut ... and so generally at variance with both the explicit and implicit characteristics and limitations of the criminal law as to the onus of proof and mode of proof, that it is not so much a question of ruling unconstitutional the type of offence we are now considering as identifying the particular constitutional provisions with which such an offence is at variance."

Drugs Offences

16

The prohibition on the possession, use, manufacture and supply of various substances is common throughout the world. In some cases, certain substances are banned on religious or cultural grounds, whereas in others, they are restricted on public policy and health grounds. In Ireland, the principal legislation dealing with the control of certain drugs is the Misuse of Drugs Act 1977 (the "1977 Act"), as amended by the Misuse of Drugs Act 1984. In addition to the Misuse of Drugs Acts, the Criminal Justice (Psychoactive Substances) Act 2010 (the "2010 Act") prohibits the sale of psychoactive substances as defined in that Act. Broadly speaking, these are substances that became popular and were sold in so-called "head shops". The ingredients used are not illegal in themselves and are often plants and other natural organisms used for other, legitimate purposes. The 2010 Act prohibits the sale, advertisement or promotion of these substances. It is also an offence under the 2010 Act to provide information on how to obtain them.

This chapter sets out the two main offences contained in the Misuse of Drugs Acts. The preparation and supply of medicines is governed by the Pharmacy Act 2007. This, in effect, permits suitably qualified professionals to dispense substances for medical purposes under a licensing system provided for under that Act.

Section 2 of the 1977 Act sets out the concept of "controlled drugs", which are contained in the Schedule to the 1977 Act. This Schedule may be added to whenever the Government deems it necessary to do so. The effect of this is that the substance in question will then be included in the offences set out in the legislation. Section 5 of the 1977 Act permits the Minister for Health to make regulations for the purpose of preventing the misuse of controlled drugs.

The two main types of offences that are committed in the context of illicit drugs are possession, and possession for the purpose of unlawful sale or supply. It is an offence under s.3 of the 1977 Act to be in possession of a controlled drug unless the drug has been prescribed for use by that person or has been exempted by Ministerial Order. The actus reus is being in unlawful possession of a controlled drug.

The 1977 Act differentiates between cannabis/cannabis resin and other controlled drugs and this is reflected in the range of penalties which are set down in s.27 of the 1977 Act, as amended by the Fines Act 2010. In summary, these are:

- Possession of cannabis/cannabis resin:
  - First and second offence: summary conviction—maximum fine of €1,000; on indictment—maximum fine of €2,500.
  - Third and subsequent offence: summary conviction—maximum fine of €2,500 and/or up to 12 months' imprisonment; on indictment—unlimited fine and/or up to three years' imprisonment.

- Possession of other controlled drugs excluding cannabis/cannabis resin:
  - Summary conviction—maximum fine of €2,500 and/or up to 12 months' imprisonment.
  - On indictment—unlimited fine and/or up to seven years' imprisonment.

The more serious of the two main offences is contained in s.15 of the 1977 Act and is committed by anyone who has a controlled drug in his possession with the intention of selling or supplying it to another person. Section 15(2) provides that the quantity of the drug found in the accused's possession is a matter which the court is entitled to regard as relevant to the issue of whether the drugs were for the personal use of the accused. The prosecution bears the burden of proving possession, and s.15(2) creates a rebuttable presumption that permits the court to infer from the quantity of drugs found that they are not for the "immediate personal use" of the accused. The onus will be on the accused to rebut this presumption to the court's satisfaction, and although the 1977 Act is silent on the issue of the standard of proof, it is usually the case that in criminal law matters, where the onus of proof shifts from the prosecution to the defence, this is discharged on the civil standard of proof—the balance of probabilities.

The 1977 Act was amended by s.4 of the Criminal Justice Act 1999, which inserted s.15A into the 1977 Act. The offence under s.15A is very similar to the offence under s.15, in that it involves the possession of a controlled substance, whether lawful or otherwise, with the intention of selling or otherwise supplying it to others. The difference between both offences is that s.15A is aimed at larger scale, commercial transactions involving drug dealing. If the market value of the drugs found in the accused's possession is deemed to amount to or be in excess of €13,000, a custodial sentence of at least 10 years must be imposed, unless there are exceptional and specific circumstances relating to the offence or to the offender that warrant the court's deviation from this. The 10-year sentence is described as a mandatory minimum sentence, although it is probably more accurate to describe it as presumptive. A sentencing court must regard the 10-year sentence as its starting point and, having regard to the circumstances, reduce it accordingly. In *DPP v R.*, unreported, Court of Criminal Appeal, 23 November 2011, the approach of the courts was described in the following terms:

> "What is even more instructive is legislation which, as in the present case, fixes a mandatory minimum sentence. Even though that sentence may not be applicable in a particular case the very existence of a lengthy mandatory minimum sentence is an important guide to the Courts in determining the gravity of the offence and the appropriate sentence to impose for its commission."

Market/Street Value

The question of how to evaluate the "market value" of drugs has come before the courts on a number of occasions. In *DPP v Finnamore* [2009] 1 I.R. 153, the Court of Criminal Appeal stated: "There is no principle or rule of law known to this court which requires that in each and every case, every package found must inevitably be individually analysed before a conviction can be considered safe."

In that case, the court accepted that the presence of amphetamines could, as a matter of probability, be extrapolated from analysis carried out on a representative sample of the drug packages found.

However, in *DPP v Connolly* [2011] 1 I.R. 755, the Supreme Court adopted a far less lenient stance on the matter and stated:

> "I would note the need to keep in mind that proof of value is an essential ingredient of the offence under section 15A. It is what distinguishes it from the offence of possession for sale or supply of an unquantified and unvalued amount of drugs. Most importantly, it is what has caused the Oireachtas, subject to exceptional mitigating circumstances, to mark the offence as one of extreme seriousness such as to require the court, in sentencing a convicted person, to impose a penalty of a minimum of ten years' imprisonment. This is, of course, subject to the exceptions mentioned in the section. The ingredient of value must be proved to the satisfaction of the jury beyond reasonable doubt."

What is "Possession"?

Liability for possession of a prohibited item is based on the connection between the accused and the item in question. The term is broader in scope than mere physical proximity to the item and incorporates an element of control coupled with an awareness of this on the part of the accused. In *Warner v Metropolitan Police Commissioner* [1969] 2 A.C. 256, the court outlined the essence of possession as follows:

"Ideally a possessor of a thing has complete physical control over it; he has knowledge of its existence, its situation and its qualities: he has received it from a person who intends to confer possession of it and he has himself the intention to possess it exclusively of others. But these elements are seldom all present in situations with which the courts have to deal, and where one or more of them is lacking, or incompletely present, it has to be decided whether the given approximation is such that possession may be held sufficiently established to satisfy the relevant rule of law."

Although it will be easy to establish possession in circumstances where an accused has actual physical control over the item, establishing possession in other circumstances is not as straightforward. In this instance, an accused who controls the prohibited item without having actual physical custody of it may be fixed with liability on the basis of constructive possession. The High Court of Australia explained the concept of constructive possession in the following way in *Williams v Douglas* (1949) 78 C.L.R. 521:

"Possession does not mean actual physical possession or manual detention. 'Suppose I request a bystander to hold anything for me, it still remains in my possession. So also possession may be required or retained over goods which are in the manual detention of a third person': R v. Sleep (1861) Le and Ca. 44 per Willes J. And the phrase possession and control denotes the right and power to deal with the article in question."

In addition to the requirement of control, to be held legally liable for possession of an item, the accused must have knowledge or awareness of the item in question. In this regard, the High Court in *Minister for Posts and Telegraphs v Campbell* [1966] I.R. 69 held:

"Normally speaking, a person can properly be said to be in possession of the contents of his own dwellinghouse but only if he is aware of what it contains. He cannot properly be said to be in control or possession of something of whose existence and presence he has no knowledge."

Section 1(2) of the 1977 Act clarifies the concept of constructive possession for the purposes of the Act by providing as follows:

"For the purposes of this Act any controlled drug, pipe, utensil or document of which a person has control and which is in the custody of another who is, either under the person's control or, though not under the person's control, acts on his behalf, whether as an agent or otherwise, shall be regarded as being in the possession of the person".

Control and Knowledge

An accused exercises control over an item if he, or someone acting on his behalf, is in a position to deal with the item from a distance, for example, to sell or otherwise dispose of it. This is the external part of the offence. The mens rea consists of an intention to control the item together with knowledge or recklessness as to what the item is. In the context of drugs offences, an accused would be required to know that the item in his possession was an illicit drug or be reckless as to that fact. On that point, the Privy Council held in *DPP v Brooks* [1974] A.C. 862 that unless provided for by statute, an accused could not be convicted of possession of illegal drugs unless he was aware that the item in his possession was a drug. Section 29 of the 1977 Act (as amended) sets out a defence to a charge of possession which places a burden of proof on the defence to show that the accused did not know, and had no reasonable grounds to suspect, that he was in possession of a controlled substance. In *DPP v Smyth* [2010] 3 I.R. 688, the Court of Criminal Appeal held that the burden of proof placed on the accused under s.29 of the 1977 Act is discharged when the defence shows the existence of reasonable doubt. This had been held in *DPP v Byrne* [1998] 2 I.R. 417.

KEY CASES AND LEGISLATION

DPP v R., unreported, Court of Criminal Appeal, 23 November 2001—Mandatory minimum 10-year penalty must be regarded as the starting point in imposing sentence under s.15A of the Misuse of Drugs Act 1977, as amended.

DPP v Connolly [2011] 1 I.R. 755—Severity of penalty under s.15A requires high standard of proof in proving "market value" of drugs.

17 Corruption Offences

The Irish law on corruption is contained in a number of statutes going back to the late 19th century. These Acts have been amended on many occasions with the result that the law governing the issue is fragmented and in need of consolidation. In 2012, the Government published the Heads of the Criminal Justice (Corruption) Bill 2012, which aims to consolidate the law on corruption by replacing and reforming the existing statutory framework.

Many, if not most, of these Acts have been passed following revelations of malpractice by holders of public office as set out in the reports of numerous tribunals of inquiry. Increased media scrutiny and public awareness have resulted in calls for greater openness and transparency and this, coupled with obligations under various international conventions, has resulted in numerous statutory changes, including the Freedom of Information Acts 1997 and 2003 (now the Freedom of Information Act 2014), the Ethics in Public Office Act 1995, the Standards in Public Office Act 2001 and the Commissions of Investigation Act 2004, to name but a few.

There is no statutory definition of "corruption" in Irish law. The Prevention of Corruption Act 1906 (the "1906 Act") deals with the punishment for "corrupt transactions", which essentially is the crime of bribery. In *R. v Whittaker* [1914] 3 K.B. 1283, bribery was explained in the following terms:

> "When an officer has to discharge a public duty in which the public is interested, to bribe that officer to act contrary to his duty is a criminal act. To induce him to shew favour or to abstain from shewing disfavour, is to induce him to act contrary to his duty: where this is done corruptly it is an indictable misdemeanour at common law which abhors corruption and fraud."

The offence is committed by offering a person who is a public official an inducement of some kind for the purpose of securing some form of benefit for the briber. The subject matter of the bribe must be connected with the official duty of the receiver of the bribe. In *HM Advocate v Dick* (1901) 3F (Ct. of Sess.) 59, the court held that unless the bribe was connected to the official functions of the receiver, no offence had taken place. The offence is also committed by the person receiving the bribe if he is aware that the inducement is being given in order to obtain some benefit as a result. Although the common law offence has not been repealed in Ireland, it is rarely, if ever, prosecuted.

The statutory offence of bribery was set out in the Public Bodies Corrupt Practices Act 1889 (the "1889 Act"), which rendered it an offence for a member, officer or servant of a public body to offer or accept or solicit gifts or benefits as an inducement to do, or refrain from doing, some act connected with the functions of the public body. The scope of the 1889 Act was quite narrow, and an attempt to remedy this came about with the enactment of the 1906 Act. The 1906 Act extended the scope of the earlier offence by extending criminal liability to relationships of agent and principal. The 1906 Act applied to:

(a) an agent obtaining some form of payment or other benefit as an inducement for doing any act in relation to his principal's affairs;
(b) any person providing the agent with a payment or benefit as an inducement to act in relation to his principal's affairs;
(c) any person or agent who knowingly falsifies documents with the intention of deceiving the principal.

The 1906 Act also extended the application of the corruption legislation to all public officials, including officials of international bodies. It also includes bribery in the private sector.

A further amendment to the corruption legislation came with the enactment of the Prevention of Corruption Act 1916. This Act introduced a presumption that payments made to employees of public bodies by individuals who want to obtain contracts from those bodies are corrupt payments. The presumption is rebuttable and it involves a reversal of the burden of proof. The burden can be discharged by the accused on the civil standard.

The Prevention of Corruption (Amendment) Act 2001 (the "2001 Act") was enacted in order to enable the ratification of three international agreements. In addition, the definition of "agent" contained in the 1906 Act was significantly extended. Consequently, the following are all agents for the purposes of the Prevention of Corruption Acts:

(a) any person employed by or acting for another;
(b) office holders, directors, employees and special advisors of public bodies;
(c) holders of specified offices, namely, Members of both Houses of the Oireachtas, MEPs, the Attorney General, DPP, Comptroller and Auditor General, the judiciary and any other person employed in/or acting on behalf of the public administration of the State;
(d) officials employed in equivalent positions in any other State.

A further amendment to s.1 of the 1906 Act is contained in the Prevention of Corruption (Amendment) Act 2010 (the "2010 Act"). This extends the category of "agent" to include people who are acting on behalf of foreign States and people who work for international organisations.

The wording of the offence contained in s.1 of the 1906 Act was also revised by the 2001 Act. The new wording provides that an offence is committed by a person who "corruptly gives or agrees to receive" or "corruptly offers" any gift/consideration to any person for the benefit of that person, his agent or anyone else, as an inducement to, or reward for, any action or inaction by the agent in relation to his office or to his principal's affairs or business. Simply put, anyone who offers a bribe or who pays a bribe in order to derive some benefit from doing so is guilty of an offence. The section also criminalises any person or agent who gives/uses any type of falsified receipt or other document with the intention of deceiving the principal. The 2010 Act clarifies that the conferring of "an advantage" is included in the offence. This means that the offence may be committed even if no financial reward was offered or given.

Sections 3 and 4 of the 2001 Act deal with presumptions. Section 3 applies in the context of proceedings for offences of corruption involving people elected to office or candidates for election. If an accused in those proceedings has received a financial donation exceeding the threshold for disclosure set out in the Electoral Act 1997 or the Local Elections (Disclosure of Donations and Expenditure) Act 1999, and it is established that he has not declared it and the donor was someone who had an interest in the accused's performance of his functions, a presumption of corruption on the part of the accused arises. Another presumption arises under s.4 of the 2001 Act. In this case, an accused who is one of the office holders set out in s.2(5)(b) of the 1906 Act will be presumed to have acted corruptly if he is prosecuted under the Prevention of Corruption Acts 1889–2010 and there is proof that the accused received money or other benefit from a person who has an interest in how the accused's official functions are carried out. Both presumptions involve a reversal of the burden of proof, which requires the accused to prove, on the balance of probabilities, that the payment was not corrupt.

The corruption offences outlined above require at least two participants. This left a lacuna whereby a person acting alone, in a corrupt manner in order to derive a benefit for himself or another person, did not commit an offence under the 1889–2010 Acts. Section 8 of the 2001 Act creates a new offence of "corruption in office". This offence is committed where a public official does something or omits to do something with the intention of corruptly obtaining some type of advantage for himself or another person. Section 8A of the 2001 Act was inserted by s.4 of the 2010 Act. The purpose of the new section is to provide immunity from civil liability to a whistleblower who reports, in good faith, his belief that an offence of corruption may have been or is being committed. The opinion must be communicated to an "appropriate person" who, in Ireland, is a member of An Garda Síochána and, in the event that the opinion is formed in the course of the person's employment, the employer. If the matter arises in another State, the law enforcement authorities or consular official are the appropriate persons for the purpose of s.8A. A person who acts in accordance with s.8A cannot be penalised for having done so. This means that, in addition to being immune from civil suit where he normally would be vulnerable to civil action, the person cannot be made to suffer a detriment at work due to acting in accordance with s.8A. The immunity provided by the section is dependent on the person acting in good faith. A person who communicates his belief that another person has committed an offence under the Prevention of Corruption Acts 1889–2010, in the knowledge that the allegations are false, misleading, frivolous or vexatious or reckless in that regard, loses the immunity provided by the section and commits an offence under the 2001 Act.

18 Inchoate Offences

The inchoate offences are attempts, conspiracy and incitement. Although sometimes referred to as incomplete offences, this is a misnomer, since inchoate offences are complete offences in themselves. All that is meant by the term "incomplete" in this context is that the substantive offence that was the subject of the attempt, conspiracy or incitement may not have been carried out. This in no way reduces liability in respect of the inchoate offences. All three forms of inchoate offence are creatures of common law in Ireland, none of them having been given statutory expression. A person convicted of an attempt may be punished as though the substantive offence had actually been completed.

Attempt

The actus reus of an attempt is some conduct on the part of the accused which is sufficiently proximate to the intended offence to incur liability. If the conduct of the accused is too remote or is merely preparatory in nature, the accused will not be convicted. In *R. v Eagleton* (1855) 169 E.R. 66, the accused was convicted of obtaining money by false pretences. The basic principles of the offence of attempt were outlined by the court and may be summarised as follows:

- (i) Intention is not a sufficient basis upon which to establish the offence.
- (ii) There must be some act(s) accompanying the intention.
- (iii) The act(s) must be in some way immediately connected to the substantive offence.

The Court of Criminal Appeal ruled along similar lines in *People (Attorney General) v Thornton* [1952] I.R. 91, defining the term "attempt" as

> "an act done by the accused with a specific intent to commit a particular crime; it must go beyond mere preparation and must be a direct movement towards the commission after the preparations have been made."

Two distinct and competing approaches to establishing the actus reus of attempt have evolved from *Eagleton*, namely the "proximate act" and the "last act" approaches. The former is premised on the requirement that the conduct of the accused is not too remote, whereas the latter approach is based on whether the accused committed the final act that is required in order to enable the commission of the substantive offence being attempted. Essentially, both approaches are concerned with setting the appropriate threshold which must be reached before liability for attempt can be imposed.

The leading Irish case on attempt is *People (Attorney General) v Sullivan* [1964] I.R. 169, where the Supreme Court stated that the decisive factor in determining whether the offence of attempt had been committed was whether the actions of the accused were "merely as a preparation for the commission of offences or whether they constituted acts sufficiently proximate to amount to attempts to commit the substantive offences".

Proximity

The difficulty of ascertaining the exact point at which an act has gone beyond mere preparation and becomes sufficiently proximate to incur liability is not altogether clear, and will largely depend on the facts of each case. In *People (Attorney General) v England* [1947] 1 Frewen 81, the Court of Criminal Appeal held that words alone could not amount to an attempt and that some positive action was required. In *People (Attorney General) v Sullivan* [1964] I.R. 169, the accused, a midwife, was charged with attempting to obtain money by false pretences. The basis of the allegation was that she had devised a scheme whereby she would receive payments in respect of fictitious patients. An additional allowance was payable when the number of patients she treated went above 25. The accused duly submitted claim forms but it was not clear whether the fictitious patients were among the first 25. The Supreme Court held that for an act to be considered an attempt, it must be sufficiently proximate to the commission of the substantive offence, and that where an act is the first in a series of similar actions, all carried out in furtherance of the commission of an offence, each action could be deemed sufficiently proximate to result in a conviction for attempt.

Another approach that has been used in determining proximity is the so-called "last act theory". This approach is posited on the notion that where the accused has committed the last act before the substantive offence is committed, he is guilty of attempt. In *DPP v Stonehouse* [1977] 2 All E.R. 909, the accused was charged with, and convicted of, attempting to enable another to obtain money. The accused, a former Government minister, took out a number of life insurance policies and then faked his own death. He was subsequently discovered very much alive, although the insurance had not been claimed by his wife, who was not part of the scam and believed the accused to be dead. The House of Lords upheld his conviction for attempting to commit the offence on the basis that he had done everything he could possibly have done to enable the offence to be committed, or, in the words of Lord Diplock, "the offender must have crossed the Rubicon and burnt his boats".

The mens rea for all attempts is the intention to commit the substantive offence. This is the case even where recklessness would be sufficient mens rea for the substantive offence. In *DPP v Douglas and Hayes* [1985] I.L.R.M. 25, the court held that the accused could be convicted of shooting with intent to commit murder, an offence under the Offences against the Person Act 1861, where it could be shown that they had an intention to kill. If the intention to kill could not be proved, the accused could not be convicted. The relevant section of the 1861 Act provided for a species of attempted murder. The modern law on attempted murder requires that the accused intended to kill; an intention to seriously injure will not suffice, even though the substantive offence of murder can be proven where the accused intends to seriously injure the victim.

Impossibility

If the accused attempts to do something that is either legally or physically impossible, he cannot be convicted of attempt. Impossibility, therefore, is a defence to a charge of attempt. In *Haughton v Smith* [1975] A.C. 476, it was held that the accused could not be convicted of handling stolen goods where the goods were not in fact stolen.

Similarly, if something is a physical impossibility, it will not result in a conviction for attempt. If, however, the accused intends to commit an offence and fails to succeed in his endeavour due to his own ineptitude, he will not be able to rely on the defence of impossibility.

It would appear that abandonment is not a defence to a charge of attempt on the basis that the offence is committed where the accused intends to commit the substantive offence and carries out acts sufficiently proximate to that offence.

Conspiracy

At common law, conspiracy occurs where two or more people enter into an agreement to commit an unlawful act, which can sometimes include civil wrongs. It is important to note that the actual offence need never be committed, and an accused can still be convicted where the objective of the conspiracy is not achieved, as was the case in *DPP v O'Brien*, unreported, Court of Criminal Appeal, 17 June 2002. This point was also made by the High Court in *Minister for Justice and Equality v T.E. (No. 2)* [2014] IEHC 51. The essence of the offence is the concluded agreement between the parties to commit an offence, a matter which can be inferred by the jury from the conduct of the accused.

The actus reus of conspiracy is the agreement *concluded* between the parties. It is essential that the agreement is more than a mere discussion of the offence. In *R. v Walker* [1962] Crim. L.R. 458, it was held that a conspiracy requires an agreement between the parties to commit the substantive offence. Mere discussions or preparatory negotiations will not be enough.

The mens rea is the intention to commit the substantive offence. The accused need not be aware of the precise details of the substantive offence, but he must have knowledge of the nature of the intended offence. In *R. v Orton* [1922] V.L.R. 469, it was held that an accused could be convicted of conspiracy even where he did not know the precise details of the offence. The court held that where the accused was aware that the activity being planned was a crime, it did not matter that he did not know all the details. A similar ruling was given in *R. v Porter* [1980] N.I. 18.

Where there are a number of individuals accused of conspiring with one another, it need not be the case that each individual knew about all the others. Where someone joins in a conspiracy already hatched by others, he will also be convicted. This can be seen in the case of *Attorney General v Oldridge* [2000] 4 I.R. 593. In this case, the accused had agreed to participate in a fraudulent scheme which had already been put into operation by others.

A statutory offence of conspiracy was created by s.71 of the Criminal Justice Act 2006, which applies to conspiracy in the context of the offences governed by that Act. Accordingly, where the offence does not pertain to criminal organisations, the common law offence of conspiracy applies.

Impossibility

If the agreement entered into relates to a specific endeavour which is impossible to achieve, no conviction will follow. In *DPP v Nock* [1978] 2 All E.R. 654, the accused were charged with conspiring to produce cocaine. Unknown to one of the accused, the material with which he was working did not contain any cocaine and consequently, he could not have produced the drug. The convictions for conspiracy were quashed by the House of Lords, where it was held that where the agreement between the defendants was to achieve a specific result and where that result was an impossibility, the defendants could not be convicted. The House of Lords also pointed out that where the indictment was drafted in very specific terms, no conviction could result. Where the indictment was drafted in more general terms, the court held that a conviction could be possible.

Where a party to a conspiracy subsequently pulls out of the agreement, this may amount to a mitigating factor. It would seem that a conviction could still be forthcoming, since the withdrawal from the agreement is dependent on being part of the agreement to begin with.

INCITEMENT

Incitement occurs where the accused persuades or influences another person to commit an offence or where a person is induced to commit an offence as a result of duress exerted by the accused. In *R. v Fitzmaurice* [1983] 1 All E.R. 189, it was held that incitement could be by a suggestion, proposal or the promise of a reward. In *R.R.B. v Applin* [1974] 2 W.L.R. 541, the court held that incitement can also occur where the accused uses threats to induce a person to commit a crime.

The actus reus of incitement is encouraging another person, by whatever means, to engage in the commission of an offence. In this way it is similar to solicitation. The leading Irish case on incitement is *People (Attorney General) v Capaldi* [1949] 1 Frewen 95. The accused enquired of a doctor whether something could "be done" for a pregnant woman. Implicit in the enquiry was the willingness of the doctor to perform an abortion. The doctor was also assured that money was no object, whereupon the doctor refused and asked the accused to leave the surgery. The accused was convicted of incitement and appealed. The Court of Criminal Appeal held that incitement involved more than the mere expression of a desire. However, in this case, the accused had gone further than simply articulating a desire and had offered a financial incentive. On that basis, the court upheld his conviction for incitement.

The incitement must be communicated either to a specific person or to a group of people. The accused cannot be prosecuted for attempted incitement where the communication fails for some reason. Additionally, where a person incites another to commit an offence and that other person agrees, both can then be charged with conspiracy. It had been the case that where the person being incited by the accused was deemed incapable of committing a criminal offence by reason of doli incapax, the accused could not be convicted of incitement. The age of criminal responsibility is now governed by s.52 of the Children Act 2001, as substituted by s.129 of the Criminal Justice Act 2006. The mens rea for incitement is intention. The accused must intend that the person being incited will commit the offence. He must also be aware of the different elements of the offence. Therefore, there can be no incitement if the accused knows that the incitee lacks the legal capacity to commit the offence. The accused will also not be liable where the person carrying out the crime commits a different offence. For example, if A incites B to rob a bank but, instead, B commits a totally different offence, A cannot be said to have incited that other offence. In *R. v Whitehouse* [1977] 3 All E.R. 737, the accused was charged with incitement to commit incest. The incitee was his 15-year-old daughter. Since the offence of incest by a female could only be committed by a female above the age of 16, the accused could not be convicted of incitement.

Impossibility

The defence of impossibility operates in much the same way with regard to incitement as it does to the other inchoate offences, and its success will depend on whether the incitement relates to a specific type of act or a more general one. Impossibility may be a defence in the former context, but will not be a defence in the latter. It should be noted that where the incitee goes further than what was actually incited, the accused will not be guilty of incitement in relation to this further offence.

Punishment on conviction

Punishment for incitement depends on whether the substantive offence is actually committed. Where the accused is charged with incitement of a summary offence which is committed, the accused is prosecuted as a principal offender in accordance with s.22 of the Petty Sessions (Ireland) Act 1851. In the case of indictable offences, the relevant statutory provision is s.7(1) of the Criminal Law Act 1997. Where the substantive offence is not actually committed, the matter of punishment is at the judge's discretion.

Statute

A statutory offence of incitement is provided for by the Prohibition of Incitement to Hatred Act 1989, which prohibits the publication, distribution or broadcast of any material that is threatening, abusive or insulting, with the intention to incite hatred against a group of people or being reckless as to whether hatred is incited. These offences may be committed by corporations as well as individuals.

19 Introduction to Criminal Defences

In order to discharge the onus of proof, the prosecution must not only prove all the elements of the offence(s) with which the accused is charged, but also negative or disprove any and all defences and explanations that are consistent with the accused's innocence. This is part and parcel of what was referred to as "the golden thread" in *Woolmington v DPP* [1935] A.C. 462.

Criminal defences may be categorised in a number of ways. Some defences are available only to a charge of murder and are partial defences only. A partial defence is one which will result in a conviction for a lesser offence than that with which the accused is charged. In the case of provocation, excessive self-defence and diminished responsibility, if successfully raised, the accused will be convicted of manslaughter, having initially been tried for murder. Some defences may be raised for any offence *other than* murder. Other defences such as insanity are general defences available for all offences.

It is also common to categorise defences according to the rationale behind them. Some defences excuse the accused's conduct whereas others justify it. An excusatory defence effectively forgives the accused for his conduct on the basis that to punish him would amount to an injustice. A justificatory defence, on the other hand, is premised on an acceptance that conduct of the accused was justified in the circumstances of the offence. An example of the former is insanity while provocation is the clearest example of the latter.

This section of the book deals with the defences available in Irish law to an individual facing trial for a criminal offence.

Defences Specific to Murder

20

There are three defences in Irish law which operate as partial defences applicable only to murder. These are provocation, excessive self-defence, and diminished responsibility. This chapter deals with the first two. Diminished responsibility is included in the chapter on insanity. The Criminal Law (Defence and the Dwelling) Act 2011, which clarified the law on the use of force following the decision of the Court of Criminal Appeal in *DPP v Barnes* [2007] 3 I.R. 130, provides a full, statutory defence where force, including lethal force, is used in defence of one's home. That defence is dealt with in the chapter on use of force.

The defences of provocation and excessive self-defence are partial in nature insofar as they will never result in an acquittal, but will reduce the offence from murder to manslaughter. From the point of view of an accused, this is important in a number of respects. First, under Irish law, a conviction for murder will inevitably and invariably result in the imposition of a life sentence. This is a sentence permitting of no judicial discretion regardless of any mitigating factors that might exist. Secondly, the offence of murder is regarded as the most serious offence in Irish criminal law. Where the offence was committed in circumstances which are covered by one or other of these defences, the moral culpability of the accused is reduced and his actions are viewed as being justifiable or excusable.

In the case of offences other than murder, provocation and excessive self-defence are relevant mitigating factors which may result in a lesser sentence, but they are not defences per se to any charge other than murder. In order to be able to raise the plea of provocation, the trial judge must be satisfied that there is evidence of provocative conduct on the part of the deceased which might have caused the accused to lose control. If no such evidence is adduced, or if the trial judge rules that it is insufficient, the defence cannot be raised before the jury.

Provocation at Common Law

The common law has long regarded individuals who act in retaliation to the provocative conduct of others as being somewhat less culpable for their actions. No such allowance is made for those who act in a cold-blooded fashion. In *R. v Duffy* [1949] 1 All E.R. 932, provocation was defined as

> "some act, or series of acts, done by the dead man to the accused, which would cause in any reasonable person, and actually causes in the accused a sudden loss of self-control, rendering the accused so subject to passion as to make him or her for the moment not the master of his mind".

The common law encompasses, therefore, both objective and subjective elements, although the English courts have traditionally employed an objective test. The difficulties with a solely objective test can be clearly seen in *Bedder v DPP* [1954] 2 All E.R. 801, where the House of Lords rejected the argument that the particular traits of the accused should be taken into account when deciding what the reaction of the reasonable man would have been to the provocative act. In that case, the accused was assaulted and taunted by a prostitute because he was impotent. *Bedder* was highly criticised on the basis that to ignore the particular traits of the accused and to judge him by reference to the reasonable man who did not possess the same traits was absurd. The English judiciary took a different approach in the later case of *R. v Camplin* [1978] 2 All E.R. 168, and essentially held that regard should be had to those characteristics of the accused that were relevant to the case in ascertaining whether he had acted as the reasonable man would have. The accused in *Camplin* was a 15-year-old boy who had been seriously sexually assaulted by an older man who had then laughed at him. The accused retaliated by hitting the man over the head with a pan, killing him. It is not entirely clear whether *Camplin* was decided on the basis that the decision in *Bedder* was incorrectly decided, or because by the time *Camplin* had come about, s.3 of the Homicide Act 1957 (the "1957 Act") had introduced a subjective element to the test into English law.

Which characteristics are relevant?

In *Bedder*, the court rejected that the accused's impotence was a relevant issue. Clearly this would not be the position post-*Camplin*, and under s.3 of the 1957 Act, in England. In *R. v Newell* (1980) 71 Cr. App. Rep. 331, it was held by the Court of Appeal that for a characteristic to be relevant, it had to be something significant that set the accused apart from the general population, and that the characteristic in question had to be in some way connected to the provocation.

PROVOCATION IN IRISH LAW

The leading case on the issue of provocation in Irish law is *People (DPP) v MacEoin* [1978] I.R. 27. Before considering the *MacEoin* decision and its impact on provocation in Irish law, three observations can be made:

(1) Given that the issue of provocation was governed by the common law, a question arises as to the constitutionality of the test laid down in *MacEoin*. The constitutionality of the common law rule regarding provocation had not been challenged and, despite the number of decisions following *MacEoin* which all appear to have accepted the test formulated therein, it remains arguable that *MacEoin* is of dubious constitutionality. Notwithstanding the matter of the court's entitlement to reject the common law test, the same court in *DPP v Noonan* [1998] 2 I.R. 439 endorsed the subjective test.

(2) The decision in *MacEoin* and, in particular, the test laid down by the Supreme Court in that case has been the primary basis for most, if not all, of the appeals taken against convictions arising from directions given by trial judges on the application of the *MacEoin* test. This is (or should be) a clear indication that the *MacEoin* decision itself and the test laid down in it is confusing at best, if not unconstitutional. The Irish courts have, on numerous occasions, highlighted difficulties with the *MacEoin* test, with the Court of Criminal Appeal stating in *DPP v Curran* [2011] 3 I.R. 785 that:

> "There is a clear and pressing need for a comprehensive review of this area, and its interaction with other areas of the law of homicide, and at a minimum, a statutory regulation of the scope of the defence of provocation."

(3) Given that provocation is a partial defence to a charge of murder only, with the consequence that the accused will be convicted of the lesser offence of manslaughter, thus leaving the issue of sentencing to the judge's discretion, the argument might be made that if the distinction between murder and manslaughter were to be removed, the confusion over the application of the *MacEoin* test would be resolved. The full range of sentencing options would then be available to the judge, who could still impose a life sentence in the appropriate case.

People (DPP) v MacEoin [1978] I.R. 27

The accused was charged with the murder of his flatmate with whom he had been in a long-term friendship. Prior to the killing, both men had consumed a significant amount of alcohol. The deceased, in particular, had a tendency to become aggressive while drunk. On the night of the killing, the accused returned home drunk and went to bed. He was subsequently attacked by the deceased, himself drunk. A struggle ensued, resulting in the accused losing control and hitting the deceased repeatedly with the hammer with which the deceased had initially attacked him. He was convicted of murder and appealed on the basis that he had been provoked by the deceased. The Court of Criminal Appeal rejected the common law objective test, and stated that it was no longer part of Irish law. The test, according to the Court of Criminal Appeal, was an entirely subjective one which required the jury to decide whether or not the accused had been provoked to the point where he had lost self-control. Accordingly, the test for provocation was set down by the Court of Criminal Appeal in the following terms:

> "[T]he trial judge at the close of the evidence should rule on whether there is any evidence of provocation which having regard to the accused's temperament, character and circumstances, might have caused him to lose control of himself at time of the wrongful act and whether the provocation bears a reasonable relation to the amount of force used by the accused."

The requirement that the provocation bears a "reasonable relation" to the force used by the accused has led to further confusion, in that it appears to introduce an objective element into what was effectively a rejection of the "reasonable man" test in the context of provocation. Subsequent cases have seen the courts attempt to explain the matter with limited success. In *DPP v Mullane*, unreported, Court of Criminal Appeal, 11 March 1997, the court decided that the inclusion of the "reasonable relation" element was not for the purpose of introducing an objective element to the *MacEoin* test but rather that, "[t]he impugned sentence in MacEoin really comes down to credibility of testimony rather than to any suggestion that the accused's conduct is to be once more judged by an objective standard".

This interpretation was later endorsed by the Court of Criminal Appeal in *Noonan.* In *DPP v Davis* [2001] 1 I.R. 146, the Court of Criminal Appeal commented on the difficulties presented by the *MacEoin* definition of the defence of provocation and suggested that a restatement of the defence may be required. More recently, in *DPP v Curran* [2011] 3 I.R. 785, the Court of Criminal Appeal, whilst stating that the test in *MacEoin* is wholly subjective, called for "a comprehensive review of this area, and its interaction with other areas of the law of homicide, and at a minimum, a statutory regulation of the scope of the defence".

What is provocation post *MacEoin*?

Provocation is essentially the same as it had been under the common law. Indeed, the court reiterated the definition cited above with the objective part of that definition omitted.

Must the provocation be immediate?

The essence of the defence is a sudden and temporary loss of control on the part of the deceased. However, it appears that "sudden" need not necessarily be "immediate", but, the greater the lapse of time between the provocative conduct and the retaliation, the more difficult it will be to sustain the defence, and may indicate revenge rather than a sudden loss of control, in which case, the defence will fail.

Cumulative provocation

The issue of cumulative provocation has arisen primarily in the context of killings that occur in the context of spousal abuse. The English judiciary had initially been reluctant to accept that cumulative provocation could satisfy the requirement that the accused had to suddenly lose control due to the provocative conduct of the deceased. In *R. v Ahluwalia* [1993] 4 All E.R. 88 and *R. v Thornton (No.2)* [1996] 2 All E.R. 1023, the accused in each case had been victims of spousal abuse who had killed their husbands. In neither case did the accused react immediately to the provocative conduct. On appeal, the conviction in *Ahluwalia* was overturned, albeit on grounds other than the issue of cumulative provocation, and a fresh appeal was allowed in the case of *Thornton*. In *Thornton*, the court held that "battered woman's syndrome" was a relevant factor to be considered when deciding whether the accused had been provoked. The Irish courts appear to have accepted the concept of cumulative provocation and will look at the most recent episode of provocation in the overall context of a longer period of abuse. Following *MacEoin,* it would appear that where the accused is the victim of long-term abuse, this will be a relevant consideration given the subjective nature of the test.

What amounts to provocative conduct?

The common law referred to an act or series of acts and consequently, it would appear that any act, lawful or otherwise, could amount to provocation. In *R. v Doughty* [1986] Crim. L.R. 625, the Court of Appeal held that a baby's crying should have been considered by the jury where the accused had been charged with the baby's murder. The defence had argued that the accused had put a pillow over the child's head in a bid to stop the child from crying. In *MacEoin*, the court referred to "wrongful acts" which could be taken to mean that the provocative conduct had to be some unlawful act. However, if the test is that of the effect of the act on the accused, there would not appear to be any logical reason to limit these acts to those that are unlawful. In *DPP v Kehoe* [1992] I.L.R.M. 481, the accused killed his former girlfriend's new partner for no apparent reason other than his presence at the house of the accused's former girlfriend. In *MacEoin*, the court also stated that words can be capable of constituting provocation.

Who must provoke?

At common law, the provocation must have emanated from the deceased and not from a third party. It is also the case that where the accused brings about a situation and then claims to have been provoked by the deceased, he cannot rely on the defence, since the provocation was self-induced.

Proportionality

It was stated in *MacEoin* that "if the prosecution can prove beyond reasonable doubt that the force used was unreasonable and excessive, having regard to the provocation, the defence of provocation fails". This would appear to be a rather bizarre requirement when one considers that the essence of the defence is that of the complete loss of self-control in the heat of the moment on the part of the accused.

In *Mullane*, the Court of Criminal Appeal held that the jury might have been led to believe, from the directions given by the trial judge, that the amount of force used should be evaluated objectively, and that this was wrong on the basis that the *MacEoin* test is a subjective one. A similar situation arose in *DPP v Noonan* [1998] 1 I.L.R.M. 154, where again, the jury appeared to have been directed to employ an objective test in relation to the question of proportionality. The court allowed the appeal on this basis. The subjective nature of the test in relation to the proportionality of the force used was also stated in *DPP v Bambrick* [1996] 1 I.R. 265, *DPP v Kelly* [2000] 2 I.R. 1 and *DPP v Heaney*, unreported, Court of Criminal Appeal, 17 January 2000.

Excessive Self-Defence

Like the defence of provocation, excessive self-defence is a partial defence to murder only and, if successfully pleaded, will reduce murder to manslaughter.

It may be a mitigating factor in respect of other offences, resulting in a lesser sentence, but is not a defence per se.

Excessive self-defence occurs where the accused uses more force than is objectively necessary, but which the accused believed was necessary. Where the accused used no more force than he honestly believed was necessary, he is entitled to be acquitted of murder. The onus is on the prosecution to prove that the accused knew he was using a disproportionate amount of force. In *People (Attorney General) v Commane* [1975] 1 Frewen 400, the Court of Criminal Appeal upheld the conviction for murder of an accused who used force knowing it to be excessive in the circumstances. The accused had been attacked by the deceased and had struck the deceased in self-defence. Having knocked the deceased unconscious, the accused then strangled him.

In *People (Attorney General) v Dwyer* [1972] I.R. 416, the accused stabbed the deceased in the course of a brawl. He claimed that he did so because he believed that the deceased had a knife and was, consequently, afraid for his life. The Supreme Court held that the accused's subjective belief was sufficient to reduce the offence from murder to manslaughter.

There are parallels to be drawn between this defence and the statutory defence set out in the Criminal Law (Defence and the Dwelling) Act 2011 (the "2011 Act"). The difference in the effect of both defences could not be starker, however. Excessive self-defence will not justify an acquittal, whereas the 2011 Act provides a full defence where lethal force is used to protect life and/or property, in accordance with the provisions of the 2011 Act.

The position in English law is different, and in that jurisdiction, excessive self-defence will not reduce murder to manslaughter, but may go towards mitigation of sentence. The House of Lords held in *R. v Clegg* [1995] 1 All E.R. 334 that a British soldier who had shot and killed a passenger in a car which had driven through a checkpoint in Belfast could not argue excessive self-defence when he was charged with the murder. His defence had been that he had fired four bullets at the passing car in order to defend a colleague who was standing nearby, and that excessive self-defence should be accepted on that basis. Forensic evidence revealed that the fatal bullet had been fired after the car had passed the soldiers, and the accused was convicted.

KEY CASES

(1) Provocation—Partial Defence

R. v Duffy [1949] 1 All E.R. 932—Definition of "provocation".

People (DPP) v MacEoin [1978] I.R. 27—Leading case in Ireland.

R. v Ahluwalia [1993] 4 All E.R. 88 and *R. v Thornton (No.2)* [1996] 2 All E.R. 1023—"Cumulative provocation".

KEY CASES

(2) Excessive Self-Defence—Partial Defence

People (Attorney General) v Dwyer [1972] I.R. 416—Subjective belief of accused.

Use of Force in Self-Defence

21

The common law has always recognised the right to use a reasonable amount of force in order to defend oneself or a close relative from attack and for the purposes of preventing the commission of a criminal offence. In *People (Attorney General) v Keatley* [1954] I.R. 12, the Court of Criminal Appeal stated that there was no need, in this jurisdiction, to show that the accused had any special relationship with the person whom he sought to protect from attack. In general, the justifiable use of force is provided for by ss.18 and 19 of the Non-Fatal Offences against the Person Act 1997 (the "1997 Act"), as amended by the Criminal Law (Defence and the Dwelling) Act 2011. A question arises as to whether the common law rules in relation to self-defence have been totally abolished or merely abolished within the meaning of ss.18 and 19. Section 22(1) provides as follows:

> "The provisions of this Act have effect subject to any enactment or rule of law providing a defence, or providing lawful authority, justification or excuse for an act or omission."

Section 22(2) provides as follows:

> "Notwithstanding subsection (1) any defence available under the common law in respect of the use of force within the meaning of section 18 or 19, or an act immediately preparatory to the use of force, *for the purposes mentioned in section 18(1) or 19(1) is hereby abolished*" (emphasis added).

The limitations on the use of self-defence were set out in *DPP v O'Connor* [2014] IECCA 39 by the Court of Criminal Appeal, where O'Donnell J. stated:

> "First, there must be an unlawful attack – or assault. The defence is not available to persons who simply engage in a fight. Second, the use of force must be to repel the assault and for the purposes of defence. The defence is not available to immunise someone who takes the opportunity of a minor assault to launch an attack with perhaps lethal

consequences. Third, the reasonableness of the force used is relevant in two respects. A jury must consider whether it has been established that the force was objectively unreasonable and if so whether it has been established that the accused knew it to be so."

Justifiable Use of Force

Section 18 of the 1997 Act provides that where the accused uses force for any of the reasons listed in the section, he will not be guilty of an offence provided that the amount of force used is reasonable in the circumstances as the accused believes them to be. The test, thus, is clearly stated in subjective terms but this is nonetheless confirmed in s.18(5), which provides that the matter of whether the accused was operating under one of the above grounds will be determined according to the accused's subjective view of the situation. Section 18 also provides that "crimes" and "criminal acts" include those which would be deemed criminal even where an accused could be acquitted on grounds of involuntariness, duress, intoxication or insanity. The use of reasonable force by a person is permissible in any of the following circumstances:

"(a) to protect himself or herself or a member of the family of that person or another from injury, assault or detention caused by a criminal act; or
(b) to protect himself or herself or (with the authority of that other) another from trespass to the person; or
(c) to protect his or her property from appropriation, destruction or damage caused by a criminal act or from the trespass or infringement; or
(d) to protect property belonging to another from appropriation, destruction or damage caused by a criminal act or (with the authority of that other) from trespass or infringement; or
(e) to prevent crime or a breach of the peace."

Section 18 clearly permits the use of force to protect a third party from injury, assault or detention caused by a criminal act. In doing this, the 1997 Act gives statutory expression to the common law position. In *Keatley*, the accused had been convicted of the manslaughter of a man who had attacked the accused's brother. The conviction was appealed on the grounds that the trial judge's direction to the jury had been incorrect. The Court of Criminal Appeal held that the jury should have been told that the use of force to prevent a crime was permissible provided that the amount of force used was not excessive.

The use of force to protect a third party is not permitted in some other jurisdictions unless it can be shown that there is a close relationship between the accused and the person whom he sought to protect. This can be seen in *Devlin v Armstrong* [1971] N.I. 13, where charges of incitement to riot and of breaches of public order were brought against Bernadette Devlin. Her defence argued that she had been acting in legitimate defence of herself and other residents of Derry's Bogside. The court refused to accept the defence on the grounds that there was no special relationship between the accused and those whom she had purported to defend.

At common law, an accused who uses force in response to a mistaken belief as to the existence of a threat is entitled to be judged according to his subjective (albeit mistaken) view of the circumstances.

Section 18(7) of the 1997 Act provides that, generally, an accused will not be able to rely on the defence where he has caused or brought about a state of affairs with the intention of using force to resist its consequences. An exception to the general rule exists where the accused is engaged in lawful conduct even where he knows that it may provoke an unlawful response from others.

Section 19(1) of the 1997 Act allows for the use of reasonable force to carry out a lawful arrest and provides that "the use of force by a person in effecting or assisting in a lawful arrest, if only such as is reasonable in the circumstances as he or she believes them to be, does not constitute an offence". Section 19(3) provides that the lawfulness or otherwise of the arrest will be judged according to the subjective view of the accused. This allows for the accused to be judged according to a mistaken belief.

Force

Section 20 of the 1997 Act defines "force", and provides as follows:

> "(a) [A] person uses force in relation to another person or property not only when he or she applies force to, but also where he or she causes an impact on, the body of that person or that property;
> (b) a person shall be treated as using force in relation to another person if—
>   (i) he or she threatens that person with its use, or
>   (ii) he or she detains that person without actually using it; and
> (c) a person shall be treated as using force in relation to property if he or she threatens a person with its use in relation to property."

Section 20(3) further provides that a threat of force may be reasonable although the actual use of force may not be. Where the accused had an opportunity to retreat before resorting to the use of force, s.20(4) of the 1997 Act provides that this is a factor to be taken into account in deciding whether the use of force by the accused was reasonable. In *R. v McInnes* [1971] 3 All E.R. 295, the Court of Appeal held that while there was no absolute duty to retreat at common law, failure to do so could be taken into account in determining the reasonableness of the use of force by the accused. This ruling was approved of in this jurisdiction in *People (Attorney General) v Dwyer* [1972] I.R. 416. The defences under ss.18 and 19 also apply to acts that are immediately preparatory to the use of force.

Defence of Property

Article 40.5 of Bunreacht na hÉireann forbids the forcible entry of a dwelling, save in accordance with law. Given the constitutional protection of the dwelling, the question arises as to what lawful level of force may be employed to repel an unlawful entry. Clearly, the status of the dwelling in constitutional terms and in terms of its importance to the well-being of the citizen will justify the use of greater force than could be used in repelling a threat to personal property. A further consideration arises in the context of the dwelling and that is whether a person whose dwelling is being unlawfully entered is, or even should be, obliged to retreat.

As previously noted, s.20 of the 1997 Act provides that failure to retreat is a factor that must be taken into account in determining whether the force used to repel a threat was reasonable, but this must be interpreted as applying solely in the context of the offences covered by that Act. The defence of the dwelling centres around the principle referred to as the "Castle Doctrine", a full analysis of which greatly exceeds the scope of this book. Put simply, the doctrine distinguishes between situations where an individual is attacked outside of his home and those in which the attack occurs in the person's home. The duty to retreat applies to the former but not to the latter on the basis that a person's home is their sanctuary. At the same time, Art.40.3.1° imposes an obligation on the State to defend, as far as practicable, the personal rights of the citizen. This has been a dilemma for the courts in circumstances where lethal force is used in response to an attack arising from unlawful entry into a dwelling.

The Court of Criminal Appeal quashed a conviction for manslaughter and ordered a re-trial in the case of *DPP v Nally* [2007] 4 I.R. 145. The original conviction for manslaughter arose from the killing by the accused of an intruder on his property. The trial judge had directed the jury that they could consider self-defence as a partial defence only and that he would accept only a verdict of murder or manslaughter in light of the excessive nature of the force used by the accused. The Court of Criminal Appeal quashed the conviction and ordered a re-trial on the basis that the trial judge had effectively encroached upon the role of the jury.

In *DPP v Barnes* [2007] 3 I.R. 130, the Court of Criminal Appeal had cause to respond to the precise issue of the competing rights of householder and burglar. At issue in *Barnes* was whether a burglar, having entered the dwelling of the deceased, could successfully invoke self-defence. The accused gave evidence that the deceased had attacked him and that he acted in self-defence. While stressing that it was not lawful in this jurisdiction to kill a burglar simply because he is a burglar, the court in *Barnes* held as follows:

(i) Every burglary in a dwelling is an act of aggression and, as an aggressor, a burglar may expect to encounter retaliatory force.
(ii) In assessing whether the degree of force used in response to the burglary was lawful, the courts will apply a test comprising subjective and objective elements.
(iii) The aggressor must take his victim as he finds him and the amount of force used by the victim in response to the attack will have to be of a grossly disproportionate nature or be accompanied by actual malice before liability will attach to the victim.
(iv) Regardless of the force with which the burglar is met, he can never be seen as *entirely* without blame in the killing of the householder or other lawful occupant of the dwelling.
(v) Self-defence must be available as a defence to the burglar, but because of his "initial, grave aggression", the killing of a householder in the course of a burglary can never amount to anything less than manslaughter.

The ruling in *Barnes* gave rise to at least two important implications in the context of self-defence. First, it raised the status of the defence as it applies to the use of force to repel an attack within the dwelling by linking it to the respective constitutional rights of the householder and the intruder, and in so doing, incorporated the "Castle Doctrine" into Irish law. Secondly, it could, arguably, have created a species of self-defence arising from what might be termed "self-generated necessity", whereby a burglar faced with disproportionate force in response to his "initial, grave aggression" may use force in defending himself. This latter point was addressed in *Barnes*, prompting the following comment:

> "Considering the heinous and inherently aggressive nature of the crime of burglary in a dwellinghouse, there is an air of improbability about the burglar, the initial aggressor, relying on the defence of self-defence when he has violently killed the householder."

This issue was discussed by the Court of Criminal Appeal in *DPP v Farrell* [2014] IECCA 42 where the court accepted that there might be circumstances in which a burglar could use force, although this issue did not arise on the facts of the case.

The Criminal Law (Defence and the Dwelling) Act 2011 (the "2011 Act") clarifies the matter and effectively gives statutory expression to the ruling in *Barnes.* Section 2(1) of the 2011 Act deals with justifiable use of force and sets out the applicable statutory test:

> "It shall not be an offence for a person who is in his or her dwelling, or for a person who is a lawful occupant in a dwelling, to use force against another person or the property of another person where—
> (a) he or she believes that the other person has entered or is entering the dwelling as a trespasser for the purpose of committing a criminal act, and
> (b) the force used is only such as is reasonable in the circumstances as he or she believes them to be—
> (i) to protect himself or herself or another person present in the dwelling from injury, assault, detention or death, caused by a criminal act,
> (ii) to protect his or her property or the property of another person from appropriation, destruction or damage caused by a criminal act, or
> (iii) to prevent the commission of a crime or to effect, or assist in effecting, a lawful arrest."

The test laid down in the 2011 Act contains objective and subjective elements. The force used may only be as much as is reasonable in the circumstances as the occupier believes them to be and, additionally, may only be used to protect against injury or death, to protect property, or in the context of crime prevention or lawful arrest. The occupier of the dwelling must also believe that the intruder is a trespasser on the property for the purpose of committing a criminal act. It is irrelevant that the belief is justified, so long as it is a belief that is honestly held by the occupier. In deciding the issue of reasonableness, the jury must give consideration to the question of whether there were any reasonable grounds for holding the belief. In accordance with *Barnes*, s.3 of the 2011 Act clarifies that there is no obligation on the occupier of the dwelling to retreat.

The occupier who uses force in accordance with the 2011 Act will have a full defence, even where the force used is lethal. There is no explicit requirement under the 2011 Act that the force used must be proportionate, and this creates an anomalous situation when the defence is compared with the defences of provocation and excessive self-defence, both of which provide partial defences to murder. It seems counterintuitive that an accused is expected to retain sufficient self-control in these cases, even where his life is under threat outside the dwelling, but is entitled to use lethal force within the dwelling without committing any offence, provided the test set out in s.2 of the 2011 Act is satisfied. An even starker example may be seen where an accused who, having satisfied the statutory test, uses lethal force in response to a threat to property will have a full defence available, whereas a person pleading provocation or excessive self-defence arising out of an assault on them will be convicted of manslaughter.

KEY CASES AND LEGISLATION

DPP v Nally [2007] 4 I.R. 145 and *DPP v Barnes* [2007] 3 I.R. 130—Justifiable use of force, including lethal force. No requirement to retreat if attack takes place in dwelling. Ruling in *Barnes* given statutory expression in Criminal Law (Defence and the Dwelling) Act 2011.

22 Intoxication

There is no general defence of intoxication at common law. Indeed, it is arguable that it is not a defence at all on the basis that it might more accurately be described as evidence of the lack of ability on the part of the accused to form mens rea, and it is invariably the case that where intoxication is raised by the defence, it is done for the purpose of establishing that due to intoxication, the accused lacked capacity to form mens rea. At the outset, it should be stressed that intoxication is *not* the same as drunkenness. Whereas the former may well have a bearing on liability, if it can be shown to have deprived the accused of the capacity to form the required intent for the offence with which he is charged, the latter will, almost invariably, be regarded as an aggravating factor with the consequent implications as regards sentencing.

The rationale behind the defence is based on a mixture of principle and policy. It is not desirable that a person could be convicted of an offence where he could not have formed the intention to commit it. Equally, it is accepted that the public should be afforded some form of protection against the actions of those who become so intoxicated as to pose a threat through criminal activity. The defence of intoxication may, therefore, be viewed as a form of balancing act between these two considerations. Certain limitations are imposed on the application of the defence.

Distinction between Crimes of Basic/Specific Intent

An offence of basic intent is one which requires no more than the performance of a particular act, for example, rape or assault. The mens rea of any offence of basic intent is recklessness. An offence of specific intent is one which requires an intention to bring about a particular outcome. The clearest example of a crime of specific intent, sometimes known as a result offence, is murder.

In *DPP v Beard* [1920] All E.R. 21, the House of Lords held that while drunkenness is never a defence, intoxication could be where the accused was rendered incapable of forming the specific intent to commit the offence in question. In this case, the accused had been charged with murder, which is an offence of specific intent. The issue was further considered in *DPP v Majewski* [1976] 2 All E.R. 142, which case has come to be regarded as the leading authority on intoxication. In *Majewski*, the accused had been charged with numerous counts of assault occasioning bodily harm. Prior to the incident, the accused had consumed a considerable quantity of alcohol and drugs and then sought to rely on the fact that he could not have formed mens rea due to intoxication. The House of Lords reiterated the position that at common law there was no defence of intoxication, but that there were some exceptions to this general rule. The main point made by the House of Lords in *Majewski* was that where an offence was one of specific intent, intoxication could be a defence if it had the effect of depriving the accused of the capacity to form mens rea. Offences of basic intent were held not to be covered by the defence on the basis that they could be committed recklessly, and since becoming intoxicated was, in itself, reckless, the defence could not apply.

The *Majewski* decision was criticised as being illogical on the basis that the distinction drawn between offences of specific and basic intent was artificial. The Lords themselves acknowledged that drawing a distinction between the two types of offence was illogical, but that public policy considerations tipped the balance in favour of doing so. *Majewski* was not followed in all common law jurisdictions, having been rejected by the High Court of Australia in *R. v O'Connor* (1980) 146 C.L.R. 64 and eventually by the Canadian Supreme Court in *R. v Daviault* [1994] 3 S.C.R. 63.

VOLUNTARY/INVOLUNTARY INTOXICATION

Voluntary intoxication occurs where the accused consumes or ingests some form of intoxicant of his own volition, as occurred in *Majewski*. An intoxicant may be alcohol or may be some other form of drug. In *R. v Lipman* [1970] 1 Q.B. 152, the accused had taken LSD and killed his girlfriend due to the belief that he was being attacked by snakes. This belief was caused by the hallucinogenic effects of the drug. He was convicted of manslaughter and appealed on the basis that he had no idea what he was doing and had not intended to kill the victim. The Court of Appeal upheld the conviction on the basis that manslaughter can be committed through the commission of an unlawful and dangerous act and that, because it was not necessary to have specific intent, self-induced (voluntary) intoxication was not a defence.

In *R. v Hardie* [1984] 3 All E.R. 848, the accused took a number of Valium tablets because he was upset about breaking up with his girlfriend. Rather than becoming calm, the accused became aggressive and ended up starting a fire in his former girlfriend's apartment. Having taken the tablets voluntarily, the question arose as to whether he could rely on the defence of intoxication. In this case, the court held that the accused could not have known that the tablets could cause aggression and, therefore, could not have been voluntarily intoxicated. The accused was deemed to have been involuntarily intoxicated, but the court stated that had he known that the drug could have induced aggressive behaviour, the defence would not have been available.

Involuntary intoxication arises where the accused takes an intoxicating substance unwittingly. In these cases, the accused will have the defence of intoxication available even for crimes of basic intent. In *R. v Allen* [1988] Crim. L.R. 698, it was held that the defence is not available if the accused knows that the substance is an intoxicant, but is unaware of its potency. The defence is not available in cases where intent is not actually negatived. Most, if not all, intoxicating substances lower inhibitions. Consequently, where the accused has formed the intent to commit an offence, albeit because his inhibitions were reduced due to the consumption of an intoxicant, the defence will not be available on the basis that, according to the court in *R. v Kingston* [1994] 3 All E.R. 353, "a drugged intent is still an intent".

Dutch Courage

Intoxication will not be a defence where the accused has taken alcohol or drugs in order to give him the courage to carry out an offence. In *Attorney General for Northern Ireland v Gallagher* [1961] 3 All E.R. 299, the accused, having formed the intention to kill his wife, consumed a considerable amount of alcohol in order to give him the courage to do so. He then argued that he had been intoxicated to such an extent that he lacked capacity to form the required intention, and that even though he had formed such an intent earlier, the mens rea and the actus reus did not coincide at the time of the killing. His conviction for murder was upheld by the House of Lords where it was held that intoxication was not available as a defence in a case of Dutch courage and that the killing could be viewed as a continuing act, the mens rea still being operative at the time of the killing.

Intoxication in Irish Law

The question of whether the *Majewski* decision had any application in this jurisdiction had been the subject of some confusion. The issue of intoxication has not been raised very frequently before the Irish courts. In *People (Attorney General) v Manning* (1953) 89 I.L.T.R. 155, the court stated that the effect of drink had to go much further than to lower the accused's inhibitions. It also appears that the court in *Manning* drew a distinction between crimes of specific and basic intent, and stated that in terms of a defence to murder, intoxication would only have the effect of reducing the charge to one of manslaughter. Similarly, in *DPP v McBride* [1997] I.L.R.M. 233, the Court of Criminal Appeal seemed to accept the principle that intoxication could be relevant in terms of the accused's ability to form mens rea.

The question of whether *Majewski* is applicable in this jurisdiction was eventually answered in the affirmative by the Court of Criminal Appeal in *DPP v Reilly* [2005] 3 I.R. 111.

In this case, the accused was charged with murder and argued that he was intoxicated to the extent that he could not have formed the mens rea for the offence. No dispute arose over the fact that the accused remembered nothing of the incident, in which an infant was found dead beside the accused. The child had died from multiple stab wounds inflicted by a knife owned by, and in the possession of, the accused. On the night in question, the accused had been drinking heavily in his cousin's house, and had fallen asleep in the early hours of the morning in the sitting room. A cot of sorts had been made up for the baby using two armchairs. The child's mother got up the next morning and went to check on the child, only to discover that he was dead. The accused was asleep in the couch with the knife nearby. He was convicted of manslaughter and appealed.

The Court of Criminal Appeal not only acknowledged the inherent illogicality of the distinction drawn between crimes of basic and specific intent in *Majewski*, but went further and stated that issues arising in the case could not be determined by pure logic. The court looked to the decision of the High Court in Australia in *R. v O'Connor*, and to the decisions of the Canadian Supreme Court, which had initially accepted the *Majewski* ruling in *Leary v The Queen* (1977) 74 Dir. (3d) 103 and in *R. v Bernard* [1988] 2 S.C.R. 833, but later overruled these in *R. v Daviault*. The Court of Criminal Appeal refused to follow the rulings in *O'Connor* and *Daviault* and held instead that the ruling of the trial judge, which had been based on *Majewski*, was correct. The position of intoxication in Irish law, therefore, is that which was laid down by the Court of Criminal Appeal in *Reilly*, which is the same as the position in England and Wales under *Majewski*.

KEY CASES

DPP v Majewski [1976] 2 All E.R. 142—Intoxication a defence to an offence of specific intent only. *DPP v Reilly* [2005] 3 I.R. 111—Ruling in *Majewski* followed by Court of Criminal Appeal.

Attorney General for Northern Ireland v Gallagher [1961] 3 All E.R. 299—Where accused ingests an intoxicant to provide him with Dutch courage, the defence will fail.

23 Automatism

The defence of automatism overlaps in certain respects with the defences of insanity and intoxication. Insanity, as will be seen in the following chapter, if successfully invoked, will lead to the detention of the individual under the Criminal Law (Insanity) Act 2006, whereas the defence of automatism will, if successfully pleaded, result in an acquittal. The defence bears the evidential burden of laying the foundations of the defence, and where this is done, the burden of proof rests with the prosecution, who must disprove it.

Definition

The leading case on automatism is *Bratty v Attorney General for Northern Ireland* [1961] 3 All E.R. 523, where automatism was defined as "an act done by the muscles without any control by the mind such as a spasm, a reflex action or a convulsion, or an act done whilst suffering from a concussion or whilst sleep-walking". In its most basic form, the defence of automatism arises where the accused had no control over his body. It is the involuntary nature of the actions that gives rise to the defence, and the defence will fail where there is anything less than a total loss of control. This was held in *Attorney General's Reference (No.2 of 1992)* [1993] 3 W.L.R. 982, which followed the decision in *Broome v Perkins* [1987] Crim. L.R. 271.

In this jurisdiction, in *O'Brien v Parker* [1997] 2 I.L.R.M. 170, the High Court held that the defence of automatism can only succeed where the defendant suffers from a total loss of control. Where partial control is retained or is impaired, the defence will fail. *O'Brien* involved civil proceedings in which the defendant was being sued for negligence in the context of a road traffic accident. He argued that he had suffered an attack of epilepsy immediately prior to the attack, but had testified to the effect that he had retained some element of control, albeit impaired, reduced or partial. Having accepted that automatism could be pleaded in civil proceedings, the High Court applied the principles set down in *Bratty* and *Broome v Perkins* and held that the defence required a total destruction of voluntary control on the part of the defendant.

INTERNAL AND EXTERNAL FACTORS

Where the automatic state is brought about by an internal factor, whether a physical or mental condition, it is viewed as being a disease of the mind and is consequently regarded as a form of insanity. This type of automatism is, therefore, insane automatism. In this situation, the *M'Naghten* rules apply, and if successful, this will lead to a verdict of "not guilty by reason of insanity", in accordance with the Criminal Law (Insanity) Act 2006, as amended by the Criminal Law (Insanity) Act 2010.

External factors are those that occur outside the body of the accused but which cause him to respond reflexively. In this type of situation, the defence of automatism, if accepted by the jury, will result in an acquittal on the basis that the accused had no control over his actions. Where an external factor causes an internal factor, it is open to the jury to find that the automatism was caused by the external factor. In this situation, much depends on the facts of any given case.

In *R. v T.* [1990] Crim. L.R. 607, the accused had been suffering from post-traumatic stress disorder brought about by being the victim of rape. She was charged with robbery and the court held that the issue of non-insane automatism should have been left to the jury on the basis that the post-traumatic stress disorder (internal factor) had in fact been caused by the rape (external factor).

Further confusion arises where the accused is suffering from some medical condition and commits an offence whilst in a state of automatism arising from that condition. In particular, cases involving diabetics have given rise to questions about whether the automatism is due to an internal or external factor and whether the automatism could be said to be self-induced.

SELF-INDUCED AUTOMATISM

Automatism is self-induced where an accused has brought the automatic state about due to the consumption of alcohol or other intoxicant. Where this occurs, the matter is essentially one of intoxication, as was held in *R. v Lipman* [1969] 3 All E.R. 410. The decision of the Court of Criminal Appeal in *DPP v Reilly* [2005] 3 I.R. 111 is relevant to this issue on two grounds. First, the decision in *Reilly* is an acceptance by the Irish judiciary of the ruling in *DPP v Majewski* [1976] 2 All E.R. 142, and secondly, the defence of automatism was raised in *Reilly*. The accused had consumed a substantial quantity of alcohol and had fallen asleep. At some point during the night, a baby, sleeping on a nearby chair, was stabbed repeatedly and killed by the accused, who had no recollection of the incident. A key element of the defence's argument was that even though the accused had fallen into a deep sleep due to the consumption of alcohol, the cause of the automatism was the deep sleep, and not the intoxication. It was argued that this ought to have been put to the jury and that if the jury accepted this proposition, an acquittal should have followed. In clarifying the issue for the jury, the trial judge stated:

> "You have heard a lot of expert evidence in relation to things happening during sleep and if you do something that you have no control over, say the epileptic or the diabetic in a hypo or a hyper as the case may be, if they do something that they absolutely have no control over then they do not have criminal liability for that. You must do something by having a free choice, even a drunken free choice, to have criminal liability for it ... I left it open to you that if you find a free standing situation in which the accused had no control over his actions, then he would not be criminally liable and he would be entitled to a verdict of not guilty. But if that situation has come about because of his voluntary consumption of alcohol then you look instead to the law of intoxication."

The jury went on to convict the accused of manslaughter, and the key issue for the appeal court was whether the trial judge's direction to the jury was a correct statement of the law. The Court of Criminal Appeal held that the trial judge's direction had been correct and that where the accused, at the time of the killing, had no control over himself, and his lack of control had been caused by his voluntary consumption of alcohol, the matter, thus, was to be decided on the basis of *Majewski*.

The older cases concerning diabetics are relevant to this issue also. In *R. v Quick* [1973] 3 All E.R. 347, the accused, a diabetic, had taken insulin, had then not eaten properly and had consumed too much alcohol, causing him to suffer from hypoglycaemia, a medical condition caused by having lower than normal levels of blood glucose. Whilst in this condition, he assaulted the victim. His defence argued that he had been in a state of automatism. The trial judge stated that insanity was the more appropriate defence. On this basis, the accused entered a plea of guilty and subsequently appealed his conviction. It was held on appeal that his condition had been brought about due to taking insulin (an external factor) and not due to the diabetes (an internal factor). This being the case, the court held that the jury should have been given the opportunity to consider the defence of automatism. The court also held that automatism would not be a defence where the accused consumed drink or drugs or where he had done or omitted to do something, the result of which could reasonably be foreseen.

In *R. v Bailey* [1983] 2 All E.R. 503, facts similar to those in *Quick* were considered by the court, the main difference here being that the accused was charged with an offence of specific, rather than basic, intent. The defence argued that he lacked capacity, due to automatism, to form the necessary intent, and that the defence of automatism applied even where it was self-induced. In *Bailey*, the court held that the decision in *Quick* as regards the application of the defence with regard to offences of basic intent was correct, and that in such cases, self-induced automatism was no defence. The court drew a distinction between situations in which the consumption of alcohol or drugs brought about an automatic state and those in which the automatic state was brought about inadvertently; the defence being unavailable for the former and available for the latter. Crucial to this matter was the foresight of the accused. The court held that the effects of insulin coupled with the effects of not eating properly might not be known to the accused, and that knowledge of these could not be assured. Where the accused knew what might happen and had gone on to take a risk, he would have been reckless and could then be convicted of an offence of basic intent. Where this was not the case, and even where the accused did not eat properly after taking insulin, he would have a valid defence. The difference between the two cases appears to be that in *Bailey*, the offence was one of specific intent, to which self-induced automatism is a defence, whereas *Quick* involved an offence of basic intent, to which it is not.

KEY CASES

Bratty v Attorney General for Northern Ireland [1961] 3 All E.R. 523—Leading case in which "automatism" defined by court.

O'Brien v Parker [1997] 2 I.L.R.M. 170—For defence to succeed, the accused must have lost all control.

R. v Lipman [1969] 3 All E.R. 410—Where automatism is the result of the voluntary consumption of an intoxicant, accused must rely on intoxication.

R. v Quick [1973] 3 All E.R. 347 and *R. v Bailey* [1983] 2 All E.R. 503—"Insulin Cases".

24 Insanity

Until the enactment of the Criminal Law (Insanity) Act 2006 (the "2006 Act"), the law governing insanity was a combination of 19th century statutes and common law rules, notably those set out in *R. v M'Naghten* [1843] All E.R. 229. These rules were radically altered by the 2006 Act, which repealed most of the old legislation, with the Criminal Lunatics Act 1800 and the Trial of Lunatics Act 1883 being repealed in their entirety. Prior to the enactment of the 2006 Act, the law on insanity was of relevance in two ways in the context of the criminal law. The first of these was with regard to the fitness of the accused person to stand trial, and the second related to the application of the insanity defence itself. As a defence, insanity is of general application in Irish law and was, until the enactment of the 2006 Act, an "all or nothing defence". The 2006 Act has been amended by the Criminal Law (Insanity) Act 2010 (the "2010 Act").

The Criminal Law (Insanity) Acts 2006 and 2010

Section 4—Fitness to be tried

There has always been a rebuttable presumption at common law that an adult is sane and, thus, responsible for their actions. An accused person cannot be tried if he is not fit to plead; to do so would be in flagrant breach of the rights of the accused to have a fair trial. Prior to the enactment of the 2006 Act, the term "fitness to plead" was used, but this term has now been replaced with "fitness to be tried". The question of an accused person's fitness to be tried may be raised by the defence or the prosecution. It may also be raised by the court of its own volition. It is also possible to raise the matter at the opening of the case by the defence. As amended by the 2010 Act, s.4 provides as follows:

> "An accused person shall be deemed unfit to be tried if he or she is unable by reason of mental disorder to understand the nature and course of the proceedings."

The term "mental disorder" is defined in s.1 as including "mental illness, mental disability, dementia or any disease of the mind but does not include intoxication". The accused will be deemed unfit to be tried if, by reason of mental disorder, he is unable to do any of the following:

(i) Plead to the charge;
(ii) Instruct counsel;
(iii) Elect for trial by jury where the offence with which he is charged is an "either-or" offence;
(iv) Make a proper defence;
(v) In the case of a jury trial, challenge a juror to whom he may wish to object;
(vi) Understand the evidence.

The criteria laid down in s.4 regarding the test of the accused's fitness to plead are based on those laid down by the courts and particularly those outlined by the Supreme Court in *State (Coughlan) v Minister for Justice* (1968) I.L.T.R. 177, where it was held that the question to be answered is whether the accused person has "sufficient intellect to comprehend the course of the proceedings of the trial, so as to make a proper defence, to challenge a juror to whom he may wish to object, and to understand the details of the evidence". Section 4 therefore mirrors the decision in *Coughlan* very closely.

The amended s.4 sets out the procedural requirements for determining the defendant's fitness to be tried. The determination of fitness to be tried is to be made by the court. Where a question of fitness to be tried arises, the court may request specialist psychiatric evidence from an approved medical officer for the purposes of deciding whether to adjourn the trial so that the accused can receive any care or treatment necessary for his welfare. The court may also make a determination as to whether the accused is fit to be tried or may order that the accused is sent to the Central Mental Hospital for no longer than 14 days and must undergo examination at that centre. The court will then receive a report from the approved medical officer stating whether the accused is suffering from a mental disorder and requires treatment.

The proceedings will then be adjourned until further order of the court. The issue of fitness to plead relates to the mental capacity of the accused at the time of the trial—not at the time of the commission of the alleged offence. Section 7 of the 2006 Act provides that an appeal may be made against the decision under s.4 of the 2006 Act. An appeal against a decision of the District Court lies to the Circuit Court and to the Court of Appeal in the case of the Circuit, Central Criminal, and Special Criminal Courts.

SECTION 5—VERDICT

Prior to the enactment of the 2006 Act, the verdict in the case of an accused person who successfully invoked the insanity defence was "guilty but insane". The verdict sounded contradictory due to the use of the word "guilty", although it was held in *DPP v Gallagher* [1991] I.L.R.M. 339 to be, in fact, an acquittal. Section 5 provides that where, at the time of the commission of the alleged offence, the accused was:

(i) suffering from a mental disorder; and
(ii) the mental disorder was such that the accused person should not be held responsible because he did not know the nature and quality of the act or did not know that what he was doing was wrong or was unable to refrain from committing the act,

the court shall return a special verdict to the effect that the accused is "not guilty by reason of insanity". Section 5 of the 2006 Act therefore incorporates aspects of the *M'Naghten* rules, which will be dealt with below, and also the concept of irresistible impulse. An appeal against the verdict may be made pursuant to s.8 of the 2006 Act which sets out three grounds on which such an appeal may be made:

- that it had not been proved that the accused had committed the offence;
- that it had not been proved that the accused had been suffering from a mental disorder at the time of the commission of the offence; or
- that the court should have found the accused unfit to plead.

An appeal against the decision of the District Court lies to the Circuit Court and to the Court of Appeal in the case of the Circuit, Central Criminal, and Special Criminal Courts.

SECTION 6(1)—DIMINISHED RESPONSIBILITY

Where the charge against the accused is one of murder and the court finds that at the time of the killing, the accused was suffering from a mental disorder which would not justify a finding of not guilty by reason of insanity, but which affected the accused in such a way as to significantly reduce his responsibility for the act, the court will find the accused not guilty of murder, but guilty of manslaughter. Diminished responsibility is, therefore, a partial defence to murder only with the same result, if successfully pleaded, as provocation or excessive self-defence. Section 6 of the 2006 Act requires the defence to establish that:

(i) the accused committed the alleged act;
(ii) the accused was, at that time, suffering from a mental disorder; and
(iii) the mental disorder would not justify a verdict of not guilty by reason of insanity but was sufficient to diminish the accused's responsibility for the act.

The term "mental disorder" is defined in the 2006 Act and must be substantial. In *DPP v Tomkins* [2012] IECCA 82, the Court of Criminal Appeal stated:

> "To afford a defence under s.6, the mental disorder must be substantial; clearly that is something more than trivial or minimal, though ultimately the test must be one of common sense which lies within the province of the jury."

In accordance with s.6(2) of the 2006 Act, the onus is on the defence to establish that the accused was suffering from a mental disorder at the time of the offence. This is subject to s.5(4), which provides that where the defence is raised, the prosecution must be given the opportunity to adduce evidence to the contrary, and the court may give directions as to when such evidence may be adduced.

Section 6(3) provides that a woman found guilty of infanticide may be dealt with under s.6(1). Even before the enactment of the 2006 Act, it is likely, following the decision in *Doyle v Wicklow County Council* [1974] I.R. 55, that an accused could rely on the defence of insanity in situations where his ability to exercise judgement was in some way diminished. In *Tomkins*, a conviction for murder was quashed on appeal because the trial judge had not explained to the jury that whilst evidence of premeditation may negative the defence of provocation, such evidence is not necessarily inconsistent with diminished responsibility. In *R. v Matheson* [1958] 2 All E.R. 87, Goddard L.C.J. stated that premeditation could well co-exist with diminished responsibility, noting as follows:

> "Here it is said there was evidence of premeditation and undoubtedly there was, but an abnormal mind is as capable of forming an intention and desire to kill as one that is normal; it is just what an abnormal mind might do."

Although the Irish defence of diminished responsibility differs from its counterpart in England and Wales under the Homicide Act 1957, the above quotation was cited with approval by MacMenamin J. in *Tomkins*. The Court of Criminal Appeal dealt with sentencing in the context of manslaughter by reason of diminished responsibility in *DPP v Crowe* [2010] 1 I.R. 129, and quashed the sentence of life imprisonment. The accused had been sentenced following a plea of guilty on grounds of diminished responsibility to a charge of manslaughter, attempted murder and assault causing harm. The court handed down a sentence of life for manslaughter and 15 years and five years respectively for attempted murder and assault causing harm. On appeal, the life sentence was varied to a term of 20 years' imprisonment on the charge of manslaughter. The other sentences were allowed to stand. The court held that the accused could not be treated in precisely the same way as an accused who was fully responsible for his actions. The seriousness of the offence and the circumstances surrounding it were sufficiently serious to warrant a life sentence had the issue of diminished responsibility not been raised, notwithstanding a plea of guilty.

The Mental Health (Criminal Law) Review Board

In keeping with obligations imposed by the European Convention on Human Rights, s.11 provides for the establishment of An Bord Athbhreithnithe Meabhair-Shláinte (An Dlí Coiriúl)/The Mental Health (Criminal Law) Review Board (the "Board"). The Board is an independent body with responsibilities and powers conferred on it under the 2006 Act, as amended.

Those powers are set out in s.12, and include the regular review of the detention of individuals detained following the passing of the special verdict, or those who are detained in designated centres following a finding of unfitness to be tried.

The Board, in carrying out its functions, may, among other things, direct in writing the consultant psychiatrist responsible for the care and treatment of a patient whose case is being reviewed by the Board to arrange for the patient to attend before the Board, or direct in writing any person whose evidence is required by the Board to attend before the Board to provide such evidence. Failure to comply with the directions of the Board and, further, anything done in relation to the proceedings before the Board which, if done in relation to proceedings before a court by a witness, would amount to contempt of court, is an offence punishable on summary conviction by a term of up to 12 months' imprisonment and/or a class B fine.

The 2006 Act provided for a periodic review of detention and for the conditional release of people detained following a determination of unfitness to be tried or as a result of a verdict of not guilty by reason of insanity. The 2006 Act was silent, however, on the means by which any conditions attached to release could actually be enforced. In *J.B. v Mental Health (Criminal Law)*

Review Board [2011] 2 I.R. 15, the High Court held that despite the omission of any statutory powers of enforcement, the Board was not obliged to order the release of a prisoner in circumstances where it could not take steps to ensure that the conditions attached to his release were being complied with. This was remedied by s.6 of the 2010 Act.

THE DEFENCE OF INSANITY UNDER THE *M'NAGHTEN* RULES

Where the accused, having been deemed fit to stand trial, wishes to raise the defence of insanity, the burden of proof shifts to him, and this burden may be discharged on the civil standard of proof (i.e. on the balance of probabilities). The burden then shifts back to the prosecution, who must disprove the defence beyond a reasonable doubt. The defence as it is known today emerged in *R. v Hadfield* (1800) 27 St. Tr. 1281. The accused believed that he had to kill himself in order to save mankind but, believing suicide to be a sin, he elected to shoot the King instead in the hope that he would be hanged. He was charged with treason, which was a capital offence.

The court held that he was insane and he was duly acquitted. The rules governing the issue of insanity were formulated by the Law Lords following the acquittal on grounds of insanity of the accused in *R. v M'Naghten* [1843] All E.R. 229. The accused, while suffering from a delusion that he was being persecuted by the Tory Party, decided to shoot Sir Robert Peel, but shot and killed Peel's secretary instead. He was acquitted on the basis that he was insane. The subsequent public outcry prompted the trial judge to pose a number of questions regarding the matter to the House of Lords. The responses to those questions are known as the "*M'Naghten* rules" and are the exclusive test of insanity in English law.

In *R. v Windle* [1952] 2 All E.R. 1, the accused was convicted of the murder of his wife, believing, due to mental illness, that it was morally right to do so. The accused did, however, know that his conduct was legally wrong. He sought to rely on the defence of insanity, but was precluded from doing so because he knew that he had been acting unlawfully, and consequently could not avail of the *M'Naghten* rules. The court held that as far as the law in England is concerned, the defence of insanity is based entirely on the *M'Naghten* rules. In Ireland, the *M'Naghten* rules are the primary test but are not the "sole and exclusive test". This was held by the Supreme Court in *People (Attorney General) v O'Brien* [1936] I.R. 236 and was upheld in *Doyle v Wicklow County Council* [1974] I.R. 55.

THE *M'NAGHTEN* RULES

Any discussion of the application of the *M'Naghten* rules from the point of view of Irish law must proceed on the basis that, first, they are *not* the sole test for insanity in Irish criminal law, although they have been the primary test, and secondly, they must now be construed in light of the provisions of the 2006 Act. The *M'Naghten* rules are as follows:

(1) Where the accused is suffering from a *partial delusion* but knows, despite the delusion, that his actions are unlawful, he will have no defence.
(2) Every person is presumed to be sane, but this presumption is rebuttable. The presumption is rebutted on the civil standard of proof, which is the balance of probabilities.
(3) The accused must show that when he committed the offence, he was suffering from a defect of reason caused by a disease of the mind, and that he did not know the nature and quality of his actions or, if he did appreciate the quality of his actions, that he did not know they were unlawful.
(4) An accused person suffering from a partial delusion should be treated as though the facts of his delusion were real.

DEFECT OF REASON FROM A DISEASE OF THE MIND

Defect of reason from a disease of the mind in this context can include conditions arising from other medical conditions. In *R. v Kemp* [1957] 1 Q.B. 399, the accused attacked his wife with a hammer. He was found to have been suffering from a defect of reason from a disease of the mind brought on by arteriosclerosis, a medical condition which had caused congestion of blood in his brain. In *Ellis v DPP* [1990] 2 I.R. 291, the accused was charged with murder and sought to rely on the defence of automatism on the basis that he was suffering from the effects of epilepsy at the time of the killing. The judge directed the jury to disregard the issue of automatism and to consider the issue of insanity. The accused was found to be guilty but insane.

In *R. v Quick* [1973] 3 All E.R. 347, the accused was a diabetic, who neglected to follow medical advice in relation to his condition. While suffering from hypoglycaemia as a result, he committed an assault. He argued that he should be acquitted on the basis of automatism, but the trial judge directed that his defence was that of insanity. On that basis, he entered a plea of guilty and subsequently appealed his conviction. The Court of Appeal held that the condition of the accused had been brought about by his failure to follow medical advice. As this was an external factor, there was no disease of the mind and, consequently, the accused could not avail of the defence of insanity.

In *R. v Sullivan* [1983] 2 All E.R. 673, the opposite conclusion was arrived at in the case of an epileptic who committed an assault. In this case, the court followed the decisions in *Kemp* and *Quick* and found that epilepsy, being an internal factor, gave rise to a defence of insanity.

The defence is not available to someone who, through lack of care or through absentmindedness, commits an offence. In *R. v Clarke* [1972] 1 All E.R. 219, the accused tried to assert that forgetfulness, caused by depression, had caused her to shoplift. At her trial, it was held that this could give rise to the defence, but the proposition was rejected on appeal where the court held that the defence avails those who have, through a defect of reason from a disease of the mind, lost the power to reason, and did not apply to those who simply failed to exercise that reason.

Nature and quality of the act

In addition to the foregoing, the accused must also show that he either did not know the nature and quality of the act or, if he did, that he did not know it was unlawful. The lack of knowledge regarding the nature and quality or unlawfulness of the act must have been caused by the defect in reason.

In *R. v Codere* (1916) 12 Cr. App. Rep. 21, a soldier was convicted of the murder of a fellow soldier. He had argued that "nature" and "quality" suggested that there were different factors to be considered in the context of insanity. "Nature", he argued, referred to the physical aspect of the act, while "quality" referred to its moral character. The Court of Appeal held that the belief of the accused with regard to the moral aspect of the act was of no consequence. He could still be convicted if he knew he was killing someone, regardless of what his reasons for doing so might be.

In *R. v Dickie* [1984] 3 All E.R. 173, the accused knowingly started a fire. The fact that he was suffering from a manic-depressive condition at the time was held not to be relevant; what mattered was that he was aware of the nature and quality of his action.

The wrongful nature of the act

The accused must also have been aware of the wrongfulness of his actions. Wrongfulness in this context means unlawful. Where the accused knew that his actions were unlawful, the defence will fail. In *R. v Windle* [1952] 2 All E.R. 1, the accused killed his wife by giving her an overdose. She had frequently asserted that she wished to commit suicide and there was evidence that she was insane. The court even accepted that the accused might have been suffering from a form of insanity communicated to him from his wife.

Despite this, the defence failed, because the accused had stated to the police "I suppose they will hang me for this". This statement by the accused showed that he appreciated that his actions were unlawful, notwithstanding the probability that he himself was suffering from some form of mental disorder.

IRRESISTIBLE IMPULSE

In English law, the issue of irresistible impulse can be viewed as a form of diminished responsibility in cases of murder only. The effect of the defence is to reduce a charge of murder to one of manslaughter. Outside of that limited situation, irresistible impulse is not covered. The *M'Naghten* rules exclude the concept, and this point has been made in a number of English cases. In *R. v Kopsch* (1925) 19 Cr. App. Rep. 50, the notion that the accused could not prevent himself from strangling his aunt was described as "a fantastic and subversive theory". The point was made in even starker terms in *R. v Creighton* (1909) 14 C.C.C. 349, where the accused was informed that, "if you cannot resist an impulse in any other way, we will hang a rope in front of your eyes, and perhaps that will help".

The Irish position on the matter is different. As stated previously, the *M'Naghten* rules are *not* the sole and exclusive test of insanity in this jurisdiction and, in the context of irresistible impulse, the Irish judiciary have accepted that this can be viewed as a form of insanity. This has now been put on a statutory footing in s.5(1)(b)(iii) of the 2006 Act, which expressly provides for the concept of irresistible impulse. In *People (Attorney General) v Hayes*, unreported, Court of Criminal Appeal, 30 November 1967, the Court of Criminal Appeal held that in the case of an accused person who had killed his wife in circumstances where he could not stop himself from doing so, the defence of insanity should be available, notwithstanding the fact that the accused was aware of the nature and quality of his actions and knew they were wrong, but was unable to prevent himself from committing them due to a defect of reason caused by a disease of the mind. In *Doyle v Wicklow County Council* [1974] I.R. 55, the Supreme Court reiterated this position. In *People (Attorney General) v McGrath* [1960] 1 Frewen 267, the Court of Criminal Appeal rejected the argument that a conviction ought to be overturned on the grounds that the accused was acting under an irresistible impulse. Although the appeal failed, it was not because the court would not accept that irresistible impulse was a form of insanity, but rather because there was no evidence to support the claim that the accused had in fact been suffering from it. In *Hayes*, Henchy J. held that the defence of insanity could not be denied to an accused where, due to an irresistible impulse, caused by mental illness, he had killed his wife. This was upheld in *Doyle*, where the Supreme Court held that it would be unjust to deny the defence of insanity in the case of an accused who, suffering from mental illness, was unable to resist the impulse to burn down an abattoir.

THE CONSEQUENCES OF THE PLEA OF INSANITY

In *DPP v Gallagher* [1991] I.L.R.M. 339, the Supreme Court held that the verdict of "guilty but insane" was in fact an acquittal. Prior to the passing of the 2006 Act, an individual found guilty but insane was detained under s.2(2) of the Trial of Lunatics Act 1883, "during the government's pleasure".

The accused in *Gallagher* sought release from detention on the grounds that he had recovered from his insanity, but was unsuccessful. He eventually absconded and left the jurisdiction. Extradition proceedings were mounted but were unsuccessful due to the fact that he had not been convicted of any offence which would have justified his extradition back to this State.

The Supreme Court in *Gallagher* also stated that the issue of the release of such an individual is a matter for the Executive, but that the individual so detained could apply to be released on the grounds that he was no longer insane or a danger. The Government or the relevant Minister would then be obliged to enquire into the continued detention, and the conclusion reached would not be reviewable by the courts. It would appear that the refusal to conduct such an enquiry might give rise to judicial review proceedings. It does seem odd that a person, who by definition was sane, having been deemed fit to stand trial, could have been detained indefinitely (or at all) following the verdict under s.2(2) of the Trial of Lunatics Act 1883.

The 2006 Act makes provision for the detention of accused persons found not guilty by reason of insanity:

> "If the court, having considered any report submitted to it ... and such other evidence as may be adduced before it, is satisfied that an accused person found not guilty by reason of insanity ... is suffering from a mental disorder (within the meaning of the [Mental Health Act 2001]) and is in need of in-patient care or treatment in a designated centre, the court shall commit that person to a specified designated centre until an order is made under section 13."

Section 5 of the 2006 Act deals with the review of detention. The fact that "mental disorder" is to be construed within the meaning of the Mental Health Act 2001 means that a person suffering from a condition such as diabetes is unlikely to find themselves detained following a verdict of not guilty by reason of insanity.

KEY CASES

R. v M'Naghten [1843] All E.R. 229—Case which led to the *M'Naghten* rules.

Irish law on insanity radically amended by the Criminal Law (Insanity) Act 2006.

People (Attorney General) v O'Brien [1936] I.R. 236 and *Doyle v Wicklow County Council* [1974] I.R. 55—*M'Naghten* rules *not* the sole and exclusive test of insanity in Irish law.

DPP v Tomkins [2012] IECCA 82—Case involving "diminished responsibility". Court held that "mental disorder" is defined in the 2006 Act and must be substantial.

Duress and Necessity

25

The defence of duress is available to an accused person who has been charged with an offence other than murder, attempted murder, and treason. It applies where the accused acted as he did due to threats made against him or a third party. The threat must be of a serious nature and the duress must be operating at the time of the commission of the offence. The determining issue here is not whether the accused had formed mens rea, but rather whether his will was overborne to the point where he could not be blamed for acting as he did.

The leading Irish case on duress is *People (Attorney General) v Whelan* [1934] I.R. 518, where the accused was charged with receiving stolen money. He stated that threats of extreme violence had compelled him to act as he did. The jury agreed and the matter was referred to the Court of Criminal Appeal, which was asked whether or not, given the finding of the jury, the accused was guilty or innocent of receiving stolen property. Murnaghan J. in the Court of Criminal Appeal held as follows:

> "Threats of immediate death or serious personal violence so great as to overbear the ordinary power of human relations should be accepted as justification for acts which would otherwise be criminal. The application of this general rule must, however, be subject to certain limitations."

The test laid down in *Whelan* appears to be objective, referring as it does to the "ordinary power of human resistance" and not to the power of the accused to resist. The test further requires that the threat should be immediate so that a threat to inflict injury at some future juncture will negative the defence, since the accused could hardly argue that his will could be overborne to such an extent by a remote threat. *Whelan* is also accepted as authoritative in many other common law jurisdictions. Subsequent decisions have cast some doubt as to whether the proper test is objective or subjective. For example, in *DPP v Dickey*, unreported, Court of Criminal Appeal, 7 March 2003, the court did not overrule the direction given by the trial judge to the effect that the personal characteristics or frailties of the accused should be taken into consideration by the jury. The better view appears to be, however, that the test is more likely to be objective.

In *DPP v Patchell,* unreported, Court of Criminal Appeal, ex tempore, 10 June 2013 the court declined to overturn *Whelan*, stating that such a change in the law was a matter for the legislature. More recently, the Supreme Court in *Dunne v DPP* [2016] IESC 24 was asked to consider whether duress can be raised as a defence or partial defence to a charge of murder. In holding that it cannot, the Supreme Court stated that

> "... what the appellant seeks here is not the development or extension of existing principles. It is the uprooting of a rule embedded for some hundreds of years in the common law and the creation of an entirely new rule to apply, as the Court sees fit, to a greater or lesser extent. This is not put forward on the basis of any claim of constitutional right, but purely on the basis that some other courts of other jurisdictions have preferred the policy of the proposed new rule and the argument that this Court is free to follow that policy."

The duress must not be self-induced. In *R. v Shepard* (1987) 86 Cr. App. R. 47, the accused had joined a gang who engaged in shoplifting. When he tried to break free of the gang, he was subjected to intimidation. In the circumstances, the court held that the jury should have been given the opportunity to consider the effects of duress on the accused. However, a different conclusion had been reached in *R. v Fitzpatrick* [1997] N.I. 20, where the accused had been charged with murder, membership of an unlawful organisation, and robbery. In this case, the defence of duress was not accepted, and on appeal it was held that where an accused joins an unlawful organisation voluntarily, he cannot then assert that he was entirely free from moral culpability and as a consequence, cannot rely on the defence of duress. The House of Lords examined the law on duress as it operates in English law in *R. v Hasan* [2005] 4 All E.R. 685, stating:

> (1) Adults of sound mind are ordinarily liable for crimes committed by them.
> (2) Since the 14th century, a limited exception to this general rule has been recognised in respect of those who commit criminal offences against their will due to duress caused by the threats of another.
> (3) The defence is one of excuse rather than justification and "is now properly to be regarded as a defence which, if established, excuses what would otherwise be criminal conduct".
> (4) The defence, if not disproved by the prosecution, provides a complete exoneration of the accused. The burden of disproving the defence rests with the prosecution and is discharged on the criminal standard of proof.
> (5) The defence is subject to a number of limitations:

(i) It is not available where the offence charged is murder, attempted murder and "perhaps, some forms of treason";
(ii) There must be a threat to cause death or serious injury;
(iii) The threat must be directed against the accused, his immediate family or someone close to him.

(6) The relevant tests to be applied are, in general, objective in nature with reference to the reasonableness of the accused's conduct and perceptions, rather than with primary reference to the subjective perceptions of the accused.
(7) The defence applies only where the conduct of the accused has been directly caused by the threats.
(8) The accused cannot rely on the defence where he has voluntarily laid himself open to the duress.
(9) The accused must not have had any evasive action available to him which he could reasonably have been expected to take.

Necessity

The existence of a general defence of necessity is not universally accepted among legal scholars and jurists. Some argue that the defence is not one of general application but may arise in the context of some offences, whereas others take the view that there is a general defence of necessity, albeit subject to limitations. Debate also surrounds the issue of whether it is an excusatory defence or a justificatory one.

The defence has certain similarities to that of duress and is subject to many of the same limitations. Both defences arise in circumstances where the accused is forced to opt for one course of conduct over another, where one involves the commission of a crime and the other involves grave consequences to the accused or a third party. Simply put, the defence arises where prevailing circumstances compel the accused to act in a particular way, and he elects to commit a criminal offence on the basis that it is the lesser of two evils. The difference between the two defences is that the defence of duress applies where the criminal offence is committed due to a *threat*, whereas the defence of necessity arises where the criminal act is committed due to the *circumstances* in which the accused finds himself. Accordingly, the defence is sometimes referred to as "duress of circumstances".

There had been reluctance on the part of the courts of England and Wales to accept that a general defence of necessity existed. In *R. v Dudley and Stevens* (1884) Cox C.C. 624, the two accused were convicted of murder and sentenced to death, although the sentence was later commuted to six months' imprisonment. The accused had been on a lifeboat for a number of weeks with two others and had killed one of the others and eaten his body. It was accepted that had they not done so, they would all have died. In their defence, it was argued that the deceased would have died anyway and that the accused had acted out of necessity. The court held, however, that a decision such as had been made by the accused would be one that would be made by the strongest at the expense of the weakest and that it was the function of the law to protect the weak from the strong. The accused were, accordingly, convicted.

The decision in *Dudley and Stevens* was later affirmed by the House of Lords in *R. v Howe* [1987] 1 All E.R. 771. Later cases show a move away from this position and, in *R. v Pommel* [1995] 2 Cr. App. R. 607, it was held that the defence of necessity was available. In *Pommel*, the accused had been charged with being in unlawful possession of a firearm. He argued that he had taken the weapon in order to prevent a murder. The court, in *Pommel*, set out a number of limitations on the application of the defence which are identical to those that apply in the context of duress. The accused must have no alternative action available to him and must go no further than is necessary to avoid the greater of the two evils. Further, the defence cannot be relied upon where the offence is committed after the circumstances which brought it about have ended. Like the defence of duress, the defence of necessity may not be invoked where the accused brings about the prevailing circumstances.

In *R. v Martin* [1989] 1 All E.R. 652, the Court of Appeal held that the defence of necessity was available only if, from an objective standpoint, the accused could be said to have acted reasonably and proportionately in order to avoid a threat of death or serious injury. The test for necessity laid down in *Martin* is a two-stage test, with the jury being required to determine:

(a) Did the accused act as he did due to a reasonable belief that he faced death or serious physical injury if he acted otherwise?
(b) Would a sober person of reasonable firmness, sharing the characteristics of the accused, have responded in the same way as the accused?

If either question is answered in the negative, the defence fails. The defence also arises in cases of medical necessity. In *Re A. (Children) (Conjoined Twins: Surgical Separation)* [2001] 2 W.L.R. 480, the Court of Appeal held that an operation to separate conjoined twins would be lawful even though the separation would result in the death of one of the twins. Evidence was given that both twins would die within six months if the operation did not go ahead.

However, in *Quayle v R., Attorney General's Reference (No.2 of 2004)* [2005] EWCA Crim 1415, convictions for possession of cannabis resin contrary to the Misuse of Drugs Act 1971 were upheld because there was no objective evidence to show that the accused were acting reasonably and proportionately to the threat of injury. The accused suffered from various medical conditions and had argued that the use of cannabis was required to minimise side effects. The court held that the threat of injury had to emanate from an external source and be immediate and imminent in order to successfully invoke the defence, and that to permit the use of illegal drugs on the basis of necessity would defeat the purpose of the Misuse of Drugs Act 1971.

The court also held that there had been no breach of the accuseds' rights under art.8 of the European Convention on Human Rights which permits interference with an individual's right to respect for private life if the interference is lawful and necessary in a democratic society for the prevention of crime, the protection of health or morals or in order to protect the rights and freedoms of others.

KEY CASES

People (Attorney General) v Whelan [1934] I.R. 518—Leading Irish case on duress and accepted as authoritative in many common law jurisdictions.

R. v Pommel [1995] 2 Cr. App. R. 607—Defence of necessity is available but the accused must have had no other alternative.

26 Mistake

There is no general defence of mistake per se, but the law recognises that there may be situations in which the accused ought not be convicted of an offence where he acted under a mistaken belief as to the facts of his situation. The Latin maxim *ignorantia facti excusat; ignorantia juris non excusat* encapsulates the general rule that a mistake of fact will be excused, whereas a mistake of law will not.

Where an accused acts under a mistake of law, he will generally be liable for his conduct. In *DPP v Healy* [1990] 1 I.L.R.M. 313, the court stated that to allow an accused to be absolved of liability on the basis that he had made a mistake of law would be "to put a premium on ignorance".

At common law, an unreasonable mistake would not absolve an accused of liability for his conduct. In *R. v Tolson* (1889) 23 Q.B.D. 706, the accused married a man honestly and reasonably believing that her husband was dead, and was charged with bigamy when it transpired some years later that her husband was in fact alive. She was acquitted on the basis that she had made an honestly held reasonable mistake. In *DPP v Morgan* [1975] 2 All E.R. 347, the House of Lords held that a genuinely held belief, regardless of how unreasonable it might have been, meant that an accused could not have formed the mens rea for the offence of rape but that the jury could consider the reasonableness of the mistake in order to decide whether it had been genuine and honest. In *Morgan* the convictions were upheld on the basis that no jury properly directed would have concluded that the accused genuinely believed that the woman had consented.

In *R. v Kimber* [1983] 3 All E.R. 316, it was held that a genuine mistake of fact could lead to an acquittal in cases other than rape. The accused will, in most cases, be judged according to his mistaken belief, but the court must have regard to the presence or absence of reasonable grounds for the belief. An example of this may be seen in s.2(2) of the Criminal Law (Rape) Act 1981, which provides that in considering whether the accused believed that the complainant had consented to sexual intercourse, the jury is to have regard, in conjunction with other relevant matters, to the presence or absence of reasonable grounds for such a belief. In *C.O'R. v DPP* [2016] IESC 64, the Supreme Court held that in the case of rape under s.2 of the Criminal Law (Rape) Act 1981, an accused person who believes genuinely, even if unreasonably, that the woman was consenting, must be acquitted. The jury must use "shrewdness and commonsense" to decide whether the mistaken belief on the part of the accused is genuine, having regard to their view of what a reasonable person would have realised in the circumstances.

Mistake of fact will not always lead to an acquittal. Where an offence is one of absolute or strict liability, mistake is irrelevant, since no mens rea is required, proof of actus reus being sufficient to impose liability.

KEY CASES

DPP v Healy [1990] 1 I.L.R.M. 313—Mistake of law is no defence.

C.O'R. v DPP [2016] IESC 64—An accused person who genuinely believes that a woman is consenting must be acquitted even if his belief is unreasonable and the woman does not consent. Jury must be told that the belief must be genuine and that they are not obliged to believe a story that is obviously false.

27 Consent

Whether consent is a defence to a criminal charge depends on the nature of the charge and the capacity to give consent of the person from whom consent is sought. The actus reus of some offences, such as rape, assault, and theft, involves the absence of consent, and in these situations, the presence of consent will be a defence.

In *R. v Brown* [1993] 2 All E.R. 75, a number of individuals were charged with various counts of actual bodily harm under the Offences against the Person Act 1861. The defendants had participated in sadomasochistic activities which they had recorded. The recording came into the possession of the police, who prosecuted the defendants. The defendants were convicted and, on appeal, argued that they were adults who had willingly consented to participation in the activities. Various injuries were sustained, but it was the defendants' contention that they had consented. By a majority of three to two, the House of Lords dismissed this argument and held that it was not possible to give consent to the infliction of assaults of the nature involved. The judgment has been heavily criticised, chiefly on the basis that the House of Lords ruled on moral issues rather than strictly on the law. The defendants subsequently brought a case to the European Court of Human Rights, alleging that their right to a private life under art.8 of the European Convention on Human Rights had been breached. The European Court of Human Rights dismissed the challenge, holding that the level of injuries inflicted by/on the defendants brought their activity out of the realm of that which could be regarded as private and immune from State scrutiny (*Laskey, Jaggard and Brown v UK* (1997) 24 E.H.R.R. 39).

Consent is irrelevant for other offences. For example, an accused charged with an offence under s.2 or s.3 of the Criminal Law (Sexual Offences) Act 2006 will be convicted notwithstanding the fact that the person with whom he had sexual intercourse purported to consent to it, unless he had genuinely believed that the person was over the age of consent. Equally, an accused who ends another person's life, even at that other person's request and with their consent, will still be convicted of murder.

Index